ROGER TAYLOR

THE OFFICIAL AUTOBIOGRAPHY

THE MAN WHO SAVED
WIMBLEDON

ROGER TAYLOR
THE OFFICIAL AUTOBIOGRAPHY

THE MAN WHO SAVED WIMBLEDON

With Marcus Buckland

First published by Pitch Publishing, 2025
1

Pitch Publishing
9 Donnington Park,
85 Birdham Road,
Chichester, West Sussex,
PO20 7AJ
www.pitchpublishing.co.uk
info@pitchpublishing.co.uk

© 2025, Marcus Buckland

Every effort has been made to trace the copyright.
Any oversight will be rectified in future editions at the
earliest opportunity by the publisher.

All rights reserved. No part of this book may be reproduced,
sold or utilised in any form or transmitted in any form or by
any means, electronic or mechanical, including photocopying,
recording or by any information storage and retrieval system,
without prior permission in writing from the publisher.

A CIP catalogue record is available for this book
from the British Library.

ISBN 978 1 83680 146 7

Typesetting and origination by Pitch Publishing

Printed and bound in the UK on FSC® certified paper in line
with our continuing commitment to ethical business practices,
sustainability and the environment.

Printed and bound by CPI Group (UK) Ltd, Croydon, CR0 4YY

Contents

Acknowledgements 9
Prelude – 1973 11

1. 5 July 1973, Wimbledon Semi-Final. Roger Taylor v Jan Kodes (Part A). 13
2. Life in a Northern Town. 15
3. 5 July 1973, Wimbledon Semi-Final. Roger Taylor v Jan Kodes (Part B). 24
4. A Young Man at the YMCA. 26
5. 5 July 1973, Wimbledon Semi-Final. Roger Taylor v Jan Kodes (Part C). 31
6. Beetling about in the South of France 32
7. 5 July 1973, Wimbledon Semi-Final. Roger Taylor v Jan Kodes (Part D) 38
8. The Boycott 39
9. 5 July 1973, Wimbledon Semi-Final. Roger Taylor v Jan Kodes (Part E). 53
10. So Near and Yet so Far. 55
11. Fred and Andy – the Best of British 58
12. The Good, the Sad and the Ugly 64
13. Nasty but Necessary 78
14. The Times Are A-Changing. 86
15. The Handsome Eight 90
16. Rocket to the Moon – Wimbledon 1970. 102
17. Double Doubles Glory. 107
18. The Art of Beating Arthur. 111
19. Jimmy and the Tie-Break 116
20. Him Again. 121

21.	A Short Chapter but the Longest Match	123
22.	The Winner Takes It All.	126
23.	The Name's Bond, James Bond. (Or at least it nearly was).	131
24.	We Are Superstars	135
25.	Uncovering a Very Private Life	142
26.	A Headline Waiting to Happen	150
27.	Even the Blind School Could Have Beaten Them.	162
28.	No Whitewash at This Wightman Cup	185
29.	Bjorn Again in Spain and Portugal	192
30.	Being a Double Act Is More Fun!	205
31.	Roger Taylor at Queen's as Opposed to Roger Taylor of Queen	211
32.	Not Always Cosy, but Always Special	214
33.	Acting the GOAT	220
34.	Super Brits or Super Brittle?	234
35.	Me in the 2020s!	238
36.	Life and Death for Real	243
37.	Roger and Out	249
Index		252

Dedication

To Mum, Dad and Vivian. For all those wonderful times in Weston Park at the start of the adventure.

Acknowledgements

ONLY WHEN we delved deeply into the intricacies of the Wimbledon 'boycott' did it become clear just how challenging and damaging an experience the summer of 1973 proved to be for Roger. I'm so grateful that he trusted me to help him make sense of what went on and chart, with honesty, courage and total co-operation, his unique story.

I'd like to thank his family for their support, in particular Alison who was invaluable in remembering some of the key dates that occasionally threatened to become a little confusing!

So many people have gone out of their way to assist us – in particular Liz and Michael Mischker, Dickie Dillon, Bob Hill, Gordon Lazenbury, Richard Evans, Mark Cox, Sue Mappin, Tony Mitchell, Nick Walden, Vivian Waite, Olivia Buckland and the AELTC library. Special thanks also to Jason Bartholomew at the BKS agency and Pitch for guiding us along the way and to Phil Cuddeford for his invaluable advice and input.

And thank **you** for buying the book. We sincerely hope you enjoy it.

**Marcus Buckland,
London, spring 2025**

'There is something immoral about abandoning your own judgement'

John F. Kennedy, October 1962

Prelude – 1973

IT WAS Stan Smith who delivered the threat. Big Stan, all 6ft 4in of him, with long blond hair and a bushy moustache. A man who'd already reached the top of the tennis tree and would go on to become even more famous for selling his Adidas shoes around the world. And who looked as though he'd happily kick me where it hurts while wearing a pair of them. Looking me firmly in the eye I could sense the fury churning inside him.

'Roger, you'll never play tennis again if you don't join the boycott.'

Message received. Message understood. Message most unwelcome. This was rapidly turning into a very ugly fight.

He wasn't joking. But neither was I. I'm not one to seek confrontation. Never was, never will be. But I've always been my own man, which has meant doing, and saying, what I feel is right, irrespective of the consequences. And that meant there was no way I was going to be bullied into submission.

The Wimbledon boycott was a nightmare vividly brought back to life when I walked through the gates of the All England Club in the summer of 2023, the 50th anniversary of a controversy that came close to splitting tennis in two.

Oh, and it was also the year I really should have won Wimbledon. Should have, could have, but for, if only. Don't worry, this isn't going to be a sob story, but it's time to get a few things off my chest.

Chapter 1

5 July 1973, Wimbledon Semi-Final. Roger Taylor v Jan Kodes (Part A)

THERE'S NO point denying it. I'm nervous. Ridiculously nervous. My mind keeps playing tricks and my stomach won't settle. Stick to the usual routine everyone says. It's just another match.

It's not, though.

It's a semi-final at Wimbledon. Another semi-final.

I've lost two of them before but, in the face of so much adversity, here I am again. And, despite all the turmoil, there's the backing of a success-starved nation. You can do this, Roger, they all say. Of course you can.

Of course I can.

But the doubts persist.

I've stuck to the routine as closely as possible. The house is full but breakfast nice and quiet. Toast and coffee plus a couple of eggs. A quick glance at the papers. My face plastered over the back pages. There's a lot on the match but I put them back down. Don't want to be distracted. Then the drive to Queen's Club. I live in Wimbledon but warm up at Queen's. Always have, even before the falling-out. I feel more valued there, having made the final twice.

It's all a bit of a blur. I go through the motions. Try to loosen up and focus on the game plan. Concentrate on what I'm good at and where he struggles. It lasts about an hour. Back in the car the traffic is surprisingly light. We're through the barrier at the All England Club in double-quick time.

And into the spotlight.

Photographers are waiting. A camera crew is recording everything. Relax, Roger, or at least try to. The entrance to the locker room is only a short walk away. Bag on shoulder I shake hands with a few well-wishers and smile. Do my best to look calm, almost nonchalant. Then I head inside. To where I am now. Sitting quietly. Trying to control my breathing. Trying to forget what it's all about. What the last two weeks have been all about.

Chapter 2

Life in a Northern Town

IN MANY ways it was a miracle I ever played at Wimbledon at all. My parents were competitive people but didn't know much about tennis. Don't forget that, born in October 1941, I was growing up during the post-war era in an area far removed from the manicured lawns of SW19.

Mum and Dad were as supportive as possible without realising what I was doing, and was potentially capable of going on to do. It was only after I became British number one and reached those three Wimbledon semi-finals that my mother expressed regret.

'If only we'd known how good you are.'

I will never forget her saying that. Can't blame her, though. I didn't know how good I was and had no real way of finding out.

In all my years as a player I didn't have any coaching. None at all. As a youngster, aged around 14, I did once have a 'hit' with a Yorkshire coach called Michael Evans but nothing developed from that and I had to learn everything by myself.

In the early days I'd play with my mum, Lilian, regularly. She loved the game and knew how to hit a ball. That's how I developed a technical understanding of sorts and an appreciation of what the sport was all about. We'd practise in one part of Weston Park with my father, Mark, a couple of hundred yards away in the lower park playing bowls. He was pretty good and wanted to win but didn't approve of the perhaps overly competitive spirit that clearly bubbled inside me. I used to get very angry when I didn't beat my mother and he'd tell her not to play with me if I was going to behave like that.

Dad worked three different shifts for British Steel; mornings for one week, afternoons the next and then nights, in a constantly repeating pattern. In those days your mother looked after home life while dad took care of the finances. I don't want to sound like a stereotypical Yorkshireman from a certain generation complete with cloth cap and lots of 'eee by gums' but the world was very different back then and certainly a lot less complicated.

I had, and still have, one older sister. Vivian was born 14 months before me. We lived in Bromley Street, Sheffield, a road very similar to one made famous by the *Coronation Street* soap opera. Demolished many years ago, there was a bombsite just around the corner, and the house was a two-up two-down, with a passage that led to the bottom of the garden and an outside toilet. Very basic, but it was a simple, happy life. I'd run out to play after school every afternoon and evening, usually on what was called 'the tip'. Football was, inevitably, the main sport. I was pretty good and, like most active kids my age, wanted to spend as much time as possible out and about, often hiding in the bushes when mother came looking to bring me home for a clean-up before tea, which would precede what became our regular hit on the tennis court. I always had to have a clean face and neck before we could set out for that.

My sister and I were lucky to have such a wonderful upbringing and we remain close to this day. There was always a sense of fun in the house and no shortage of love. Mum and Dad had met at school and were so happy together. You'd hear her singing in the kitchen as they did the washing-up in tandem, after which the door would open and they'd come into the living area, often dancing a waltz and having a giggle. Then they'd sit down and hold hands, a picture of contentment. Arguments were almost unheard of. They had the most loving, caring and respectful relationship and knew exactly how to bring out the best in one another. If there was an issue, it was quickly resolved, usually with a touch of humour. Dad was very slow to fit a new sink once, which started to infuriate my mother. 'That's it,' she said eventually, 'I've had enough of this. I'm off!' She was joking and we all knew it. Dad went upstairs and came back down with her suitcase. 'It's all packed,' he joked. 'Off you go and good luck.'

That type of good-natured ribbing served them well for decades. Mum lived to the age of 95, Dad to his late 80s, and they never changed. Not the sort to hang around in the local pub, drinking beer and having a gossip, they'd be quick to take us out if anything notable was going on, particularly to sporting events like a Test match, the football at Bramall Lane or international table tennis, whatever was happening in the area. We were rarely left at home and it felt great to be part of such a tight-knit family.

I was quite a cheeky so-and-so growing up. Mum was always chasing me around the house while trying to get me to do this and that. I'd joke that she could never catch me but I was also careful not to take things too far. Vivian learnt to play tennis as well but was more into her dancing and went to a dance academy for a number of years, where she excelled. We may not have had a lot of money but we were better off than many others, with nothing to complain about. Mum was so talented. She was an outstanding swimmer in her youth, an indication of the sporting genes running through the family, and was also a fabulous seamstress. She made some beautiful wedding dresses and ballroom costumes and her determination to succeed in a number of different areas was reflected by the manner in which she taught herself to play tennis. Wanting what was best for her family, she went the extra mile to help us on our way.

My first racket, given to me aged around eight or nine, was a Grays with nylon strings. I was desperate not to break it. Luckily that was nigh-on impossible because it was like a fishing rod. I'd just stand around watching whoever my mum was playing plus anyone else on the adjoining courts and copy what I saw, good or bad. Most of them were pretty unorthodox with their approach but, employing some logic and common sense, certain tactics and patterns of play began to form in my mind. There were no magazines to study, no YouTube to turn to, absolutely no points of reference at all, other than what was going on in that park in South Yorkshire. It was a case of making do or buggering off to try to become the next Sheffield United centre-forward. United, not Wednesday of course!

There was one guy with a big three-piece design racket which was meant to maximise power and control. His name was Barney Rosen and he was THE man to watch in the area. God knows how he even lifted that bloody racket, it was so heavy. But I eventually started to compete against this unique group of individuals in the park, having developed a set routine with my mum every night after school. We used to head up to the park with some honey sandwiches she'd made and hit for as long as we could before it got dark. During the winter that would be around 20 minutes max. My plan of attack was always to be sensible when it came to shot selection but, naturally as a youngster, I also wanted to hit the ball as hard as possible. Slowly but surely, blessed with a fair degree of natural ability, I started to improve.

Mum was inspirational and arguably the player I've admired more than anyone else. Passionate, enthusiastic and very hard-working, I owe everything to her and vividly remember the day she became Sheffield Parks champion, which was a sought-after title in the area. It was brilliant and demonstrated to an impressionable, sports-mad youngster that anything was possible. Funnily enough there was quite a big crowd milling around the place that day, though not to see Mum in action. Behind the court was the main London to Scotland railway which the *Flying Scotsman* operated on. Invariably at weekends there'd be a fair few trainspotters taking notes and they were out in force, oblivious to a moment of sporting folklore in the Taylor family. I must confess to turning my back on the match and running up to the fence when the most famous train of that era flew by in the blink of an eye. Other than that moment, though, I watched the entire match and developed a 'lucky' single clap for every winner she came up with.

It does make me laugh when I see how today's youngsters come through the ranks with talent ID, county training, constant one-to-one coaching and all the tournaments that are run pretty well by the Lawn Tennis Association (LTA) at junior level, even if it's a costly exercise for the parents involved. We knew nothing about junior tournaments as I grew up and there was no mini-tennis with red or orange balls to help facilitate the start of the journey. Nowadays, if you haven't begun to develop your technique by around the age of six or seven, you're already playing catch-up. Only a few notable exceptions, such as Kyle Edmund, wait until they're ten or 11 before taking it seriously and then go on to make an indelible mark.

A brick wall next to the reservoir was my only hitting partner away from the courts. If I missed that, I had to climb over an iron fence and retrieve the balls from the water. Hardly glamorous but I was a determined little so-and-so and knew no better.

Gradually, I started to get noticed and heard about some tournaments in the area. Buxton was, I think, one of the first places I competed at in my early teens. Then there was Bradford and eventually the Yorkshire Championships at Scarborough. That led on to the North of England Championships, also staged in Scarborough, which was the sum total of my circuit. I never travelled south to places like Norfolk and Tunbridge Wells, which I heard lots of people talking about. They sounded like locations on a different planet. We didn't have a car. Every journey was by bus, often two or three of them at a time, so it was a mission to make relatively short journeys.

By now, though, the bug had bitten, big time. I started to play some titanic county matches, more often than not in the wet and the rain, for Yorkshire against Lancashire. These were hard court winter singles. I started off as the lowest listed player at number six but didn't take long to climb the ranks.

From there we moved on to County Week, which Yorkshire had never won, after which I was included in the squad for an amazing 'Whit' tour trip. That really opened my eyes as it took me to London for the very first time. We stayed at the Strand Palace Hotel and thought we were in wonderland: the lights of the city, the glamour and plenty of fancy food. There were matches against Oxford and Cambridge and, most significantly, the All England Club. Amazing!

A few years ago, I spoke at the members' autumn dinner at Wimbledon. One of the older guests introduced himself and started reminiscing about this young, dark-haired Yorkshireman from that week all those years ago who'd serve four double faults immediately followed by four aces. He was quite right. I was so rough and ready but clearly had a lot of potential. These days, youngsters can attempt to mirror their heroes. I was copying what I had seen in the park and, not surprisingly, a lot of it was rubbish. There was no coach to tell me anything constructive (or destructive) but I had a visual understanding of what could and should work for me. It was fairly basic common-sense tactics but having a clear picture in my mind enabled me to develop an increasingly reliable game plan. Some people can't see it. For whatever reason, the pictures elude them, but they were crystal clear to me, which was a gift.

By now I'd developed a close friendship off court, and a successful one on it, with Dickie Dillon, who also came from Sheffield. Dickie was the same age and we were both taken on that trip to London to gain some experience and keep each other company alongside the older players. In truth, we were only there as back-up reserves and didn't have any real idea how to be effective as a doubles team. But, following some poor results by the seniors against Oxford and Cambridge, we were thrown into action and decided to lob like crazy. Hit it high and, if they got it back, lob and lob again. It worked.

We won a couple of matches and the county hierarchy started to take proper notice of us. By now I was also playing a few senior tournaments and giving a pretty good account of myself against some of the best players in the region.

Shortly after that excursion a fellow called Bert Bishop approached my mother. His son also played and he was quite influential on the local tennis scene. In sporting terms, Sheffield, as you may know, is divided between the Sheffield Wednesday and Sheffield United ends of the city. There were a couple of courts in a club situated in Wednesday territory where another mate, Bob Hill, who I'm in touch with to this day, lived. Bert ran various events there and knew people. He obviously saw something in me that he liked despite the eccentricity and naivety of my game. I didn't have much of a serve for a long time and there was no logic to the way it developed. I was a lefty despite doing everything else right-handed. It just felt natural and that was it. But I continued to build on what I had, not what was lacking, and it finally started to get me noticed with those who had some influence.

By the mid-1950s my game was good enough to see me qualify for the Junior National Championships, which were held on the outdoor clay courts at Wimbledon. Having been knocked out in the first round in 1955 I made the semis 12 months later and the final in 1957. Mike Harvey, who I recall came from somewhere near Birmingham, beat me that year but I was still young enough to play again in 1958. Except that I forgot to enter in time! You had to send your application in three weeks before the tournament but, for whatever reason, my letter arrived a day late and the LTA refused to listen to my pleas for leniency. I even persuaded Bob Hill to write to them and say it was all his fault and that he'd forgotten to post the letter in time but it made no difference. I would have been hot favourite to win that year; another one that got away! The only consolation was that I decided to go and play an under-21 event in Eastbourne instead and managed to win that.

In my mid-teens and off the back of some other impressive wins, I was invited on to an LTA course at St Faith's school in Cambridge. It was run by national selector Dan Maskell who went on to become a household name through his television commentary for the BBC. Tim Phillips, later a chairman of the All England Club, was also there along with a number of other young protégés. To be honest, the coaching was limited and it was all pretty basic stuff. I really could have done with a proper backhand and probably should have been taught a new grip, which I never actually changed throughout my entire career.

Ahead of a serving practice session Dan asked us all to put our rackets down and throw some tennis balls as far as possible to test our strength. I threw the first one a heck of a long way into the balcony, at which point he said that was enough of that and we moved on to something completely different! I threw it right-handed so God knows how he was able to make any evaluation about my service technique!

What I remember most about that week was the presence of some LTA councillors, most of whom looked as though they were in their 80s and enjoying a nice little jolly. We'd have a sweepstake each evening to predict which one would fall asleep first during dinner. One of them always did! Now 80-plus myself, I feel a tinge of guilt about that!

As underwhelming as the experience was from a learning perspective, it felt good to now be a 'nominated young player'. I certainly wasn't out of my depth on court and, having had a taste of life at that level, wanted more.

There wasn't to be another opportunity, though. Back I went to Yorkshire to hone my skills, hoping I'd be invited to train at Queen's Club during the winter, which was the prize for the country's top juniors. The offer failed to materialise and I never received another invitation from the LTA. What I didn't know until after she died was that in November of that year my mother wrote to the secretary Basil Reay asking whether I could be part of the winter squad. He replied saying they didn't feel I had made the necessary progress, thank you very much and goodbye.

The bottom line was that Dan, the national selector, didn't appear to rate me. To him my game wasn't of the 'Oh I say, what a peach of a shot' level, which was desperately frustrating from a personal point of view because I was never given a proper opportunity to demonstrate what I had and find out what I needed to work on to make real progress. Of course, that happens to so many players not blessed with a perfect set-up, week in, week out, year in, year out. There are coaches standing next to greatness who often can't see past their own shoelaces. You need a really good, driven coach and supportive parents with an ability to appreciate what's inside a player and what is required at each step of a horrendously complicated and long journey to have any chance of getting somewhere.

Dan had been a professional ball boy at Queen's and was part of the establishment there. When, a few years later, I did begin training at Queen's on a regular basis, I realised there remained a hierarchy dictated by society. A few of the lads from Fulham, who I became friendly with, would have coaching roles with the members (some of whom were limited in terms of ability, to say the least) and, while practising on one court, you'd hear things like 'lovely shot, my lord', and look across to see the coach giving you the wink while trying not to fall about in hysterics. It was an amateur set-up open only to the chosen few.

It's so easy to fall by the wayside in your mid-teens as a player. These days the little funding offered to promising youngsters is normally taken away at 14 unless they are one of the 'elite'. My determination and belief allowed me to deal with the tough times and keep coming back for more, supported by two brilliant parents, but I understand why so many youngsters turn away from tennis before they've been given a proper chance to see what might be achievable. It's such a waste and the LTA should be ashamed of a system that lets so many promising youngsters drift away too soon.

Chapter 3

5 July 1973, Wimbledon Semi-Final. Roger Taylor v Jan Kodes (Part B)

IT'S LONELY inside the locker room. That's always the case towards the end of the fortnight. There's only four of us left from the original 128. I'm aware of Jan's presence over in the far corner but we haven't acknowledged each other and I don't intend to. Nothing personal but I've nothing to say to him. I'm sure he feels the same.

The clock seems to be ticking so slowly. Unlike my heartbeat. A part of me wants to get out there now. The other part wants the clock to stop. There's no one for me to talk to. I don't have a coach. Or a trainer. Or a physio. Or a manager. You get the picture. It's me alone. Always has been. Guess it always will be.

The weather's not great. It's unseasonably cold and the forecast suggests rain later. No point worrying about that, though. I've learnt not to concern myself with factors outside my control. Instead, I change into my playing gear and begin a light stretch. The past few days have been stressful both physically and mentally, but I pride myself on being as fit as possible. I run around Wimbledon Common on Christmas Day and every day thereafter to ensure I'm ready for whatever seven matches might take out of me at the Championships. No excuses. I'm all set.

'Taylor on court in five minutes' comes the cry. Captain Mike Gibson, referee here since 1962, is not my cup of Yorkshire tea. I've heard him described as imperious. I can think of several other adjectives. He lacks empathy but a lot of the officials are like that. I check my bag. Everything

5 July 1973, Wimbledon Semi-Final. Roger Taylor v Jan Kodes (Part B)

is where it should be. One more visit to the gents and I'm primed. Ready for that short walk from the locker room and through the members' area. We pause by the door that opens up on to Centre Court. I'm aware of Kodes next to me but we still haven't officially acknowledged one another. What's the point? We'll shake hands on court so let's leave it at that.

And then the door opens. The buzz of the crowd hits me first. I'm used to it, having played countless matches on Centre Court. This is different, though. There's a heightened expectancy. And the expectation is on my shoulders. A cheer is followed by thunderous applause as the crowd spots us for the first time. It's overcast as we walk on to the greatest court in the world. A court that is so intimate. So special. I head for my chair, remembering to turn and show due respect to those in the Royal Box. Put the bag down. Take out my racket and walk to the net. Now we're eye to eye. Ready to shake hands. Don't blink, Roger. Look the part, Roger.

'Play,' says the umpire. And we do. For the right to be in the Wimbledon final.

Chapter 4

A Young Man at the YMCA

DESPITE BEING ignored by the sport's governing body I continued on an upward trajectory. Having made a mark at those Junior National Championships and elsewhere, I then went to the Chapel Allerton tennis club in Leeds for what was called a 'sifting' process. Twelve months earlier I hadn't even been aware that this talent ID scheme existed but I won a junior match at the Sheffield Hallam club, which was the best of its kind in the city, and a fellow called Ernest Hampson happened to be watching. He liked what he saw, told me about the 'sifting' and then drove me to Leeds for it.

Dan Maskell was in charge, which didn't bode well for my chances. Crucially, he was being assisted by a new coach from Australia, George Worthington, who had been an excellent player and was someone all of us youngsters were excited to be around. George was very approachable and really liked my game. He watched me a couple of times and then told my parents I simply had to go to London to maximise my talent, insisting there was no way I'd achieve anything in the sport if I stayed at home. His advice, echoed by others, was enough for Mum and Dad to agree the time had come.

It can't have been easy for them but Mum went to see my headmaster, hardly the warmest or most encouraging of individuals, and refused to have her mind swayed when he highlighted the potential downfalls of such a move. Herbert Wadge always made it clear he was the boss and delivered a rather condescending speech at their meeting. 'Some boys come up here, Mrs Taylor,' he announced, lifting his hand to a certain height. 'Others,' he went on, 'may be capable of getting there.' His hand was now raised several inches higher, 'but they can't all get there.' The inference was clear but Mum stood her ground. 'I'm sure you are quite right, headmaster, but I want my Roger to have a chance of getting as high as he possibly can.' And that was that. I was on my way.

Mum and Dad felt it was their duty to give me every possible chance to succeed and I'm blessed to have had that type of support. They were always there for me too, even when I was on the other side of the world. I used to get very sore feet through the rubber on my tennis shoes. The only thing that helped were special insoles with cork on the bottom. Every month, wherever I was, a package of these insoles would be delivered to make sure I was okay and give me a little reminder that they were thinking about me from afar.

There was never any jealousy between Vivian and me, even though I was the one able to follow my dreams. Short as it proved to be, her competitive dancing career was fulfilling too and we have never fallen out. The parental message to both of us was clear. We want you to be fulfilled and do whatever makes you happy. I'm so proud of Vivian. She has three wonderful children and seven grandchildren who adore her and will do anything she asks. Her ability to mould a loving family unit is worth its weight in gold and I really couldn't wish for a better sister. Our paths don't cross as often as either of us would like but we know we're there for each other if required and fate tends to play its part. I'll never forget going to visit Vivian in the early 80s when, unknown to anyone else at the time, I was in the throes of divorcing my first wife, Frances. With a sisterly intuition she immediately asked what was wrong. When I told her, she looked at me and laughed. 'Can you believe it,' she said, 'I've just been to see a solicitor and I'm divorcing Brian!' Her first husband, she went on to tell me, was not the father she wanted for her children.

There we were, together again just like children, this time helping one another deal with a truly horrible adult issue.

I think she found it quite funny when I started to make a bit of a name for myself. 'Is that your brother?' became a regular question. 'Ooh, he's quite good-looking isn't he!' I know how proud of me she was, though, and I know how proud I am of her.

Anyway, I've jumped the gun a bit. George Worthington went out of his way to find a job for me at Fred Perry Sportswear in the centre of London and everything was quickly arranged. Aged 17, I packed my bags, full of excitement and trepidation, in the late summer of 1958 and embarked upon one of the most exciting chapters in my life.

Dickie Dillon came down too, which was great. There we were, waving goodbye to our families at Sheffield station and climbing aboard a steam train with smoke billowing all over the place. It could have been the setting for a post-war romantic film and I felt quite emotional as the train chugged south. Keeping in touch with family and friends was very difficult back then. I didn't see my parents, sister or local mates for weeks and sometimes months on end. Thank God I had Dickie to keep me company.

We stayed at the YMCA in Wimbledon. It was a little haven from the realities of life in the big city. Run as a Christian society, church services were available and there was also snooker and table tennis, with a real mix of people staying at the place. Back then Wimbledon Broadway itself was limited in terms of amenities. It amounted to one cinema, the theatre and a shop/café that offered eggs, sausage and chips or sausage, egg and chips or chips, egg and sausage!

Our deal was full board but, for religious reasons, there was no evening meal on a Sunday so we had to juggle a weekly salary of five pounds, two shillings and sixpence (around £75 today), a fair bit of which went on the tube fare from Wimbledon up to the West End where the Fred Perry shop was situated.

Life settled into a pattern. Wimbledon to Earl's Court on the District line. Then down the stairs for the Piccadilly line to Piccadilly

Circus and out at the Shaftesbury Avenue exit. From there we'd walk along Windmill Street, passing the Windmill Theatre, which is conservatively described on Wikipedia as being best known for its *'nude tableaux vivants'*.

There were usually a few of the often vivacious 'stars' of the show outside the theatre who would embarrass us northern bumpkins with some suggestive greetings as we wandered by but I wouldn't be telling the truth if I said I didn't look forward to those exchanges! From there we'd cross into Lexington Street where the Fred Perry warehouse was, and around the corner into Golden Square for the main office. As two fit lads we were on hand to do whatever was required in terms of unloading the stock and sorting it out in the warehouse, which was managed by Terry Lane. We'd also turn our hand to some DIY, painting or whatever else was needed. It was physical work but a pretty good substitute for being in the gym, which our modern-day contemporaries consider a basic ingredient in their tennis schedule. Rather than cross-trainers and an assortment of weights, we'd be catching heavy boxes full of Green Flash shoes, which would often split in half as they were hurled from the lorries. Or we'd be carrying heavy loads to the two big shops around the corner, Lillywhites and Simpsons. It was a laugh. Dickie and I would load up the trolleys and then have a race around the streets to see which of us could get the stuff delivered first. There wasn't as much traffic around town in those days so such antics weren't quite as dangerous as they might sound.

Lunch would consist of half a pint of milk and a sandwich so, via a lot of exercise and a pretty lean diet, we managed to get ourselves in tip-top physical condition.

What we really wanted to do of course, was play tennis as much as possible. After all, that's why we'd come down to London. Tibby Wagner, an old-school Hungarian who modelled himself on being a tough guy, leased Fred Perry Sportswear. He wasn't, shall we say, the most generous of bosses, but was quite fond of us. Tibby had shown plenty of business acumen to sign a deal with Fred and started off by giving sweatbands to players before branching out into shirts, shorts and all the rest. And it was quite something for a young player, never mind a member of the public, to be decked out in Fred Perry kit. The ultimate accessory was an alpaca jacket, which these days sell for around £140. The first time I wore one of those I really felt as though I'd made it on the tour.

Dickie and I had to clock in and out and plan our tennis commitments in great detail. So, if I had a match in, say, Surbiton, Hurlingham, Sutton or the Connaught club for example, I'd work out exactly how long it would take me to reach the tube, change trains where necessary and then run to the club. We didn't have the giant bags most players are seen with today. It would be a couple of rackets and maybe a spare shirt if you were lucky. For tournaments further afield like Guildford or Eastbourne we'd usually stay with a family and then have to make up for any hours lost at work with overtime. Terry knew exactly what we had and hadn't done so, if necessary, we'd come in at the weekend even if there wasn't much to do.

It was a fantastic time, one of those golden periods in my life that I look back on with such fondness. What training we did usually involved varying amounts of practising in Wimbledon Park or Fulham Park and lots of running around Wimbledon Common. Sometimes we'd jog past the All England Club, which tended to look bleak and unwelcoming for all but the two weeks of the year when the Championships were staged. I could go for miles. When the men's pro tournament at Wembley came around each year, I'd sometimes run back to the YMCA in Wimbledon, having gone to watch the professional stars of the day in action, a distance of about 12 miles. I know that sounds like madness today but I was brought up in a no-excuse, nothing's impossible culture and didn't mind pushing the limits when necessary. I knew I'd have to make myself as hard to beat as possible and that meant being super-fit. Blessed with a sprinkling of Yorkshire grit, the need to put in some hard graft when required was never an issue.

Chapter 5

5 July 1973, Wimbledon Semi-Final. Roger Taylor v Jan Kodes (Part C)

KODES IS a tough so-and-so. Twice a French Open champion and two-time US Open finalist, his credentials speak for themselves. I lost to him in Rome on clay back in 1969 but then beat him on the red stuff in Hilversum shortly afterwards. Clay is his best surface but he's far from being a mug on grass and no wonder, with such a complete game at his disposal. Deep, solid ground shots, a threat when coming forward and a top-quality backhand return is a pretty potent mix. Oh, and he's fast, fit and courageous too. Then again, so am I. So, let's not worry about him. Or try not to.

The first set is tight. There's nothing between us but I edge it by nine games to eight. Similar story in the second except that he wins a couple of crucial points and, eventually, the set 9-7. Back where we started and the weather's showing no sign of improving. Despite losing the set I'm feeling more relaxed now. I'm serving well and my volleys are sharp enough to keep him on the run. The crowd is playing its part. Not like in New York where things can get out of hand but I feel the support, respectful as it is for both of us. It's another tight set but I win it by seven games to five. One more to go, Roger.

I try to block the thought out but there's a sense of déjà vu. I was two sets to one up in my first Wimbledon semi. That was in 1967 against a very determined German Wilhelm Bungert in a match full of errors. We coughed up 27 double faults between us that day and he broke me early in the fourth and fifth sets to win. The quality in this match is much higher but the pattern is starting to repeat itself. One break gives him the set 6-4. We're going the distance.

Chapter 6

Beetling about in the South of France

CHANCE MEETINGS change lives and mine was turned upside down one day in the winter of 1960 when a brash, 6ft 6in Australian marched into the office at Fred Perry when I happened to be behind the counter. Barry Geraghty was loud and good-humoured, a larger-than-life character who very quickly became one of my best friends. Bazza came from Bega in New South Wales and had travelled to the UK by boat, via Aden and the Suez Canal, accompanied by a transistor radio that I don't think he ever switched off, and a guitar.

He was in the shop, trying on some clothes and started talking about a few tournaments he'd recently played in. Then he asked me if I knew anyone who might be interested in going to the South of France for the upcoming Riviera circuit that ran along the Cote d'Azur for ten weeks in the early spring.

'Erm, yes. Me!' I replied, after a lengthy pause. And our friendship blossomed from that moment.

Barry had a Volkswagen Beetle and over the next few weeks we set about laying our hands on some essentials. These basically consisted of two sleeping bags and countless tins of spam, baked beans and rice pudding, which we bought in Woolworths. There was also a small stove upon which we planned to bring our gastronomic delights to life! My mother borrowed a tent from the local school and, before I knew it, we were on our way, though not before Bazza developed something of a crush on my sister. Vivian insists to this day that nothing ever happened. But the way in which she always breaks into a wistful smile when his name is mentioned suggests to me that, perhaps, something did. Maybe I'll find out the truth one day, though Bazza is, sadly, no longer with us.

Queen Victoria put the French Riviera on the map when she first visited the area in 1882. It became a regular haunt for British royalty and, as the 20th century dawned, so did a growing love for tennis in the region. Its 'golden' period was from 1874 to the start of the Second World War in 1939 when more than 450 international tournaments were played along the Mediterranean coast in places such as Antibes, Cannes, St Raphael, Nice and Monte Carlo.

By the 1960s some of the glamour of that pre-war era had faded but, for a Sheffield lad who'd never been overseas before, this was the start of a great adventure. The plan was to stay at various campsites along the way, get into as many tournaments as possible and hope for a spot of luxury accommodation whenever that opportunity presented itself.

I almost lost Bazza before the trip really started. Crossing over from Dover to northern France the weather was still very wintry with a fair bit of snow on the ground. Coming from Australia he'd never before seen this strange white powder that was making our drive more than a little hazardous as we crossed the Alps. Out of the blue he stopped the car on a hairpin bend, grabbed his guitar and, while musically expressing his love for this part of the world, jumped into the snow for a photo, promptly disappearing from view! He'd had no idea just how deep it was. Needless to say, he didn't do it again.

Without any maps, never mind satnav, we travelled down the coast and had a little bit of success every now and then on court, though I soon realised I didn't have big enough groundstrokes to compete properly at that level.

We also didn't have a big enough tent!

On the very first night we rocked up in the dark at this near empty campsite in which one other rather luxurious-looking tent was set up 100 yards or so away. We opened up ours only to realise it was designed for little children. My mother had borrowed it from a school-teacher friend without fully appreciating its limitations! So, there we were, a giant Aussie and a relatively sturdy Yorkshireman trying to squeeze inside this tiny little space with a knee-high entrance. We rolled about the place in hysterics but it was an intimate experience, to say the least.

The following morning we crawled out with great difficulty to the bewilderment of a German family standing next to their large caravan and double-deluxe tent with big zips and all the mod cons. Once they'd stopped laughing at the sight of two grown men desperately trying to untangle themselves from a pop-up structure designed for a ten-year-old, they proved to be very friendly and wished us luck as we headed off, rather sheepishly, to the tennis. Our fanbase was developing!

Wherever possible we'd wangle our way into free accommodation and hang around whichever club was hosting that week, making the most of any food and drink that was available. It was essentially a diet of cheese sandwiches, (the Gruyere was magnificent) and a beer or two. There was no guarantee we'd play each week. Although our entry forms had been sent off several weeks earlier, you only found out the day before the tournament whether or not you'd made it into the draw. And, although we were decent young players, this was a step up in class so, even when we did get in, there weren't too many wins to celebrate along the way.

We came across some very talented individuals, including Bob Carmichael who became a top-ten player and made at least the fourth round of all the slams a few years later. He went on to coach a number of excellent players including Pat Rafter and Lleyton Hewitt and was a tough, uncompromising individual. Bob once grabbed John McEnroe by the collar and threatened to knock him out during a doubles match in Las Vegas, not a threat to take lightly. An apprentice carpenter by trade, he was nicknamed Nails. Every

Aussie had to have a nick-name and his was particularly appropriate. Bob was one of the A-grade players who operated on this circuit. They weren't really good enough to play Davis Cup or compete regularly with the very best and had a lot of limitations, yet they knew how to make the most of the weapons at their disposal and that was a valuable lesson for me. Keith Diepraam of South Africa was another in that category who caught my eye. He went on to coach Wayne Ferreira and used to hang around with his fellow countryman Robin Sanders, who I remember watching lose to Pierre Darmon of France in the Aix-en-Provence Final that year.

The trip was a real eye-opener for me. The matches were played on slow clay courts, much slower than anything I'd experienced back in the UK. It was so hard to break down opponents on that type of surface. They didn't seem to do much, yet there you were, walking off having lost again, wondering what on earth had happened.

But, aside from having to wash the clay out of your socks and shirts in a sink just about every day, it was a blast. We only had the minimum kit, with no fancy accessories. These days I have to roll my eyes when I see what the players pack into their giant bags. Former British pro Colin Beecher has more creams in his bag at any one time than I've used in my life! But space was limited. I think I had three rackets during that two-month trip with a few pairs of socks, some shorts, underwear and four shirts. We also had one smart outfit which we'd put on occasionally to visit the casinos and watch how the rich and famous passed their leisure time. Watch, not participate in, I hasten to add. We kept out of trouble, aside from the time Bazza took it upon himself to hurl a very big, aggressive Hungarian off a diving board following a bit of a set-to one afternoon around a pool. We had to beat a hasty retreat after that but everyone liked Barry and we became an inseparable double act.

The tournament at Monte Carlo concluded the swing and was an extravagant affair run by a charismatic lady called Gloria Butler. Her father had built the country club, which was badly damaged during the war. Gloria, and her mother, then restored it and made sure everyone involved was well looked after. Each year they hosted a cabaret at the end of the week with no expense spared. All the players would take part and, though the legendary German actress and singer Marlene Dietrich may not have been overly impressed had she been around, my impersonation of her while expensively dressed in vintage clothing and a pair of high-heeled shoes made in Paris, certainly captured the audience's attention. So too did Lew Hoad and I, decked out in exotic bathing costumes as a double act called Miss Stinky and Miss Down-Under.

The weeks flew by and all good things must come to an end. The LTA insisted British players had to be back in the country by early April for the Hard Court Championships, which was probably just as well because what little money we'd started the trip with had all but disappeared.

By the time we approached the docks at Boulogne our cash and petrol supplies had run out. Bazza left the car in neutral whenever we went downhill during the last 20 miles and it was a huge relief to finally get on board the ferry. We spent the crossing counting every coin we could find in various pockets and under the car seats before changing them back into English currency. Luckily Barry had hoarded money from all over the world during his trip from Australia. He produced hundreds of coins from deutschmarks and francs to ones we couldn't even identify. It didn't amount to much but provided just enough to fill up the Beetle and take us back to London. Luck was on our side there because, having driven into Earl's Court, I spotted someone I knew and managed to borrow enough cash to fill up the tank again for the journey to Sheffield. Bazza was a member of the Overseas Club in town so, with me mimicking an appalling Australian accent, we spent the night there before heading north at the conclusion of an unforgettable experience.

My friendship with Barry led to a lifelong affiliation with Aussies and the country itself. Thanks to some sponsorship help from Slazenger, I travelled down under every winter over the next few years to hone my skills while everyone shivered in Britain. I used to stay with the Geraghtys and mingled with a wild but fun-loving bunch. There were a few bar-room brawls which meant you had to be on your toes just in case something kicked off. Bazza's brother Rex was nick-named Wrecker for reasons that soon became apparent. Sharing a room with old Wrecker was an experience. He tended to come home very late and usually quite inebriated and would wake me up by grabbing his weights from under the bed and beginning a full-scale workout! There was never a dull moment on those visits and one or two romantic interludes that modesty prevents me from expanding upon. Oh, the exuberance of youth! I learnt a lot and over the new few years developed into a player capable of matching, and sometimes beating, the best.

Chapter 7

5 July 1973, Wimbledon Semi-Final. Roger Taylor v Jan Kodes (Part D)

THERE'S NOTHING between us as we move through the fifth set. And all the time it's getting darker and darker overhead. The crowd's a little restless. They're glancing towards the sky. Some umbrellas go up. I'm serving first; 1-0, 2-1, 3-2, 4-3, 5-4, no breaks and now the rain is steady, the surface slippery. And I'm one game away from the final.

'Play is suspended' comes the call from Egyptian umpire Ali Maker after three hours and 24 minutes, with the time 7.20pm.

No, not now. Not after all that's gone before. I pack my bag, give an appreciative wave to the crowd and head back to this lonely locker room. Four points from the final. It feels a hell of a lot more than that. Then again, the past few weeks have consisted of a lot more than six matches. Truth be told, the tennis has been a sideline.

Chapter 8

The Boycott

LET'S CUT to the chase. Depending on your age, you may be oblivious to the intricacies of the 1973 Wimbledon boycott. Unfortunately, it's left a hole in my heart that hasn't properly healed more than 50 years later. It's a convoluted tale so I'll try to keep things as simple and concise as possible.

I was 31 in June 1973 and keen to take full advantage of what time I had left as a top-class tennis player. Nothing more, nothing less and absolutely no politics thanks very much. I was in good shape, driven and ready to shine before Father Time put me out to grass. In those days most players hung up their rackets in their early 30s. The longevity that's been such an asset for the likes of Roger Federer, Rafael Nadal, Novak Djokovic, Serena Williams and so many others in recent times was the exception rather than the norm back then.

The biggest tournament of the year was fast approaching and I felt great off the back of a run to the quarter-finals at the French Open on my least favourite surface; further proof I was peaking at just the right stage of the season. Ilie Nastase ended my run on his way to the title in Paris but there were no complaints or concerns for me as I turned my attention to the grass-court swing.

Then, out of nowhere, a chasm opened up that looked like swallowing me whole. In an instant I became one of the pivotal figures at the heart of a ferocious battle that was a sign of the times and left me with no obvious place to turn.

That's right. Me. A Sheffield lad, whose father just happened to be a trade unionist, inadvertently caught between the wishes of a union looking to flex its muscles in the fight between professionals and amateurs on one side and the hopes and expectations of a regulated sport, and a nation, on the other.

So, what was it all about?

The newly formed men's union, the Association of Tennis Professionals (ATP), was in its infancy, keen to assert its authority against what were considered to be archaic rules that did nothing for player welfare. There was a growing disharmony between the players and the world governing body, the International Lawn Tennis Federation (ILTF), which reached boiling point in the spring of 73.

Niki Pilic, a left-hander from Yugoslavia, was at the centre of the controversy. Due to play a Davis Cup tie against New Zealand in May, Pilic also had a contract with the World Championship Tennis professional tour to compete in a lucrative tournament in Montreal the same weekend. Deciding to play there rather than represent his country, Niki was immediately banned by the Yugoslav Federation, ironically run by his own uncle, General Dusan Kovac. The ban was to last nine months and include all events controlled by the amateur governing body, the ILTF, including the Davis Cup and the Grand Slams. There was an irony to the fact that Pilic became the 'rebel with a cause' at the centre of the story. Around the same time, Arthur Ashe wrote that Niki was 'politically somewhat to the right of Marie Antoinette. He is perhaps the most conservative member of the tour, the original male chauvinist pig (Bobby Riggs is a feminist by comparison) and a chronic hypochondriac and complainer as well.' Frank Keating wrote a brilliant piece in *The Guardian* in which he described Pilic as 'broodily dark and explosive' off court and a man who 'thought anyone who even looked like a hippie should be shot, preferably through the heart, by him'.

Yet here he was, suddenly a cause célèbre.

The Yugoslav Federation's hard-line attitude provoked a very strong response from the ATP, run by ex-pro Jack Kramer, who was executive director, and its president, Cliff Drysdale, a top-class South African player with whom I'd won the US Open doubles less than a year before.

Kramer, a tough but charming American, was described in an article by the writer J.A. Allen as 'the father of modern tennis', and the 'most influential man in the sport during the 20th century'. Dressed immaculately at all times, he came across as a little self-satisfied on occasions but could never be ignored. As a player he'd been the catalyst for a 'serve-and-volley' era in the late 40s and 50s and won a number of slams, including Wimbledon in 1947, after which he turned pro. He went on to become a hugely successful promoter within the sport and built a reputation for organising high-quality events and persuading a number of amateur champions to follow in his footsteps and join the professional ranks. His competitive streak was illustrated by what is thought to have been his last tennis match in 1994. Having undergone three hip replacements and having felt the effects of an arthritic back for decades, Jack lost to one of his grandchildren and felt compelled to explain why. 'When you can't run too far, you have to overplay every ball you can hit, so you make a lot of errors.' He was 72!

Drysdale was quite something too. Inducted into the International Tennis Hall of Fame in 2013, he was considered dynamic, debonair and delightful. Good-looking and super-smooth, Drysdale could certainly be all three of those; and a few others besides. The bottom line was that Cliff wanted what was best for Cliff. We played a lot of doubles together over the years and his innovative two-handed backhand made him a very useful partner. Yet he had an unsettling habit of sometimes packing his suitcase at the hotel and bringing it to wherever we were playing. Hardly confidence inspiring at the start of the week in particular! I'd sometimes go on court wondering if he'd already booked his flight home for later in the afternoon.

He was, though, hugely successful as a player, activist within the sport (he liked to call himself a 'locker room politician') and commentator with his soft, melodic voice; Rod Laver said he 'could talk a lion into becoming a vegetarian'. We teamed up almost by chance to win what was his only slam title in New York in 72, of which there will be more later, beating John Newcombe (with whom I'd won the title 12 months earlier) and Owen Davidson 6-4, 7-6, 6-3.

However, we never defended that title. In fact, as a result of the boycott we never played together again. Or spoke to each other again.

Another key figure behind the scenes was Donald Dell. A former player, writer and lawyer, Dell was the first sports agent in professional tennis and had an impressive list of clients including Arthur Ashe, Stan Smith, Jimmy Connors and Ivan Lendl. I first came across him in the late 60s after signing for IMG. Having contested a series of events on the Caribbean circuit (no great hardship it has to be said), we then played in Dallas and Houston. Ashe was part of the line-up of pros on that tour and bore the brunt of some horrific racism that left me shocked to the core. They wouldn't, for example, let him into the clubhouse in Dallas, where the only black people permitted entry were shoe-shiners. We all got changed in a little room somewhere around the back of the building instead. The event in Houston was then cancelled because of Arthur's presence and I recall something similar happening in Buffalo as well. It was horrendous. Donald, who initially captained Ashe in the Davis Cup, was managing him then and did so for 23 years, apparently without signing a contract. Their business relationship, according to Dell, was based on a handshake.

Dell is also famous for negotiating two of the best shoe deals in sporting history. He was behind Stan Smith's tie-in with Adidas and the 'Air Jordan' sponsorship involving Michael Jordan and Nike. Of more relevance here, though, is that he co-founded the ATP and had a huge influence on Kramer and Drysdale during the dispute.

The ATP's plan of action had been crystal clear from the moment the row erupted. They would withdraw their players from the French Open and Wimbledon unless Pilic's suspension was lifted. To be fair, I could see, and support, their argument to a degree. After all, it was in my interests for players to maximise their earnings and, clearly, Pilic was going to make a lot more money in Canada as opposed to a Davis Cup tie. The question centred on whether a boycott was too dramatic a step to take and would it do anything to improve relations between both parties in the long run? Oh, and as British number one, was it right for me to turn my back on Wimbledon?

Over the next few weeks Pilic was allowed to play the French Open when, having contested his suspension, the ban was reduced from nine months to one. He brushed aside all the distractions in Paris to reach the final, before losing to Nastase. Then, due to a technicality, he was allowed to enter the Italian Open in Rome. That concluded the clay-court season but there was no escaping the fact he now had to miss Wimbledon.

At that point the ATP and Pilic filed a suit in the British High Court asking for an injunction to lift the ban, but the judge, Sir Hugh Forbes, ruled that 'there has been no breach of natural justice', and refused to reinstate him, a hugely significant development. Like it or not, you had to respect the British judicial system!

Intense debate followed. The minister for sport, Eldon Griffiths, became involved and tried to bring the sides together but all to no avail.

The ATP board met at the Westbury Hotel in London on the Thursday evening before the Championships during which a suggested compromise was proposed. Drysdale invited three non-board members, Ken Rosewall, Charlie Pasarell and Cliff Richey, to attend, without the right to vote, and suggested that, if the ILTF agreed in writing that ATP members owed first allegiance to their own association, rather than their national association, would the board then be prepared to accept an offer Pilic had made to withdraw from Wimbledon voluntarily and so render a boycott unnecessary?

It became clear very quickly the answer was a resounding no!

That stance, and the ATP's refusal to respect Mr Justice Forbes's court ruling, cost the 'rebels' the support of many involved in the crisis. They were portrayed as the 'bad guys' in the eyes of the media and strengthened the public's view that, to quote the hugely respected writer John Parsons, 'Here was a British institution under attack from a power-crazy organisation dominated by Americans.'

A final meeting on the eve of the Championships between the president of the ILTF, Allan Heyman, the chairman of the All England Club Herman David and Drysdale failed to resolve anything. That led to one final vote by the ATP to determine, once and for all, whether the boycott should be ratified or overturned. Interestingly, Stan Smith, along with two Englishmen on the board, John Barrett and Mark Cox, now voted in favour of playing. Arthur Ashe, Jack Kramer and Jim McManus backed the boycott leaving the casting vote to Drysdale. Incredibly, he decided to abstain and, without a majority decision, the boycott was now inevitable. Drysdale's strategy was considered by many a clever piece of brinksmanship. He didn't want to be held personally responsible for a boycott, but knew a tied vote meant it would go ahead. You could also argue he absolved himself of any responsibility at a critical moment, which, to some, could almost be construed as an act of cowardice. The bottom line was that, for the only time in the tournament's history, the draw had to be made again, with 81 of those originally scheduled to play packing their bags and flying home.

I had, of course, been following the story closely while trying to find peak form for Queen's and Wimbledon. To be perfectly honest, the atmosphere in and around the locker rooms was pretty horrible. Who was going to do what and how severe would the repercussions be, both in terms of player bans and long-term relationships, was all anyone wanted to talk about.

It was at Queen's that Smith, the defending Wimbledon champion, made his threat to me in no uncertain terms. Stan was a big man playing arguably the best tennis of his career and, if he could sacrifice his chances of winning back-to-back titles at SW19, he saw no reason why anyone else should not follow his example and get behind Pilic.

All very well for him but a little one-eyed in my opinion. He did, of course, go on to change his mind in that final vote at the last minute, which seems to have been conveniently forgotten over the passage of time. It's also worth noting that Smith's Wimbledon triumph 12 months earlier had come amidst another boycott. In 1972, most of the best players in the world, the so-called contract pros of which I was one, were unable to compete as a result of an ongoing dispute between the ILTF and World Championship Tennis (WCT).

In reality 73 was a test case, the first of many to be fought between the ATP and the authorities over the control of professional tennis. Mark Cox who, like Smith, changed his mind and voted to go back to the membership in that final meeting has recently talked about the anguish he felt as the debate intensified. He admitted to being 'a bit disingenuous' throughout and, despite deciding to stick with the players for what he felt was the good of the game, couldn't shake off a sense of guilt he felt for being disloyal to the club. Once things died down, he wrote to Herman David, apologising for his stance, and was subsequently banned from a few UK tournaments. He hadn't planned to compete in many, if any, of those anyway so it was of little consequence and both he and John Barrett have gone on to be major figures within the club.

Like them, I was proud to be a member of what in many ways is a magic kingdom and can't emphasise enough how much the Wimbledon fortnight meant, and still means, to me. Growing up in Sheffield, we didn't have a television set. I used to run across to my grandmother's house every afternoon after school to watch the action on her little black-and-white portable. Nothing compared to the Championships and it felt like a dream come true when I moved into the area, bought a house and started competing there.

Wimbledon was part of my DNA and all the more important for me as British number one and flagbearer for the host nation. Looking back, I realise how my day-to-day connection with the club had a direct bearing on my decision-making. Mixing with some of the old guard who made up the bulk of the membership, eminent soldiers who'd fought in the war and risked their lives for their country, led me to question who was going to stand up for this great event and not be bullied into submission. Answer: me.

As a proud Yorkshireman I was angry at the way so much pressure had been exerted on the membership by the ATP hierarchy. I did understand the principle they were fighting for. It was important for players to have more self-determination, but I had been part of the professional game for a number of years by then. Becoming one of 'the Handsome Eight', which we'll come on to later, was a brave decision in itself. It could have led to the end of my career there and then but I took a big risk and it paid off. It also paved the way for the Open Era, so I'd already done my bit in terms of player welfare and my mind was made up.

I've read several reports suggesting I never really knew what I wanted to do, or what I should do as the dispute raged on. That's simply not true, though. It was only as the point of no return materialised that the intense pressure, which had been weighing me down for so long, almost led to a change of course. We had just moved into a lovely new house in Almer Road, around the corner from the club. My father was staying with us, so too Pierre Barthes, the elegant French player with whom I'd become good friends over the years. The phone did not stop ringing, the press was constantly at the door and message after message kept arriving. I was either a villain or the bravest man in Britain with nothing in between! TV and radio coverage was constant; politicians continued to have their say. Headlines called for Kramer to be kicked out of the country. A campaign to raise funds for the YMCA cause in Wimbledon, my first home after moving to London as a teenager, was started. In essence, it was to support British tennis but was primarily a show of solidarity for me. Wherever I turned there was no escape.

The fact my father was a long-time trades unionist added another layer to the narrative. I tried to be as low-key as possible over that and keep him out of the spotlight. Never a man to force his opinion on others, he did warn me as to what would happen if I didn't join the boycott, without at any stage telling me what he thought I should do. He knew all about the power of a union and the downside of falling foul of one. 'You'll be isolated,' he said, 'nobody will talk to you.' We had long chats in our brand-new drawing room and my wife Frances had her say too. She firmly believed I should play, which obviously helped my resolve as did a telegram from the British Lawn Tennis Association.

'As an Englishman you may feel that to an even greater extent than overseas players you are under an obligation to respect the decision of a British court.'

I did.

It was early on the first morning of the Championships that I almost buckled. A thousand thoughts were racing through my mind and amidst the hysteria I looked for the easy way out. Picking up the phone I rang the referee's office to withdraw. The moment I put the phone back down I knew I'd done the wrong thing and immediately rang back to re-book my spot. That shows just how confused I'd become. Call it weakness if you like but I'm not ashamed to admit being torn in two. If you've ever been in a position where you can't win whatever you decide upon, then you'll appreciate the agony I was enduring. And still feel to this day.

Once the decision had been made, and the tennis started, I gradually began to experience a sense of calmness, and indeed righteousness, at doing what I believed was the correct thing.

There were other demons lurking inside my mind, though.

With 81 players missing and so many 'rabbits' thrust into the draw to make up the numbers came a perception from some that I was in it simply to win it. I promise you that wasn't the case at all but, subconsciously, it affected the way I felt on court and contributed to a lot of sloppy play. Too many conflicting emotions took away some of the steely focus that was invariably a trademark of my game.

There is one other aspect of the whole business that riles me to this day and that is how the club has brushed the boycott under the carpet as though it never happened. I recently had dinner with a couple of friends who are members. Keith Wooldridge and Sally Holdsworth are a similar age to me. I asked them both for their recollection of the events of that summer, to which Keith replied, 'Well, it was nothing, was it.' And that is the view of the club. Go into the museum and you'll see no mention of 73. The boycott is a subject that's been closed down and woe betide anyone wanting to rake over it again. I'll always remember standing on the members' balcony during the 1974 Championships and seeing Tim Phillips, a committee man at the time, on his way to becoming chairman, walking along the concourse with his arm protectively draped over the shoulder of who else but Donald Dell. One of the main instigators of the boycott was now being accorded all the respect in the world. Wimbledon was desperate to appease those who'd pulled out 12 months earlier, but has the club, or indeed the LTA whose event it actually is, ever shown an ounce of gratitude to me for playing that year in the face of so much opposition from my contemporaries? Not a chance.

How I played competitive tennis during that turbulent three-week period remains a mystery to me. Somehow, I retained sufficient focus at Queen's to beat John Alexander of Australia, Ashe, Drysdale in the quarter-finals and then another Aussie, Owen Davidson, in the last four, dropping just one set along the way.

That set up a showdown with Ilie Nastase and a chance to avenge my defeat at his hands in Paris a few days earlier. I received a standing ovation from the crowd as I walked out for the final and gave as good as I got in the first set before eventually having to settle for second best at the hands of the Romanian maverick; 9-8, 6-3 the final score. What I recall most about that afternoon are the bizarre antics of Jim McManus. A US Open doubles semi-finalist in 1968 and a founding member of the ATP, he was proving to be particularly outspoken amidst all the bickering. Furious at my decision to enter Wimbledon, he tried to ruin the occasion by persistently ringing the bell on the pavilion at Queen's throughout the match. (The bell is there to announce the end of play to members the rest of the year.) It was extraordinary. I deliberately ignored what he was doing and walked straight past him afterwards without so much as glancing in his direction. But it's an indication of how unpleasant everything was becoming.

It was the second time in six years I finished runner-up at Queen's. Back in 1967 I played some brilliant tennis at a venue I've always felt so comfortable at. In the end I lost to my nemesis John Newcombe that year – he beat me in 23 of our 29 encounters. But there was no time for regret at another near miss in 1973. With Wimbledon one day away I had too many other things on my mind.

The mass exodus of players meant I'd been propelled from number 16 to third seed, behind Nastase and Jan Kodes. Ilie was the biggest name remaining. He claimed that, as a member of the Romanian army, he had no choice but to compete. A conspiracy theory still prevails suggesting he deliberately went on to lose to Sandy Mayer in the fourth round but I've no idea if there's an ounce of truth in that suggestion. I was isolated from everything else happening, in a cocoon, just trying to deal with what I had to do.

Jimmy Connors, who, ironically, was banned from the French Open a year later due to his involvement with World Team Tennis, was another star on show and, despite the boycott, the eventual attendance for the fortnight was in excess of 300,000, the second highest in the Championship's history up to that point.

I received a thunderous ovation from the Royal Box, led by the Duke and Duchess of Kent, when I played on Centre Court in round one and that was repeated match by match. It meant a lot. As at Queen's the week before, I was able to play some very good tennis despite the hullabaloo. After defeating Jean-Louis Haillet of France, I comfortably beat West Germany's Harald Elschenbroich, followed by the Czech player Jiri Hrebec. American Robert McKinley provided some stern resistance in the fourth round but victory over him took me through to the quarter-finals and one of the most memorable encounters of my whole career.

Amidst the gloom of the boycott there had been one golden ray of sunshine at the Championships, provided by a young, long-haired and very good-looking Swede. Bjorn Borg first played Davis Cup for his country at the age of 15 and had already made an impression at the French Open by the time he arrived at Wimbledon that June. Under the shrewd guidance of former player-turned-coach Lennart Bergelin, the 17-year-old – too young to be an ATP member, –had all the skills required to become a superstar. The first of six French titles was less than a year away and he'd only have to wait three more summers for the first of his five successive Wimbledon crowns.

We hadn't crossed swords prior to then but I'd watched him in Paris and knew straightaway, as was the case when Carlos Alcaraz first burst on to the scene in recent years, that he was heading to the very top.

I only ever played Bjorn twice but our first match was extraordinary for a number of reasons. The setting obviously helped: a last-eight duel at Wimbledon featuring the great British hope and a thrilling new star of the game. It was a real clash of styles too. Already considered a veteran, I was reliant on my attacking serve-and-volley instincts. Borg, by contrast, set up camp on the baseline but kept me guessing with his extravagant topspin and breathtaking go-for-broke winners whenever a chance presented itself. Understandably the crowd was with me but you couldn't help but notice, and hear, the looks of adoration and screams of support from a teenage female contingent, which had been stalking him at every opportunity during the tournament, reviving memories of Beatlemania. With precious little security around the grounds in those days, that had often led to pandemonium.

I raced through the first set but, not helped by an excessive number of double faults, then found myself down by two sets to one. There was a reason for those doubles that I've already alluded to. The swirling controversy of the boycott had left me in a perpetual state of confusion and, strange as this will sound, there was a part of me that didn't want to win. At the same time, of course, I was desperate to!

Bjorn had already played two five-setters, against Karl Meiler of Germany and Hungary's Szabolcs Baranyi, so I still fancied my chances of grinding him down. Sure enough, one break to love gave me the fourth set. Bjorn swung so hard at a ball in that game he shattered his racket!

It then looked as though I was going to stroll through the decider and at 5-1, 15-40 on his serve it was all but over. Not that you can, or should, ever take anything for granted on a tennis court. He saved both match points with an acrobatic winner followed by an ace and, almost before I knew what had happened, we were level at five-all.

As a self-effacing Yorkshireman I'm not inclined to big myself up too much but determination is one of my great strengths and I promptly demonstrated that, by breaking him again to lead 6-5.

Moments later two more match points were on my racket only for me to blow the first with another double fault.

The next serve was judged by the umpire and line judge to be an ace and that, technically, was that.

'Game, set and match Taylor,' said the umpire.

Borg simply looked at him in disbelief, indicating the ball had missed the line.

And I knew he was right. I could see the serve was out.

So, what should I do? The officials clearly weren't going to listen to him. The umpire said 'Game, set and match Taylor' for a second time and there was nothing in the world to stop me from going to the net, shaking hands and looking forward to a semi-final. Yet, after everything else such a turbulent fortnight had thrown at me, the thought of claiming victory on a ball that landed even fractionally out was unthinkable.

So, I called a fault against myself, to the total bewilderment of the officials and spectators. It's not something I had ever done before, and I never did it again, but I could see no other satisfactory resolution. My heart was pounding but my head was clear. Murmurs of incredulity followed as the crowd worked out what was going on. Play eventually continued, now with an added layer of tension to heighten what had already been an electrifying atmosphere.

Borg then clubbed a backhand winner and from 40-15 got it back to deuce. I could easily have panicked but felt strangely calm, knowing I'd done the right thing. A service winner brought up match point number five and this time, thanks to a backhand error, I crossed the winning line, legitimately, 6-1, 6-8, 3-6, 6-3, 7-5.

The reaction from the press afterwards was incredibly positive. I was put on a pedestal for replaying the point in such dramatic circumstances and lauded for giving the nation a real chance to finally celebrate a home-grown champion for the first time since the war. The point was also made more than once that while many of my ATP colleagues had turned their backs on me for playing at all, for many in the UK my decision was considered an act of bravery. Several newspaper headlines branded me 'the man who saved Wimbledon'. That looked and sounded good, really good.

Chapter 9

5 July 1973, Wimbledon Semi-Final. Roger Taylor v Jan Kodes (Part E)

BACK IN the locker room I sit down with no idea what to do. Are we done for the day? Should I have something to eat in case it's only a short delay? There's no one around to ask. Over in the corner I see Jan chatting to a couple of people, one of whom is giving him a massage. Who are they and why have they been allowed inside the locker room? I'm unsettled by that. Is he breaching the rules? What the hell are they telling him?

I wait, and try to stay focused. The minutes tick by with no update. It's getting on for three quarters of an hour now. Fairly sure we'll be coming back in the morning, I get ready to jump into the shower.

Which is a bad mistake.

After precisely 42 minutes and without any warning, there's a loud cry from Captain Gibson. 'Taylor, back on court now.'

No airs and graces, no special treatment for a British number one. Just get back out there and never mind that it's dark, the court is still slippery and quite a lot of people have already decided to go home. Is that the right way to treat a man trying to end 37 years of hurt?

There's no choice. I put on one of the two clean shirts Frances went home to fetch during the delay, which have been handed to me, grab my bag and head back out.

But I've lost focus and realise it straightaway. The atmosphere's flat and my mind is wandering. He's in the zone, though, constantly going to my backhand while remaining solid and risk-averse.

Kodes holds for 5-5. Then he breaks straightaway. One minute he's serving to stay in it. Now, he's serving for it.

Eight minutes and three games after the restart, and despite saving two match points, it's over before I know what's happened.

All those hopes snatched away in the blink of an eye; a sickening sensation after everything I'd experienced and imagined. I go through the motions. Shake hands at the net while mumbling something coherent. Remember to thank the umpire. Acknowledge the crowd; retain some dignity while flinging everything into the bag. Head back inside and begin the post-mortem. Let me wake up. Tell me it's a horrible dream. It's not, though. Instead, it's the end of the dream.

Chapter 10

So Near and Yet So Far

IT TOOK the best part of three days to come to terms with that loss. Tell a lie. I still haven't really come to terms with it, or the whole boycott saga. Over the following 72 hours I kept reliving key moments. Could I have refused to go back out after the rain delay? Should I have refused? I replayed that in my mind several times during Tim Henman's rain-affected semi with Goran Ivanisevic in 2001 and again when Rafael Nadal and Novak Djokovic contested the 2012 French Open Final. On that occasion Novak was fighting back as conditions deteriorated. It started to rain and the balls got heavier, which wasn't to Rafa's liking. He put a lot of pressure on the umpire to suspend play, which is what duly happened. When they eventually resumed in drier conditions, the Spaniard regained the ascendancy and went on to win.

Of course, a show of player power and any attempts to influence the officials wasn't the 'done thing' under Captain Gibson or Colonel so-and-so: the club was full of military personnel in influential positions back then. Never trust a man who holds on to his military title in peace-time! Cruel defeats are part of the job. That goes without saying. This was the worst one, though, and it gnawed away at me at a time when the bitterness of the boycott had already had a significant effect on my psyche.

It was a miserable end to an extraordinary chapter in my life and there are painful reminders whenever I visit Wimbledon. I couldn't bring myself to watch the final against Alex Metreveli, whom I would have been very confident of beating, but know the details of Jan's 6-1, 9-8, 6-3 win because his name jumps out at me whenever I pass the honours board. Usually I look away but every now and then I stare back and wonder ... what if? A Wimbledon title would have changed my life forever but that's the beauty, and cruelty, of sport. I try not to dwell too often on what might have been. But I'm only human. A few weeks later I discovered it was one of the players I'd most looked up to as a kid, 1954 Wimbledon champion Jaroslav Drobny, who'd given Kodes a long pep talk prior to the match. A fellow left-hander, he'd kindly taken an interest in my development but knew the areas to exploit. I didn't hold it against him. As a fellow Czech he was always going to be in the opposition camp.

Niki Pilic didn't speak to me for a year after the Championships, and other relationships, notably those with Stan Smith and Cliff Drysdale, never recovered. I'd make the same decision again, though. A $5,000 fine by the ATP for breaking the boycott added insult to injury. It was a substantial sum of money, which Wimbledon took care of. I'm grateful to the club for that.

The world is full of 'politicians' who slither about the place, playing the game. I've come across plenty during my time in tennis. It's not me, though. I've always been my own man, for better or for worse, and if that's cost me along the way, then so be it. Times were very different, attitudes still largely conservative. I couldn't come out smelling of roses either way and wouldn't wish the sort of stress and aggravation I experienced on anyone. It left a scar that will never fully heal and has given me fresh nightmares while putting all this down on paper as the memories come flooding back. The subsequent lack of respect shown to me by the club hurts to this day. My decision to play, at great personal cost, should not have been overlooked then or now. Poor old Herman David died in February of the following year and I'm sure the stress of it all was a primary factor. He alone knew what I had gone through and would have backed me to the hilt as the dust settled but, under new management, the club was desperate to appease and welcome back those big names in 1974.

My part in it all was quietly forgotten. Kramer issued a hard-nosed summary in his 1979 memoirs. 'Roger,' he said, 'punished himself enough for his decision. He had been a good player – the first rank off the top – but he never amounted to a thing after Wimbledon 73.' Easy to say. And he's right to a degree. What I didn't know on that sultry July afternoon while walking back to the locker room after beating Bjorn, vaguely aware of the screams of his teenybopper army, was that I would never win another singles match at the Championships again. Jack had no idea what a damaging effect the whole wretched saga had on me and, to be honest, nor did I at the time.

Now, though, I realise just how debilitating it was and I can't help but feel angry and frustrated. Over the following weeks I turned down the chance to appear on three of the most popular shows in the country, *Through the Keyhole*, *Desert Island Discs* and *This is Your Life*. Despondent and demoralised, the world seemed a dark place and I had no wish to show my face in public. Some may point to my lack of success at the Championships thereafter as proof that, deep down, I knew I was guilty of an error of judgement in deciding to play. John Lloyd has claimed he greatly regrets his decision not to back the boycott. It's easy to say that with the benefit of hindsight but I stand by my actions. There were compelling arguments on both sides. I was caught in the middle and inevitably became a villain to some. For others, though, I was the man who saved Wimbledon and that's alright by me.

Chapter 11

Fred and Andy – the Best of British

IT GOES without saying I'd much rather have been the man to **win** Wimbledon. We had to wait an awful lot longer, before Andy Murray eventually followed in Fred Perry's footsteps on that never-to-be-forgotten afternoon in 2013. I'm lucky enough to have known our two 'greats' quite well and have an enormous amount of admiration for both, even if neither was perfect.

Fred used to turn up at the office or warehouse every now and then while I was working about the place. You'd know he was there straightaway because of the sweet smell of the tobacco used in his constantly lit pipe. Fred usually wore this long beige coat, almost like a dressing gown, and was friendly when chatting to us during those early days in London. He had a presence you'd expect from a sporting legend who won Wimbledon three years running, in 1934, 35 and 36. A tall man at around 6ft 3in, he played the game beautifully, with balance, a wide variety of shots and a huge amount of confidence. On top of those Wimbledon titles, he won the Aussie and French Opens, the US Open three times, enjoyed great success as a doubles player and represented Great Britain with distinction in the Davis Cup, winning that trophy four years running between 1933 and 36. Oh, and just for good measure he was also table tennis world champion in 1929.

There was an American lilt to his voice, which resulted from the many years he spent living across the pond. As my career developed, we became quite friendly and there were obvious similarities between us. He'd grown up as a working-class lad across the Pennines from Sheffield in Stockport, Lancashire and didn't have things all his own way tennis-wise. Fred's daughter Penny spoke about the great tennis divide that I also experienced. 'It was like being in two completely different continents – north of Watford and south of Watford.' She added that, 'Fred went belligerent with it. His defence was to go on the offence.'

There's no doubt he could be quite fiery at times, and upset the hierarchy when turning professional in the late 1930s. His decision to leave the UK and take up American citizenship just before the Second World War didn't sit well with many in the establishment but, having become a pro, he needed to make a living. He joined the US Air Force during the war but was fiercely patriotic and I vividly recall being shocked when talking about him at an All England Club lunch I attended while still a young man. I sat next to an elderly committee member who wasn't the easiest person to engage with. Looking for some safe ground I steered the conversation around to Fred and asked just how wonderful a player he had been to win all those titles. This fellow stared straight back at me, hesitated, frowned and then said, 'Fred had a bad war you know.' And that was it! I didn't know what to say but subsequently heard similar sentiments and rumours of his unpopularity within sections of the club.

Fred's Wimbledon membership was rescinded as soon as he turned pro and it was only towards the end of his life that feelings mellowed and Wimbledon commissioned the famous statue, which meant the world to him. 'I never thought I'd live to see the day when a statue was put up to the son of a Labour MP inside the manicured grounds of Wimbledon,' he wrote in his autobiography, before adding, 'There will be a few former members of the All England Club and the LTA revolving in their graves at the thought of such a tribute paid to the man they regarded as a rebel from the wrong side of the tennis tramlines.'

I was interested to see an article featuring his daughter Penny some years back in which she admitted her father might have 'felt a twinge of regret had he been alive when Andy Murray took his mantle as the last British man to win Wimbledon'. When I peaked in the late 60s and early 70s there was a feeling on my part that he saw me as a potential threat to his Wimbledon legacy. Don't get me wrong, there was never any animosity and he invariably came up to congratulate me after a good win. Maybe it was just my imagination but I couldn't help but suspect, deep down, he was backing my opponent. It was a hunch that stayed with me throughout my career. Despite all that, we stayed in contact and I'd see him on the rare occasions he came over from the States. Towards the end of his life he was due to open some new courts at Queen's Club but was too ill to attend. I gave him a call to check on his condition and we had a lovely conversation during which he said, 'I don't want anyone else other than you, Roger, to open those courts. It would mean a lot if you could take my place.' Naturally, I did, and his warmth during that call in turn meant a lot to me.

Goodness knows how many times I've been asked to name the greatest British player of all. You can only beat those put in front of you and Fred's era was so completely different to today. I'm old enough to have known Fred well, though not so old as to have been able to watch him live, I hasten to add! And I'm fortunate enough to have seen Andy Murray emerge and play his part so magnificently while facing the might of Roger Federer, Rafael Nadal and Novak Djokovic in their prime.

We'll come on to my time in charge of the Great Britain Davis Cup team in more detail later, which is when I first spoke to Andy. Ahead of a 2003 tie against Morocco in Casablanca we had some injury problems which prompted me to call Murray and see if he'd like to be involved with the squad. When I first played for Great Britain, we had a tradition of including our top juniors, not to play but to benefit from the experience of being involved, a tactic which had worked very well for the Australians in particular. At that point nobody knew just how good he was going to become. I was a little surprised when he said the pursuit of ATP points was his priority, but I didn't push him into joining up. A few months later he won the 2004 Junior US Open title to reach number one in the rankings, beating, amongst others, Juan Martin Del Potro, Sam Querrey, Mischa Zverev and Sergiy Stakhovsky in the final. Had I been aware just how talented he was at such a precocious age I'd have promised him at least one match during that Davis Cup tie rather than just the opportunity to enjoy the experience of being a hitting partner for the week but there's the benefit of hindsight for you.

Not long afterwards, I saw him playing in Didsbury, I think against Arvind Parmar, and the full extent of his ability immediately became clear. Even then I thought he'd reach the top of the game but it inevitably took a while to improve his fitness and become the iron man (with the metal hip) that, for me, made him one of the greatest competitors in the history of the sport. Following his progress was an incredible adventure but he made some strange decisions along the way. No doubt I'll be criticised for this but I never understood why he turned to Amelie Mauresmo when at the peak of his powers. What was that all about? I know Andy has always fought for gender equality and respect that completely. It was a groundbreaking appointment when they teamed up in the summer of 2014, by which stage he'd already won two slam titles and a gold medal at the London Olympics. During their two years in tandem he reached two more Australian Open finals and had some excellent results on clay. But I never understood her role. Was she going to teach him to serve and volley? Could she control his volatility on court? (The answer to that was a definite no.) You don't teach players new tricks at that level but, for them to listen and adapt in subtle ways, there has to be an infinite amount of respect or the coach becomes a mumbling wreck, leading to the whole process breaking down. Mauresmo was a wonderful player in her own right but not, in my opinion, the correct fit for Andy at that stage of his career.

His inability to stop screaming at his box over the years also surprised me. Yes, we are all hard-wired in different ways but he hated himself for doing it and I, for one, would not have put up with that sort of behaviour if I'd been part of his team. He constantly got away with it because, more often than not, he was winning, but the game needs to crack down on some of the overt on-court aggression that's almost become commonplace. I was pleased to see Andrey Rublev disqualified in Dubai in 2024 for his verbal onslaught at a line judge, though I was equally moved by his searingly honest admission early in 2025 that he has been fighting a lot of inner demons. Frances Tiafoe and Sascha Zverev are two other players who have gone way over the top. Going back some years Serena Williams sailed dangerously close to the wind several times as well. No umpire, good or bad, deserves to be on the receiving end of a barrage of abuse in a working environment, and the same goes for coaches and support staff. Unless you stamp down on it, the next generation of players assume it's acceptable and the cycle continues.

The only time Andy really got that side of his game under control was during Ivan Lendl's first coaching stint, which coincided with his very best results. The mutual respect was clear to see and paved the way for a number of other super-coaches in the game, such as Boris Becker and then Goran Ivanisevic with Djokovic, Carlos Moya, Michael Chang and Richard Krajicek. Lendl made it clear he would not accept any backchat. At the time, sports psychologist Don Macpherson commented, 'When Murray looks up at his team and his monkey mind is just about to shout abuse, he suddenly sees the brooding, unsmiling Lendl, and the monkey backs down every time ... out of respect.' And there's that keyword again. Respect. Without that, a coach has nothing.

I don't want to dwell on the negatives, though. Andy was inspirational in many other ways, became so fit, and invented defence at the next level. Whenever I think of him, I picture his extraordinary coverage at the back of the court, running along the baseline to retrieve one seemingly hopeless cause, then turning so smoothly and speedily to hare back the other way and keep a point going, before, invariably, finding a way to win it. That was phenomenal, so too his anticipation, which was a real gift, that brilliant double-handed backhand of his and the remarkable desire that burned strongly inside him to the very end of his career.

His belief and sheer bloody-mindedness used to make me think about my old mate Dickie Dillon. I never understood, until he flew over from his home in the States to see me recently, why he didn't volunteer to come with Barry and me to the south of France for our trip and also why his playing days came to an end so suddenly in his early 20s. Dickie and I were extremely competitive as youngsters and were of a very similar level. He played at Wimbledon a year before me, as a qualifier in 1959, and journeyed down to London with the same dreams and aspirations that filled my mind. But then the doubts crept in. He kept losing tight matches and the confidence drained out of him, which is horrible for anyone trying to make a living in sport. One day he was in the warehouse when Fred showed up. They had a chat, talked about how well I was doing and what a struggle it was proving to be for Dick on the back of all his recent losses. Fred turned, looked him in the eye and said, 'Dickie, you're just not enough of a bastard to be a good tennis player.' There, from one of the all-time greats, was the confirmation he needed, painful as it was to acknowledge at the time.

And I suppose it means I am a bit of a bastard!

Chapter 12

The Good, the Sad and the Ugly

THERE'S NO doubt that Dickie was my first, and greatest, friend in the tennis world. He was there for me early on, helped enormously during some of those dark months after the boycott and we remain close to this day, even though Dickie has lived in the States for several decades. I also want to give a huge shout-out to another lifelong friend Bob Hill. His father, Frank, used to drive us to various tournaments as kids and we remain in regular contact despite his decision to live in Canada, where he pursued a very successful academic career. The three of us shared some wonderful times and I'm blessed to have known two such fine men.

Inevitably, though, as my game developed so I began to forge friendships with those I met, and started to play against, many of whom would also remain part of my life for the next 50 years.

The Good

Having never had a full-time coach I relied heavily on watching and learning from those around me and was lucky to have some excellent role models. Billy Knight was six years older and a prolific winner with almost 50 career singles titles. He won the mixed doubles at the French Championships and also enjoyed a run to the quarter-finals in the singles there. Clay was his favourite surface, though he liked grass too and reached the round of 16 at Wimbledon four times having burst on to the scene as a junior in the early 50s by winning the boys' titles at Wimbledon, and also in Australia, where he beat Roy Emerson in the final. By then he'd already won the English table tennis title as well; not bad for a youngster. As impressive as those achievements were, I was surprised to see a newspaper headline a couple of years ago proclaiming that Al Pacino was going to star in *Billy Knight* the movie. It turned out that film centred on the history of cinema rather than Billy's life but he was quite a character nonetheless and Pacino would have been a good fit for the part. Tough and rugged on court, Billy knew how to scrap, particularly on clay. He was a lefty and, like me, had a weaker backhand so I learnt a lot by studying his approach whenever I could. He demonstrated the value of fighting for every point and I can vividly recall some of his victories when becoming British Hard Court champion in 1958, 63 and 64. To win the Hamburg Open on clay in 1959 was another notable achievement and I hope he looked back on his Manchester doubles title of 1963 with particular pride. Alongside Mike Sangster he beat Charlie Applewhaite and me 6-4, 8-10, 6-2 in the final.

That defeat was nothing to be ashamed of. Sangster had a fantastic serve and, with his sharp dress sense, exuded a certain charisma, having become the first British guy to win a tournament in Australia. I was back home when that happened and thought it amazing because he had to beat some of their best players along the way. Mike was a big fellow, around 6ft 2in, and compiled some really consistent results in the slams, making the semis at the French, Wimbledon and US Open and the quarters in Australia. He reached the final of the doubles in New York with Graham Stillwell in 1964 and was a really good team man as his Davis Cup record would suggest. He played 65 matches, more than any other Brit, and I'd love to know how fast he would have served in the modern era. Back then he sent one down at 154mph. It was such a ferocious weapon that even the great Rod Laver once found himself caught up in the netting at the back of the court, so far had he retreated to try to get racket on ball.

Mike, who came from Devon, could have been a footballer. He was offered a contract by West Ham before deciding to focus on tennis and developed his game under Arthur Roberts, who later guided Sue Barker to the top of the tree. Polite, respectful and such a talent, Mike died at the age of 44 while playing golf. It was a devastating blow for everyone who knew him.

Talking of talent brings me to Bobby Wilson, who had the most wonderful touch and tended to become embroiled in epic matches which would often go the distance. With his receding hair-line he always looked older than he actually was and I'm sure there are some who feel, with so much ability at his disposal, he could have achieved even more in the game, having also made an early impact by becoming Wimbledon junior champion. Bobby admitted he lacked a killer instinct and enjoyed playing more than winning which, in some ways, must be wonderful. Mind you, quarter-final runs at the French, Wimbledon four times and the US twice isn't a shabby record. Nor is reaching the Wimbledon doubles final in 1960 and representing his country in 34 Davis Cup ties. Bobby loved the sport and carried on coaching in his native north London until shortly before he passed away, aged 84, in 2020.

For those of a certain generation, the name Alan Mills will immediately evoke memories of an elegant man with a walkie-talkie popping his head out from the back of Centre Court as a precursor to rain stopping play. Alan was the Wimbledon referee for 22 years, between 1983 and 2005, and received a fair amount of grief from those who blamed him for all the bad weather during those roofless times. I remember his smooth game and quiet determination to cause an upset whenever our paths crossed.

Alan was the sort of opponent I knew I had to beat to make an impact. Usually, I came out on top but it was rarely straightforward on that British circuit, be it in Birmingham, Leamington Spa or even the Torquay Palace Hotel which staged one of the most extraordinary events during that era. How they put the tournament together I still don't know. It was a beautiful place with delightful gardens that included a putting green and two indoor wooden courts. It was staged in the middle of winter and went on throughout the day … and night! There was so little tennis anywhere else at that time of the year so we all turned up, stayed in the hotel and sometimes started matches at four o'clock in the morning. You'd go to bed and receive a call in the wee small hours saying, 'Mr Taylor, you're on court in 20 minutes.' It may sound rather relaxed and antiquated now but, although there were no points or prize money at stake, we took it seriously and I recall immense satisfaction at beating Mike Sangster in the final one year. His huge serve was a monster on those indoor courts but, somehow, I tamed it to beat the local hero.

Alan Mills was a regular in Torquay. He became the first Englishman to beat Rod Laver, in 1961, and the first man to win a Davis Cup tie 6-0, 6-0, 6-0. It took him 32 minutes and clearly wasn't a day Luxembourg's Joseph Offenheim subsequently reflected upon with any great fondness.

We were all mates and there was seldom any tension or niggles between us. Those Davis Cup ties helped the bonding process and although we had to play each other quite often during the course of a season, there was enough camaraderie to prevent any feuds or long-term bitterness. In my early days on the team I'd often be asked to play an exhibition set, which was staged in the middle of the tie. It didn't count for anything but was an opportunity to make a mark and I did well in those, which really helped me to settle. Life in general was more relaxed. I may be romanticising things but everything seemed much more straightforward back then. The first year I made the semis at Wimbledon in 67 is an example of that, and far removed from how things are now. I was staying with friends in Earl's Court and, every evening, we'd go to a pub nearby called the Hansom Cab, which is still going strong nearly 60 years on. I had a couple of pints on the first night of the Championships and, being superstitious as just about all tennis players are, it meant I had to go back every night and repeat the process. When I finally lost in the semis at the end of week two, my mate Reg Bennett checked that I'd still be going to the pub that night and, when I turned up, they gave me a tankard engraved with all my results from the fortnight. Such a lovely touch and I still drink out of it to this day. That gives you an indication of how things were. It was much more relaxed, off court at least, and I cherish the lasting friendships with so many of those I played against and keep in touch with to this day, if possible.

One of those is Mark Cox who, it's fair to say, was probably my biggest domestic rival over a sustained period in the late 60s and early 70s. We were different in a lot of ways although Mark's upbringing, initially at least, wasn't so very far removed from mine. When discussing our relative merits, most articles would make comparisons between the son of a Sheffield steelworker and the privately schooled and Cambridge-educated aristocrat, attributing that as the primary reason for an obvious lack of warmth between us on and off court. In actual fact Mark grew up in the backstreets of Leicester, living in a terraced house rather similar to mine with an outdoor toilet. The big difference was that his county supported him from a very early age, and it was through Leicestershire tennis that he ended up going to the prestigious Millfield School in Somerset before studying economics at Cambridge. That academic path was in total contrast to my 'lessons in life' degree at the YMCA and there is no doubt we shared precious little in common. Mark considered me overly competitive and antagonistic when we played and I can't really blame him. I had to fight tooth and nail and be confrontational when necessary. If there was an opportunity to get under the skin of an opponent, I'd look to do it, within the laws of the game. Every match I played had an intensity that I also took on to the practice court and my training sessions. The likes of Jack Kramer may say I was never a great player but I was definitely a great competitor and if that was unpalatable for some then so be it. Those looking for empathy wouldn't find it from me, which isn't to say I disrespected the opposition or simply spoiled for a fight. It was an essential ingredient in my make-up that I make no apology for. The great writer Rex Bellamy, himself from Sheffield, once wrote: 'Taylor is tall, dark and handsome. He is a characteristic Yorkshireman in that he is something of a loner, a man who takes an independent line without making a fuss. He comes from industrial Sheffield where a youngster learns to use his fists as soon as he can walk without a harness. Two of the most impressive things about Taylor are his shoulders. When he comes into a room you notice the shoulders first, then Taylor. He's a good man to have in your corner when trouble starts.'

That's a fair assessment. I was a bit of a loner, admit to being intensely competitive and could be quite demanding as a doubles partner. Having built up those shoulders lugging heavy boxes across town while working for Fred Perry, then why not use them to my advantage? It was survival of the fittest ... and I was always one of those.

Although I was a year and a half older, Mark had already established himself as a player by the time I found my bearings in London and he was better than me in those early days. There was no socialising at all to begin with, just an immediate awareness that he was one of the guys I had to match up with to be taken seriously. Later on, we played against and alongside each other on a regular basis but, being lefties, never formed a truly effective doubles partnership. I remember one particular team trip to New Zealand where we started opening up to one another a little more and there were never any serious clashes or fallings-out. It was just a case of two guys with very differing personalities who invariably went their separate ways at the end of a day. I liked to have a couple of beers, he didn't, but that was fine, and we had a few special moments as a doubles team at Wimbledon and also in Mexico City where we beat John Newcombe and Tony Roche. You don't have to sing from the same hymn sheet to appreciate someone and a mutual respect was always evident, even if you sometimes had to look quite hard to find it.

He actually won our first four encounters and two of the last three in 1977 but I had a good run against him in 72 and 73, which included an epic quarter-final in Copenhagen en route to my first professional title. It finished in my favour 6-4, 6-7, 7-6 and I'm not ashamed to admit there were a couple of moments of good fortune for me at the start of the deciding tie-break. But you make your own luck and that was a really big win, which meant I became only the second unseeded player to win a WCT tournament.

Mark is a genuinely nice person, which made his occasional blow-ups, and I mean proper blow-ups, on court all the more surprising. Steam did come out of his ears but he never behaved in a threatening manner and can be proud of a fine career. He may describe himself as nothing more than 'a journeyman player' but that's not true. Winning ten top-level career titles, reaching 12 in the world and being a key member of the Great Britain team that reached the Davis Cup Final in 1969 and 1978 elevates him beyond that description. However, when it comes to making an overall assessment of a British player, or indeed any player, I look closely at their Wimbledon record. It tells you a lot because the Championships tend to provide the ultimate test of character and beating the top players there requires something special. Mark's record was relatively modest. He made the fourth round on three occasions, losing to Rod Laver in 68, Billy Martin 9-7 in the fifth set in 77 and 2, 2 and 1 to Jimmy Connors in 1979. His record is similar to Greg Rusedski's, who never found his best form at SW19, reaching the quarter-finals only once despite having such a good game for grass. Maybe I was simply too fixated on those two weeks. As mentioned before, I'd train on Christmas Day with a long run around Wimbledon Common, believing that would help give me an edge six months later come the key moments in a tight contest on the grass. It meant I was always ready to give my best and I'm sure Mark was too. Everyone is different and he recorded some fantastic results. It's all about dealing with pressure when it matters, though – that's what makes the difference between really good and great players.

We continued to play together well into our 70s. It was during the World Championships in our age category a few years ago that Mark was taken ill. The format was a team event during week one followed by an individual competition. He played okay in the team part of it, watched by his wife, Susie, who has herself struggled with ill health in recent years. They then went home early and, the following Tuesday, Mark suffered quite a serious stroke. Nobody saw him for some time so I rang and offered to help in any way I could. He was keen to get back on court and we started to hit on a regular basis, playing cross-court drills with a winner and a loser to make it as competitive as possible. He improved very quickly, which was great to see. Afterwards we would have a cup of tea before he rushed off to look after his wife. I know he was both touched and surprised when I called him, later saying it illustrated a level of caring he had never previously attributed to me. I understand that because I am a hard person to get to know and kept the shutters down between us for years. Becoming friends after so long and hearing him describe me as one of the best British players of all time meant a lot. It felt great to play a positive part in the life of a man who certainly played his part in mine.

The Sad

Where to start with Christopher 'Buster' Mottram? Well, a few basic facts to begin with. He reached a career-high singles ranking of 15 in 1983, won a couple of singles titles, five more as a doubles player and finished with an excellent Davis Cup record. In 19 ties he won 27 of his 35 singles matches and four from six in doubles, beating some very good players along the way.

That was Buster the tennis player. Then there was Buster the man.

Extreme in his views, he had an affiliation to the National Front at one point and a tendency to fall out with people on a regular basis. He was complex, to say the least, and in some ways a victim of his own naivety and desire to be liked. But, for all his foibles, I did like him.

At 6ft 3in, Buster was an imposing figure who came from a tennis-driven family. His father, Tony, for many years a national coach, ensured that both he and his sister Linda, who reached the third round at Wimbledon and the Australian Open and was a doubles quarter-finalist at the All England Club as well, had excellent techniques, albeit taught in a very rigid fashion. I knew Buster as a junior initially and hit with him quite a lot at Queen's Club. It was fascinating to watch him because he wasn't naturally talented yet had the ability to listen and learn. He did everything just as the textbook would tell you, which is no bad thing. Buster spent hours and hours on court while his dad drilled him in an old-fashioned but effective way with tin cans and all the rest of it but what really made him stand out from the other British players was his excellence on clay. He could be brilliant, and I mean brilliant, on the dirt but had a hang-up about Wimbledon because he liked perfect surfaces and couldn't come to terms with some of the awful bounces you get, on grass in particular. And, let's be honest, he had a few other hang-ups as well.

Buster was a member of the Wimbledon Club, which is just across the road from Wimbledon itself. He often used to change there before coming over to play during the Championships, even if he happened to be scheduled on Centre Court. I once noticed him marching across the road with two rackets under his arm ahead of one big match and couldn't believe what I was seeing. But that was Buster! Always a little bit different. I have a theory that some of his angst stemmed from what happened in the Wimbledon Boys' Final of 1972 against Bjorn Borg. Buster recovered from a set down to lead 5-2 in the third before losing the next five games and with it the match, a hammer blow for a 17-year-old being touted as Britain's brightest prospect since Fred Perry. It does go to show just how good a player he was back then, as well as being a fine competitor.

You couldn't escape the baggage, though. Playing with him on court was rarely a problem and I enjoyed teaming up in doubles, as well as watching him beat some of the game's greats. And on a one-to-one basis I found him to be good company. He could be funny, often playing up to the caricature he quickly established for himself, especially in front of an American audience, which invariably found him very amusing. Buster never forced his extreme politics on me either but publicly expressing his opinion was, of course, a recipe for disaster in the years immediately after Enoch Powell's 'Rivers of Blood' speech. Davis Cup ties became increasingly fraught affairs with captain Paul Hutchins having to monitor his every move and check every message Buster was sending out, to avoid diplomatic incidents. There was an undeniable naivety to him. He'd share his thoughts with the press thinking they were his friends only to see a very different story appear the next day and it goes without saying that he should have known better. I remember one quote in which he declared, 'I hope Enoch Powell will never die, just as his namesake in the bible never died.' That, I believe, was a reference to Genesis 5:18-24 which states that Enoch lived for 365 years. None of us shared his politics in any way, which inevitably left the team feeling very uncomfortable while also trying to remain as protective as possible of a colleague.

I wasn't in the squad come 1978 when, against all expectations, Great Britain went on a fantastic run in the Davis Cup. Buster beat Tony Roche in the semis and Brian Gottfried after a five-set marathon in the final before the United States came out on top 4-1 with a young John McEnroe head and shoulders above the rest. Buster had returned to the team that year after an 18-month absence following a bust-up with Paul Hutchins and was at loggerheads with David Lloyd, who called him, amongst other things, 'a tennis tragic'. Now, at the time, Buster was actually campaigning for me to succeed Hutchins as captain, without my knowledge I should add. That left me in a slightly awkward position and Buster's never-ending crop of headlines kept him firmly in the spotlight. There were anti-Nazi protests at some of the Davis Cup ties that year with banners proclaiming 'Buster Mottram is a Nazi' and 'Heil Adolf Mottram'. Flour bombs interrupted the tie against Austria in June, which was staged at the Bristol Tennis and Squash Centre, and he was the subject of constant barracking by the crowd. Yet he was able to put all that to one side and lead from the front. When on song he really could play but there was a self-destruct button that has done little to assist him through the years. At times he simply couldn't help himself. Most of you have probably heard about the famous incident at Wimbledon when he told John Lloyd before a match that he was deliberately going to hit a serve into the Royal Box. And he tried to! The ball just missed, leaving Dan Maskell to utter the immortal line, 'Gosh. Dare I say that was a slight mishit!' His antics and beliefs saw him frozen out by the establishment. He never became a permanent member of the All England Club which, for a player with his record, would usually be guaranteed. In 2023, following further misdemeanours, he was banned from the place altogether. Buster spent more time there than just about anyone else and it's been very sad to watch his decline and exclusion, even if much of it has been down to his own failings. His record on court speaks for itself: 27 Davis Cup singles victories from 35 matches equates to a 77 per cent winning record. He once crushed Adriano Panatta 6-0, 6-4, 6-4 at the Foro Italico and recorded other famous wins in high-profile matches, one in particular against Yannick Noah, so there was no questioning his ability when in the right frame of mind. All too often, alas, his demons overtook him.

The Ugly – Bob Was No Uncle

One name sits atop the list of villains. Bob Hewitt's qualities could be counted on one hand with at least a couple of fingers left in reserve.

I don't want to comment on what happened to him in later life. I had no contact and no knowledge of the details of what was clearly a very harrowing tale, though the substantial prison sentence handed out to him for rape and sexual assault speaks volumes and led to him being expelled from the tennis hall of fame.

I knew him to be a fearsome and very awkward opponent. He was a fine, if limited, singles player and superb when it came to doubles. He won every doubles slam at least once in the men's and mixed events, enjoying the majority of his success with Frew McMillan who, by contrast, was a charming and intelligent fellow. Frew went on to enjoy a rewarding career in the broadcasting world and I often wonder what he really thought about Bob and having to spend so much time with such an angry man. It was always interesting when you played against them because Frew would stay quiet and never argue or reveal his emotions on court. He'd leave Bob to do what he had to do without censuring him in any way.

Hewitt's anger spilt over when I played him in Berlin in 1969 which, back then, was staged just before the French Open. He was a big guy, around 6ft 2in, and originally from Australia before he moved to South Africa. Whenever you played against him you knew there was going to be trouble and that something was going to happen. It was the quarter-finals of the singles. Bear in mind that although he's famous for being a doubles expert, he made it to six in the world as a singles player and won a number of titles, so he was no mug and could certainly handle himself.

At that point I was playing some of my very best tennis on clay. It was a golden period for me on that surface and we went at it hammer and tongs. Back then they used to have a ten-minute break after the third set. I led by two sets to one and he was angry, very angry. Reports later emerged that he pushed an old man with a walking stick out of the way as he stalked back to the locker room muttering various threats and was close to losing the plot altogether. For some reason we were in separate changing rooms, which was probably just as well, but I knew he was boiling over and adjusted my tactics a little bit. For example, just to irritate him, I walked around the net from the opposite side to the umpire's chair so he didn't have a chance to say anything to me. Little things like that can make a big difference.

Sure enough, I went on to beat him which, at the time, was a very big win. I was pumped as we came to the net but he was apoplectic and his eyes were bulging. Just as we were about to shake hands, one of the ball boys walked between us, a bit keen perhaps, and, with a pad in his hand, asked for our autographs, something that obviously wouldn't happen these days! The young kid was looking more at Hewitt, who turned to him and spat, 'Don't ask me, ask this lying, fucking cheating bastard!' Well, our heads were almost touching at this point but I tried to defuse the situation and told him to calm down; God knows what the poor ball boy was thinking! Hewitt wouldn't listen, though, and said he was going to 'get me' back in the locker rooms. I responded instinctively by saying I'd be waiting for him. Plenty of bravado, though I assumed it would quickly blow over.

So, we went back to our separate dressing rooms and, although he'd done his best to ruin my victory, I was on a high and feeling very happy with life. Now, perhaps appropriately, there were some Western-style swing doors that separated the two rooms. All of a sudden, they came flying open and in marched Hewitt, frothing at the mouth with a look of thunder on his face. Fortunately, there were a few players near me, some of them South African, able to see exactly what was going on. He bustled straight up to me, right up to my face, and, mouth drooling, launched into a lengthy verbal assault describing in some detail exactly what he'd like to do to me. Becoming more and more wound up, he then started poking me in the ribs.

I tried to put on a brave face while wondering how the hell I could extricate myself from the situation before things got really nasty but there was no time for that. A physical attack was imminent so I stood as tall as I could and calmly warned him that if he touched me again, 'it was on'. He responded to that by shoving me, so I hit him as hard as I could around his cheekbone, just under the eye. And down he went, almost in slow motion. The way he crumpled to the floor between two lockers was comical in a strange sort of way. On his way down I gave him another punch to the stomach. A few of the players intervened at that point including Ray Moore who was quick to say he'd happily testify that Hewitt was the aggressor if anything came of it.

Nothing did in terms of an enquiry, though I quickly acquired the nickname Rocky and also realised I'd done some damage to my hand while delivering the blows. It soon started to hurt. By coincidence we were due to play against each other again in the doubles that afternoon. He appeared on court with a number of stitches visible and his eye patched up, dripping with animosity. Fortunately, that match finished without further incident but, overnight, my hand became very swollen. I had to pull out of the singles and ended up missing the French Championships as well. Must have been one hell of a punch. In hindsight, I'd say it was probably worth it!

Somewhat awkwardly we then found ourselves in the same queue at the airport at the end of the week. He was just behind me and I kept waiting for some sort of attack, be it verbal or physical, but nothing happened. He was actually very calm most of the time off court and usually travelled with his wife.

The press wouldn't leave him alone for a while after news of our set-to was made public. I remember how during one match in Paris the following week, he started drilling balls towards the newspaper boys and acting like a madman. It was slapstick really but he clearly had a lot of issues.

Chapter 13

Nasty but Necessary

NOW IS as good a time as any to tell you a little more about someone else with a few 'issues'. Before I do it's worth stressing the importance of possessing a certain amount of ego to make it in an individual sport. I was never a brash, in-your-face John McEnroe-type of character but I'm from Sheffield and have some of the steel that part of South Yorkshire is famous for. Let's be honest, you aren't going to last long in terrain dominated by swashbuckling international superstars and fiercely determined, ultra-competitive opponents from all over the world if you can't stand up for yourself and look after number one.

And if that means making a few enemies, then so be it.

I had a few of those. Tennis is just like boxing, though. It's you against him and you'd better land the harder blows sooner rather than later. Worry about the rest afterwards.

I don't have any problem with players displaying their personality on court, within reason. In fact, I welcome it. Tennis, more than ever, requires the oxygen of publicity to guarantee column inches in the face of massive competition from other sports and inspire interest from the next generation, who seem to rely solely on tasty social media content for their news fix.

Back in the 60s and 70s there were plenty of larger-than-life characters. The need for a 'corporate image' wasn't the priority it is today, and with no phone cameras to capture your every move, it was much easier to relax and be yourself. And be a pain in the backside when necessary. One handsome, dark-haired Romanian was an expert in that regard; a man who crossed my path and made me cross, more than anyone else on a regular basis.

Nasty by name and often nasty by nature, Ilie Nastase knew how to play the game and make headlines, often at the same time. We contested some big matches, notably that Queen's final of 1973 and an epic encounter at the US Open in 72 that I'll tell you more about later. He invariably got the better of me, winning 12 of our 14 encounters but most of them were fairly close and tended to include more than a degree of melodrama ... though not from my side of the net I can assure you.

Nasty was incredibly talented and a nightmare to compete against, especially when things weren't going his way. Yet he was the type of player I would go out of my way to watch and, for all his histrionics, could be laugh-out-loud funny. There was so often a touch of the 'Charlie Chaplins' surrounding his demeanour on court, not least when it came to his antics with the cyclops line machine, the first electronic step on the way to Hawkeye. Cyclops was a service-line monitor that used infrared beams to determine whether a serve was in or out, and didn't always appear to function smoothly. One of Ilie's party-piece routines was to sneak up to the machine on tiptoes when he felt hard done by, almost as though it was alive. He'd look at it closely from different angles and have the crowd in hysterics.

Amusing for them but increasingly irritating if you were waiting to play the next point.

He'd think nothing of walking on to court with a couple of small rackets or a policeman's helmet, anything to provide a laugh and a distraction. I remember playing him once when he began creeping around the court, hardly moving at all. It prompted Bill Threlfall in the commentary box to quip there'd be no need for any slow-motion replays.

Then there was the time in Rome when a heated dispute between the two of us ended in bizarre fashion with around 15 spectators, including a lady with a large dog, becoming actively involved. In those days the line judges and umpires were amateurs and not to be relied upon. You'd sometimes see one of them reading a paper during the match or even fast asleep. I knew I'd found the line with a cross-court winner but Nastase, acting like an innocent choirboy, insisted it had landed wide. Players were allowed to cross the net back then for a closer look. As I walked over, some of the spectators, including this rather large, regal-looking lady with a big Labrador on the end of a lead, strolled on to the court to see what was going on for themselves! There wasn't much to talk about. The mark, clearly inside the line, was visible for all to see but Nasty did what he could to get away with it before eventually winking at me and rubbing it out with his shoe.

It was fun but it was also gamesmanship and he often crossed the line, just as John McEnroe and Nick Kyrgios in particular did a few years later. Those type of players are pretty clever when it comes to using, and abusing, umpires, officials and opponents for their own good. Having said that, I tended to look at McEnroe in a different light after having a very interesting story related to me by the respected tennis writer Richard Evans. Many years ago, Richard, as part of his research for a McEnroe biography, interviewed John's headmaster on the subject of his days as a key part of the school tennis team. In the absence of officials at that level, the players called their own lines and McEnroe was well-known for being incredibly generous towards his opponent when it came to any close calls. Supermac wanted to earn everything for himself in a fair manner. What he couldn't accept was something being unjustly taken away from him. That's why he lost the plot with many of the umpires he had no respect for and I can understand his frustration. Injustice tends to eat away at you, especially when you've been fighting tooth and nail for hours under a burning sun. That said, there's a certain code of conduct which has to be adhered to and McEnroe was guilty of breaching that far too often.

I did my best to ignore Nastase whenever things heated up but it wasn't easy. Let's not forget he was also a fantastic player who climbed to number one in the world in 1973 and 74, won the US Open and French Open along with two Wimbledon final appearances. We're talking about one of only ten men to win more than 100 titles in singles and doubles, so he didn't really need to resort to questionable tactics as much as he did. But that was the way he was wired.

He was so fast, had every shot in the book, an incredible feel for the game and served better than he was given credit for. And, of course, he was a good-looking fellow with natural charm who usually had the crowd eating out of his hand thanks to an easy-going confidence that bordered on arrogance. He could also be very funny. There's one story about him having his credit card stolen but saying he didn't bother reporting it to the police because the thief was spending less on it than his wife!

There's also a famous tale involving Jan Kodes ahead of a Davis Cup tie between Czechoslovakia and Romania. Kodes himself told me how he and the rest of the Czech team arrived in Bucharest and went to pick up their bags from the carousel. No sooner had Jan collected his than some surly-looking security guards appeared, demanding he open them all up. The atmosphere then became increasingly tense as the guards threatened to throw all his stuff on the floor and began treating him with total disdain. Jan was furious but just about managed to keep a lid on things as he headed off to present his passport at a tiny little window in the customs area. Inside the dark booth was an official in full outfit with a cap covering most of his face. He grabbed the passport and started tutting and gesticulating with his hands, indicating a serious problem. Eventually the official stamped it, threw it back and then stuck his head through the window. And who was it but Ilie himself, laughing his head off! Classic Nastase!

We had a little set-to during a match in Paris quite late in my career when I was partnering Onny Parun from New Zealand. Onny had a problem with his neck at the time that made it very hard for him to serve. For some bizarre reason he decided to tie a piece of string around his neck and held it in his mouth to try to ease the pain while, in theory, helping his service motion at the same time. It did look rather strange but Onny insisted it would work.

We were playing Nastase and Ion Tiriac, who was already hugely influential in the tennis world and went on to become a billionaire with his many business interests. Tiriac, an imposing man with a chilling stare, became Guillermo Vilas's and Boris Becker's mentor and was very used to having things his own way. Can't say I ever warmed to him and what cordiality that did exist between us evaporated that afternoon. We were playing in the veterans' event on the main court at Roland-Garros and were third match on after singles encounters featuring Henri Leconte and then a young Becker himself. Both turned out to be one-sided and were over very quickly.

We were getting ready inside the old locker rooms situated in the bowels of the stadium. They were really big with lots of different sections and alcoves so you could lose yourself in a corner, far removed from anyone else. We'd been hanging around in there for ages waiting for an update on the order of play when I suddenly noticed on the TV monitor that Nastase and Tiriac were already on court. No one had bothered to inform us. Quite clearly it was a wind-up!

We quickly gathered together our gear, had a stretch and ran down the stairs and out on to the court. The crowd immediately started booing us in typical French fashion with Nastase milking the situation and inevitably making fun of Onny's extraordinary neck brace. That set the tone for the rest of the day. The match proved to be incredibly close even though my partner was running around with a long piece of string in his mouth. We weren't playing tie-breakers that week and after a marathon battle the score was a set apiece and six-all in the third. Tiriac and Nastase suggested that, as it was getting late, we should play a breaker to decide the match but I was still fuming about being left in the changing rooms and refused. Tiriac, whose threatening demeanour and passive-aggressive behaviour made him extremely unpredictable, then came ambling up to me and started pulling out his pockets as though he had money in them and could buy whatever he wanted. He was physically intimidating but I looked him straight in the eye and said it was no problem if he didn't want to carry on … they could just default. Tiriac didn't like that at all and the temperature rose big time but we went on to beat them by 11 games to nine. Very sweet!

Tiriac's influence on Nastase was evident then and always has been. The first time I saw Ilie play was in the Davis Cup Final during the summer of 1969. I was British number one then but banned at that point having turned pro. Mark Cox, Peter Curtis and Graham Stillwell were in the Great Britain team that went into the final rubber between Cox and Nastase level at 2-2. Cox won the first set but lost in four, with Tiriac a disruptive influence in the stand. He'd whistle at Nastase as if he were a sheepdog and the two of them managed to distract Cox with a variety of ruses to get the job done.

There's a feeling amongst some that, but for Tiriac, Ilie would have become a true great. The influential Jack Kramer wrote in his autobiography that Nastase was 'a naturally enthusiastic kid' but that Tiriac tried to install in him a win-at-all-costs mentality akin to 'handing over a ticking time bomb that kept exploding in his own hands'. Tiriac had been a national hero in Romania for many years, initially as an ice hockey star, and made his mark as a tennis player through sheer determination while never coming close to being world class. He famously beat Tom Gorman during a fiery Davis Cup tie in Bucharest in 1972 and almost defeated Stan Smith as well, backed by the most volatile crowd. Tiriac tried everything, leaving Smith to tell him at the net, 'I've lost all respect for you today and I'm never going to speak to you again.' That wouldn't have bothered Tiriac in the slightest but Nastase was different. He wanted to be liked and I understand why Kramer reached the conclusion he did.

Nonetheless, part of Nastase's skill was the ability to create explosive situations and then put them to one side, rediscovering top form while his opponent struggled to regain focus. That's quite a skill. With the obvious exceptions of McEnroe and at times, more recently, Novak Djokovic, few others perform better having lost their temper; just ask Andrey Rublev. I've often wondered how many more titles Andy Murray might have won had he been able to stay more focused and spend less time berating his team. I realise it's very hard to escape from your default mannerisms once you get into the heat of battle but it's rarely a benefit to see red for any length of time.

Nastase made a career out of it, though. He'd think nothing of disappearing off court in the middle of a match if things were going badly. He memorably did that at the Royal Albert Hall when he was playing the American Clark Graebner. Sworn enemies, Clark had allegedly once called him a Romanian goat herder. Nastase retorted that Graebner was an 'animaaal' and they nearly came to blows several times.

His gamesmanship definitely had an effect on me. We played at the Royal Club in Barcelona once. It was on Centre Court and I was holding my own deep in the third set; eight-all, then 9-8 to me, at which point he suddenly ran into the crowd and vanished! Everyone started laughing but there was a long delay and I was left fuming. Eventually they called the supervisor who was also chairman of the club. Out came this very elegant-looking man in a suit and tie who could not have been more charming. I told him the situation was unacceptable but he just shrugged his shoulders and said, 'I'm sorry, Mr Taylor, but there's nothing I can do.' The umpire kept asking for Mr Nastase to please come back and finish the match but he didn't and knew exactly how long to keep the charade going. By the time he did finally reappear I'd almost snapped. The crowd was still laughing and he then started bouncing the ball time after time before deliberately letting it hit his shoe and dribble away, which produced even more laughter. Of course, he then wiped the floor with me.

I can understand why so many people liked him but he did tread a very delicate line and some of his behaviour, some of the things he said and did were totally unacceptable. The incident he became involved in with Anne Keothavong when captain of the Romanian Fed Cup team was ugly and had severe consequences for him. He asked Annie K for her room number during a press conference before the tie in 2017 and said some terrible things to Jo Konta which led to him being banned for three years and refused entrance to the French Open and Wimbledon. That would have hurt him because, only a year earlier, he'd been invited into the Royal Box and turned up in a Romanian colonel's uniform with epaulettes and a smart white cap with braid on it. Everybody wanted a photograph with him that day as he laughed and joked about the place. He was a delight to be with and genuinely charming. Sometimes, though, I suppose he just couldn't help himself and the Fed Cup controversy was clearly an example of that.

Chapter 14

The Times Are A-Changing

NOW IT'S not something I like to boast about but, back in the day, I wasn't the worst-looking fellow on the planet. Ilie Nastase claimed in his autobiography that he slept with 2,500 women (why so few?!?) and he was by no means the only top player to enjoy a spot of extra-curricular activity in what were very different times. However, if you're hoping for some salacious gossip regarding my own experiences, then I'm sorry to say you're in for disappointment. I'm a down-to-earth Yorkshireman who likes to keep certain things private and, in any case, I was hardly in the Nastase category when it came to gallivanting around the world!

Being a reasonable-looking fellow had its benefits, though, particularly in 1968, when I turned professional. Things had gone well for me the year before, notably at Wimbledon. Having made my debut in the main draw as a qualifier there in 1960, I had enjoyed a few runs to the fourth round and in 1967 I lost only 17 games to get that far again. Cliff Drysdale was my round-of-16 opponent and I beat him in five arduous sets before seeing off Ray Ruffles in three to tee up a semi against the unseeded German Wilhelm Bungert. It was a strange tournament that saw only two seeds reach the last eight and just one, the eventual winner John Newcombe, go through to the semi-finals.

Bungert was a friendly guy I had a lot of time for. Straight-backed with hardly any back-swing, he and Christian Kuhnke, a two-time Wimbledon quarter-finalist, were Germany's star players and enjoyed plenty of success together in the Davis Cup. I led Bungert by two sets to one in that semi (as, of course, was the case against Kodes in 73) but he proved to be incredibly cool-headed, eventually out-lasting me to win 6-4 in the fifth. That was Bungert's third successive five-set victory, which left him physically exhausted. Come the final, Newcombe, who'd lost only two sets all fortnight, won at a canter, for the loss of just five games. He was unstoppable that summer, as I'd discovered when losing the Queen's final to him a couple of weeks earlier.

That major disappointment aside, it had been a really good period for me development-wise but I felt as though I'd reached a crossroads. A post-Wimbledon-blues sentiment lingered in the back of my mind and I couldn't shake it off. After all the buzz and excitement of an adrenalin-fuelled fortnight, a sense of something missing, and the need for a new challenge, left me anxious and confused. Sure, there were tour events and cup competitions to prepare for but the absence of a clear pathway in the amateur game had become a growing concern for me. As were my finances. The 'prize' for reaching the semis at Wimbledon in 67 was a £30 voucher which had to be spent at Lillywhites or Simpsons. Inevitably, payments were made 'under the table' in this era of 'shamateurism' but it was hardly lucrative. And all this time the world's best players, the likes of Rod Laver, Pancho Gonzales, Ken Rosewall and Fred Stolle, who'd turned pro some years back, were operating on a different level while unable to compete in the slams because of their professional status. How could that be good for tennis?

Bill Tilden of the United States, a ten-time Grand Slam champion in the 1920s, highlighted the problem in his visionary autobiography, *My Story; A Champion's Memoirs*, which was published in 1948. In it he wrote, 'If tennis is to realise its full potential, it must find a solution to the professional/amateur problem which has plagued it for many years. Only through such a solution can there be free competition among not just a few of the great players of the world – but among all of them. The sporting public want to see the best. It doesn't give a hoot whether that best is amateur or professional.'

He was spot on and it all sounds so obvious now, but a notion that the honour of playing Wimbledon and the French outweighed the value of being paid to do so persisted. Great champions, the old-fashioned argument ran, didn't need cash prizes to validate their credentials. As a result, the split between the pros and the amateurs continued.

At this stage I had no idea the dawn of the Open Era was actually just around the corner. Immersed in tennis, all I wanted was an opportunity to play against the best – and if I could be paid for doing that, then so much the better. I'd always looked up to the top pros. As a kid I went to see them in action at Scarborough, which had a lovely centre court and two other grass courts kept in pristine condition. I was also at the Wembley event one year when living at the YMCA. To watch those guys in action was inspiring for a tennis-mad youngster like me. Tony Trabert, the Peruvian Alex Olmedo who won Wimbledon in 1959 before turning pro, Lew Hoad and Pancho Segura were among those who captured my imagination. Segura, from Ecuador, almost died after being born prematurely and had rickets as a child. You would never have guessed that from the way he played. Fleet-footed 'Segoo' was famed for his two-handed forehand which our old friend Jack Kramer once described as the greatest single shot in tennis.

So, it wasn't just money that led me towards the pro ranks but also an opportunity to reach another level. In truth, I didn't feel I had any other options. By now, in my mid-20s, it was too late for me to go to an American university, which had started to become a popular alternative. Warren Jacques, who captained the GB Davis Cup team for several years, was one of the first people I knew to go down that route, when he signed for Lamar Tech in the early 60s. These days there are amazing opportunities for British youngsters in the States, offering good degrees to fall back on if the tennis ultimately leads nowhere. In late 67 I may not have been on the road to nowhere but a change of direction was required and one unexpected call dramatically re-arranged the landscape.

I remember it all so clearly. I was staying with some friends, Reg and Mickey Bennett, in Chiswick, west London on a cold, wet night in November 1967. Reg had been a very good junior, who went to Lamar Tech but when he was playing in Australia he cut his hand on a bottle in the locker room. What seemed like a minor injury at the time continued to trouble him and he had never been able to fulfil all the early potential.

The phone rang and a man with a strong American accent asked to have a word with 'Mr. Taylor'. It was Dave Dixon, who had contacted several people to track me down. I knew very little about him but quickly discovered that, having made a lot of money in the plywood business and been involved in American football, Dave had decided the time had come to 'change' tennis forever and wanted me to be part of his revolution. He had the gift of the gab and sold his 'pitch' in the most compelling, persuasive manner. Not surprisingly, I was hooked. The essence of his message was this: backed by the Texas millionaire Lamar Hunt, Dixon planned to sign up the best players in the world, put them in coloured clothing, change the scoring system and rev up tennis crowds with a variety of innovative ideas. 'At no point will our umpires demand silence' was one of his messages. And, he told me, everything would be done in style with prize money for all, including first-round losers, quality hotels and top-class travel to 80 venues throughout the year with $100,000 up for grabs.

'Bloody hell,' I thought. 'Sign me up.'

Sure enough, he did. And, overnight, I became one of 'the Handsome Eight'.

Chapter 15

The Handsome Eight

HAVE YOU heard the one about the Englishman, two Australians, two Americans, a Frenchman, a South African and a Yugoslav? If so, please feel free to skip forward to the next chapter, but this group of new pros embarked on quite a ride at the start of 1968, which is definitely worth expanding upon.

Within two months of Dave's phone call the cast had been assembled and the show was on the road. Joining me as founding members of World Championship Tennis (WCT) was the pick of a crop not already harvested by the National Tennis League (NTL) professional set-up, who had players such as Rod Laver, Ken Rosewall, Andres Gimeno and Pancho Gonzales in their ranks.

The eight were Tony Roche, Dennis Ralston, Pierre Barthes, Niki Pilic, John Newcombe, Earl Buchholz, Cliff Drysdale and me.

Lamar Hunt, in association with his nephew Al Hill Junior, and leading journalist Frank Deford labelled us the Handsome Eight. It was a shrewd marketing exercise, even if some privately joked that Roche's inclusion put quite a strain on that description. You know I'm only kidding, Tony!

Roche, from New South Wales, won 13 Grand Slam doubles titles during his career plus the French Open in 66 and also reached the Wimbledon final in 68. After hanging up his rackets, he enjoyed a hugely successful coaching career with Ivan Lendl, Roger Federer and Lleyton Hewitt.

Dennis Ralston, a tall right-hander from California reached the Wimbledon final in 1966 and was a doubles champion there, as well as at the French and US Opens. He had a wonderful all-court game and demonstrated great skills as a coach too in partnership with Chris Evert, Yannick Noah and Gabriela Sabatini, amongst others. Dennis could be an angry man on court and was plagued by knee injuries. Late in life he had to have his left leg amputated below the knee while struggling with a series of health issues but he was a big presence and fun to be around.

Pierre Barthes and I formed a strong friendship over the years. A dark-haired elegant Frenchman, Pierre was softly spoken, thoughtful and won the US Open doubles with Niki Pilic who was a very interesting character.

Niki will always be remembered for his pivotal role in the 73 boycott but shouldn't be underestimated as a tennis player. He reached the French Open Final in 73 and became the first captain to win the Davis Cup with three different nations – Germany, Croatia and Serbia – ironic when you remember it was his refusal to play a Davis Cup tie for Yugoslavia that led to the Wimbledon boycott in the first place!

John Newcombe, as we've already learnt, was in fine fettle at this point. I used to think of him as 'the last of the Old Aussies', in that he was fiercely competitive with a 'pass me if you can' mentality but was so amenable and sociable off court and always had time for a cold beer. I loved his spirit.

Earl 'Butch' Buchholz had been a brilliant junior, winning the French, Wimbledon and Australian boys' titles. His subsequent playing career never matched those early heights but he was a two-time Wimbledon quarter-finalist and made the last four in New York in 1960. Butch did so much for the sport after retiring and founded what at the time was called the Lipton International Players Championships and is these days known as the Miami Open.

Last but not least was Cliff Drysdale, who keeps appearing in this book and was always going to be part of a revolution like this. Cliff once revealed that his prize for reaching two Wimbledon semi-finals was two pairs of shorts! 'That kind of neglect,' he went on, 'created the opportunity for Lamar Hunt and Al Hill Junior.'

And what an opportunity it created for us! Initially, though, things did not go quite according to the script.

The inaugural WCT tournament was staged in Sydney, Australia in January of 68. There was an element of humour and surprise when we stepped off the plane to meet Dave Dixon for the first time. In all the pictures I'd seen he'd been as bald as a coot but there he was wearing this ridiculous-looking wig, which nearly fell off a couple of times as the introductions were made; an early sign that things weren't quite as they appeared.

Then came news that the court had been set up in the car park of the Channel 7 television studios. Everything had been arranged so quickly and, as we were banned from any official venues, options were limited. So, a car park had to do. Despite plenty of teething issues, Dixon was a bundle of energy with all his new ideas and determination to cut out the dead time in a tennis match. He showed us this huge clock at one end of the court. Each match was designated to last for one hour, split into four quarters, and every point would be worth a certain amount of money. A Klaxon was sounded by the umpire to signal the start and, after 15 minutes, when it sounded again, we'd hare down to the other end for the second quarter, fully aware that every second was precious. There were no sit-downs or delays because the more points we played the more money we could make. From what I can remember, it was US$10 a point in the first quarter, up to $15 in the second and $30 in the third. There was then a tweak in the fourth quarter. Both players could choose the amount they wanted to play for. If you were on top heading into that last period, the temptation would be to remain cautious and protect your lead because whoever won the point picked up all the money.

So, if I was winning, I might elect to play for $30 but my opponent, who was perhaps $100 behind, would go for $50. Whoever won the point therefore picked up $80. It was a clever system that kept you guessing to the very end and we never had a tie.

Dave also had a huge box full of coloured shirts, the like of which had never been worn on a tennis court before. We had to choose a different colour and, simply because I rather liked a song, 'Snoopy vs the Red Baron,' which had reached number two in the charts a year or so earlier, I opted for red.

Despite the modest surroundings, big crowds turned up, which was no surprise with Newcombe and Roche on show. The spectators were encouraged to make as much noise as possible and it proved to be a successful week, with Roche crowned winner after beating Pilic in the final. I finished sixth, ahead of Barthes and Ralston.

From Sydney we travelled to Lamar Hunt's hometown in the US, Kansas City. This was a big deal for him but problematic again from a logistics point of view. Dave Dixon may have been full of new ideas but he somehow forgot to book the stadium in time! Instead, we were to play in the stockyards, which at one stage housed the second-biggest livestock operation in the States after Chicago's Union Stockyards. More than 200 acres in size, the stockyards used to accommodate 70,000 cattle a day plus 40,000 hogs, 45,000 sheep and 5,000 horses and mules, along with meat-packing and banking facilities. It was big business between around 1870 and 1951, when a major flood caused a huge amount of damage and signalled the beginning of the end, with the last cattle auction held in 1991.

There was a smell of cattle everywhere, which wasn't entirely in keeping with the promise of first-class facilities that had been at the heart of the WTC's original manifesto. To make things even more complicated the artificial grass court had been laid on top of an ice rink, which led to one moment of slapstick comedy, which could also have resulted in serious injury. I'll come to that shortly.

We still had the coloured shirts and, by now, some snazzy shorts had been made for us as well. Unfortunately, whoever designed them clearly had no idea that professional tennis players tend to have big thighs. They were all far too tight and none of us could fit into them. Minutes before play started there we were, the Handsome Eight, ripping our shorts along the sides before squeezing into them, hoping our dignity would be preserved, before running down a steeply angled cattle-chute and out on to the court.

The first match was between Dennis Ralston and Pierre Barthes, who both came trotting down the chute before emerging under the glare of a strobe light that followed them to the net. Dave Dixon was already out in the middle with two enormous boxes. Wielding a huge microphone he thanked the crowd for coming before launching into his sales pitch.

'Ladies, take a good look at this handsome Frenchman Pierre Barthes. If he wins tonight, you will all receive a bottle of this expensive Revlon perfume. You'll love it and you'll love him,' added Dave, who then put down the perfume he'd taken out of one box and started rummaging in the other.

'Now, guys, you're not going to let that happen, are you? Put your hands together for this mighty American Dennis Ralston. If he wins there's aftershave for all of you.'

Back in the late 60s, tennis still hadn't really taken off in America outside California and Florida so most of the crowd were clueless as to what was going on. Inevitably, though, they were caught up in the razzmatazz. Some were booing, others whistling; it was all a touch surreal, with a whiff of cattle dung reminding us where we were. It was also cold, leaving a reporter from *The Guardian* to note that 'Kansas City makes Wolverhampton look like Athens'.

The scoring system had changed for week two. This time we were playing 31-point sets with the server switching every five points. The lighting wasn't great but the real area of interest was at the side and back of the court where the line judges were sitting. One half of the officials' chairs were on the artificial court surface with the other half precariously balanced on the ice underneath. It was a recipe for disaster and, sure enough, very nearly produced a calamity when Barthes and Ralston became embroiled in a lengthy rally.

Barthes came to the net, allowing Ralston to lob him. Barthes then backed up to execute a fine smash that had Ralston on the retreat. He sent up a defensive lob which Barthes attacked with gusto sending his opponent even further back, to the extent that Ralston then collided with a line judge. One minute the poor fellow was sitting there focusing on the rally, the next his chair skidded backwards and sent him flying skywards. For a moment it looked as though he was hovering in mid-air, before he crashed back down on to the icy surface. Ralston, who was now desperately attempting to get some traction on the ice while also trying to avoid the outstretched official, finally went down in a heap as well. It was like something out of a Laurel and Hardy sketch and had us all in hysterics, but it could have led to a nasty injury for one or both. Pierre was left standing at the net, looking bewildered. '*Ooh la la*,' I remember him saying, '*c'est fou*, this is crazy.' It was certainly a far cry from Wimbledon but, with Dave Dixon and his ever-moving wig a constant source of fascination and energy in those early weeks, it was definitely memorable.

From Kansas City we went to Shreveport in Louisiana, and then Miami and Houston where Butch Buchholz recorded back-to-back titles. The crowd in Miami was almost non-existent. There were about 53 people on day one so it was no wonder the tour was already starting to rack up some big losses. There weren't any professional umpires either so, as and when a paying spectator appeared, they were asked if they fancied being a line judge! Americans are generally pretty confident so they'd usually say yes before then asking questions such as 'What happens if the ball hits the line?' It was a touch shambolic and around about then, Dave, whose wife was not well, quietly departed the scene. We carried on. New Orleans, Orlando,

Tulsa, San Diego, Los Altos, Bakersfield, Fresno and Evansville in Indiana were all part of the circuit between January and late April followed by three more tournaments in May in Minneapolis, Buffalo and Baltimore, where I finished third.

As we packed, travelled, played, slept, packed, travelled and, well you get the picture, major developments were taking place at the top of the game which ushered in the Open Era. The LTA attracts plenty of criticism these days but, to be fair to our governing body, it was their brave decision, inspired by the chairman of the All England Club, Herman David, which rapidly accelerated the process. David was fed up with those determined to keep the game amateur and had memorably stated, 'It seems we have come to the end of the road constitutionally and that the only way to make the game honest is by unconstitutional action.' Herman, who played Davis Cup for Great Britain before going on to captain the team, detested amateur tennis, describing it as a 'living lie'. His 'unconstitutional' move was to organise the Wimbledon World Professional Lawn Tennis Championships in August 1967. Eight players, Butch Buchholz, Andres Gimeno, Pancho Gonzales, Lew Hoad, Rod Laver, Dennis Ralston, Ken Rosewall and Fred Stolle, were invited to play and be paid over the course of four days. Laver defeated Rosewall in a thrilling final just a month after the hugely anti-climactic conclusion of the official Championships, when John Newcombe had crushed Wilhelm Bungert.

Having campaigned for years to change the system, Herman was not to be denied after that. In the late summer of 67 he announced Wimbledon's 'unilateral and non-negotiable' decision to make the 68 Championships open to everyone. The LTA backed him and, despite initial opposition from the International Lawn Tennis Federation, support from other federations left the ILTF under enormous pressure. They held an emergency general meeting in Paris on 30 March 1968 at which a vote to make tennis 'open' was passed unanimously.

The best doubles team I've ever seen. Mum and Dad. Top seeds for more than 60 years.

Clearly not happy after losing to Mike Harvey in 1957.

First experience of Wimbledon from the inside. 1958

Power comes from pain. A young man at the YMCA in 1959.

THE LAWN TENNIS ASSOCIATION
PATRON: HER MAJESTY THE QUEEN

SECRETARY:
S. BASIL REAY, O.B.E.

TELEPHONE: MONARCH 9051.
TELEGRAMS: LAWNTENNA, LONDON.

Barons Court, West Kensington,
~~RIVER PLATE HOUSE, FINSBURY CIRCUS,~~
LONDON, ~~E.C.2.~~ W.14.

PRIVATE & CONFIDENTIAL   11th November 1959.

Mrs. L. Taylor,
48 Bromley Street,
Sheffield 3,
Yorks.

Dear Mrs. Taylor,

    Thank you for your letter of 1st November about Roger's future. I quite understand how disappointed you must be to hear that he has not been invited to train at The Queen's Club this Winter, but let me say at the outset that there are certainly no personal or other reasons for not including him, other than the fact that the Committee do not feel at the moment that he has made the necessary progress. The list is a very restricted one and only Davis Cup or Wightman Cup players, or those who, in the opinion of the Committee, are likely to achieve Davis Cup or Wightman Cup standard have been included.

    Without doubt Roger's best plan will be to compete in as many tournaments as possible during the Summer of 1960 and obtain some good results and thus gain further recognition.

    Roger is, of course, still a Nominated Young Player and can continue to play at The Queen's Club free of charge under the arrangements for N.Y.Ps.

    I will certainly see that your letter is placed before my Committee at their next meeting.

                             Yours sincerely,

                                Secretary, L.T.A.

Mum did her best but the LTA said no. 11 November 1959.

Fred the fantastic on his way to a third successive Wimbledon crown in 1936.

One day Sir Andy will have a statue to match the man whose footsteps he followed in.

One of my first wins at Wimbledon against a disgruntled Abe Segal. June 1963. Copyright Sport and General Press Agency

Mark Cox. Surbiton 1967. Arch rival/old friend.

John Newcombe. Wimbledon champion in 67, 70 and 71. My nemesis.

The Rocket with yet another title in 1969.

Rod turns his back on me as I turn the tables on him. Wimbledon 1970.

LAVER PRAISES ROGER TAYLOR

Thinking injury might have helped towards the holder's defeat by Roger Taylor, L.T. asked:

Have you really felt confident at any time since you injured your right ankle? Did you hit your peak too soon — you played very well at Queen's Club.

"Oh no! I don't think it was that — I double-faulted the match away and it was fairly windy out there. When your serve is a little bit off in swirling conditions you don't go for quite as much accuracy as you need. Roger was playing quite well — he served quite well — he didn't put much on the ball, he kept them fairly low and with the conditions a little bit difficult you couldn't penetrate. I couldn't punch my volleys as much as I would like to and when I did they seemed to float too much".

You missed a lot of low ones today — was that because he had nothing on the ball or because you were stiff or — ?

"It all revolves around my service really. My first serve didn't have much sting on it. I guess my timing is not as good as I would have liked it. For a couple of games its fine and then I lapse for a game or two. I think this was where Roger was able to get better returns of serves — this is where I found myself following up rather than being closer and able to penetrate a little bit more".

What was wrong with your backhand in this match? Why the string of errors?

"I think Roger served quite well, the court was taking a lot of kick today rather than slice. Normally the centre-court takes slice — it doesn't kick. Today it was getting a lot of kick and lifting away sharply. You just couldn't get up over the ball. And the conditions out there are not very fast. In fact it's quite slow at the moment — when you get to the service line, it's very dusty. Such a dry summer, maybe that's why my serve isn't going so well. It's all powdery — no grass around to serve on. The ball doesn't get away; it sits up a little more".

Do you think his variations of service were clever, and his variations at the net?

"His serve did not bother me. It's just that I did not make my returns good enough. In fact I did not try to do a terrific amount with them. Sometimes I tried to move in on the ball, but with them popping and kicking quickly (even mine were doing it) and he was varying it quite well".

"It's disappointing losing. I don't like it — it's not in my nature — but I've had a good innings and Wimbledon has been a good stepping stone to a lot of things. I've had a lot of personal satisfaction".

"No I wasn't nervous — maybe that was the mistake! I felt good — I felt strong and there's not much more you can ask for".

Did you change your racket or try anything to improve your rhythm?

"No that doesn't make the difference. In fact I was stroking the ball fairly well, but at the time I wanted the point either Roger was there to make a good shot or I just missed it; a few inches can make a tremendous gap in the score. But Roger played consistent tennis and he tried hard".

Rod Laver and Roger Taylor before the upset. Is that how Taylor smiles when he is confident?
Picture: George Hourd

So sweet to rise above the Rocket. Wimbledon 1970.
Copyright George Hourd

Wedding day 1. Glasgow 1969.

Rebels with a cause: The "Handsome Eight" (standing, from left): Dennis Ralston, Roger Taylor, Tony Roche and Pierre Barthes. Seated, John Newcombe, Niki Pilic, Butch Buchholz and Cliff Drysdale.

The Handsome Eight.

Within a month of that, the first official tournament of the new era took place at the West Hants Club in Bournemouth. The star of that show proved to be Mark Cox who, still playing as an amateur, beat two professionals, Roy Emerson and Pancho Gonzales, to create massive headlines. The pros, expected by almost everyone to crush their amateur opponents, felt the strain that week, which probably contributed to some of the results. Mark eventually lost to Rod Laver, who later said, 'The pressure was entirely on the pros as it was an opportunity for the amateurs to show us how good they were.'

Despite that weight of expectation, Laver and fellow professional Ken Rosewall reached the final without dropping a set, though Muscles (so named because he didn't have any) agreed with Laver's view, saying, 'There was some thought that the pros would be better than the amateurs and I felt it did lead to a tense situation during the week.' Rosewall came out on top 3-6, 6-2, 6-0, 6-3 to pick up £2,400 and the event was a huge success with ticket sales six times greater than the previous year. A day after the final a leading British journalist at the time, Linda Timms, wrote, 'If anyone doubted that Open tennis would galvanise public interest overnight, here was their answer.'

Rosewall and Laver then contested the first Open Era slam final in Paris a few weeks later. Ken claimed that in four sets as well but the Rocket returned to winning ways at Wimbledon when he beat Tony Roche in straight sets, six years on from his last appearance there. I, somewhat disappointingly, lost in the second round to Onny Parun, but the presence of all the returning pros brought added glamour and prestige to the biggest and best tournament in the world and pointed to a brave new future.

And, without wishing to blow my own trumpet, the formation of the Handsome Eight had proved the catalyst. Sure enough, in next to no time, the quality of play rose and public interest grew enormously. That attracted new sponsorship, so boosting player income. Finally, here was the chance to earn a living while competing at the highest level.

The only remaining blot on my landscape was a Davis Cup ban that had come into effect the moment I turned pro and remained in place under the jurisdiction of the International Tennis Federation, another of the sport's governing bodies, despite the game opening up. Their ruling was that professionals could play in the competition but 'contract' professionals tied in to the NTL or WCT could not. When signing up to the Dave Dixon bandwagon I knew the consequences of my action but don't want you to underestimate how big a blow it was to be cast into the international wilderness for five long years. Representing Great Britain in the Davis Cup was the ultimate accolade as far as I was concerned and always meant the world to me. I made my debut as a 23-year-old in 1964, beating Ernst Blanke and Peter Pokorny of Austria, and vividly recall the pride of representing my nation, something I'd never considered a realistic target when growing up.

Two ties stand out in particular. The first was in May 1966, the same weekend that Sheffield Wednesday beat Everton to win the FA Cup Final. We were in Budapest to play a very tough Hungarian side. Our number one Mike Sangster, lost to their number two, Andras Szikszay, in the fourth match to leave the tie level at 2-2. It meant I had to beat Istvan Gulyas who was a legend on clay and could run all day, ably supported by legs that looked like tree trunks. We didn't start until quite late on the Sunday afternoon, knowing, somewhat uncomfortably, that our visas ran out that evening. The first set went on for an eternity with Gulyas eventually winning it 18-16. I fought back to win the next two, by which time darkness had all but descended, making it impossible for play to continue. Our captain, Hedley Baxter, was left scrambling around trying to obtain the special permits required to extend the trip, by no means straightforward at such late notice back then. Hedley finally succeeded and, the following morning, I went back out to win the match in four sets for my first really big Davis Cup triumph. The anti-climactic conclusion to all that was a narrow defeat at the hands of West Germany a month later when that man Bungert beat me. He was a pain in the backside when I come to think of it!

The other stand-out Davis Cup memory is a 1967 tie against Canada played in Bournemouth. During the course of those three days I managed to save two match points before beating Bob Bedard in the second rubber after which Bobby Wilson and I faced two more match points in the doubles against Keith Carpenter and Michael Belkin. Normally I would have partnered Mike Sangster but he'd hurt his hand quite badly when slipping on the clay during his opening singles match and couldn't compete. Now, as a lefty I almost always played in the left court but Bobby, who was prone to getting in a bit of a state at times, insisted he had to play on that side so, under duress, I agreed to switch. We promptly went two sets down before swapping around and somehow came through an absolute belter 12-10 in the fifth.

Following my ban in 1968 the team went on to reach the final in 69 before national fortunes dipped alarmingly with first-round exits in 1970, 71 and 72. During that period the chairman of the LTA, Derek Penman, visited my flat and asked what it would take for me to become an amateur again and so be able to return to the Davis Cup fold. I told him that, though I greatly missed not being involved, revoking my professional status was not an option. Finally, in 1973 'contracted' pros were re-admitted but, inevitably, the team had changed considerably and it was never quite the same again, though we did have an exciting run to the final of the Europe Zone against Italy in 1976. I lost a tight fourth rubber to Adriano Panatta that August in what proved to be my last Davis Cup match. When the curtain came down, I'd amassed a record of 29 wins and 11 defeats. Had my ban not been implemented at the end of the 1960s I would have been an integral part of the team which made that final against Romania in 1969 after victories over Switzerland, Ireland, West Germany, South Africa and Brazil. Graham Stillwell came in and played brilliantly but there's no doubt my win-loss ratio would have been boosted quite considerably. Fred Perry holds the GB Davis Cup record for most victories with 45. Mike Sangster won 43 while Andy Murray and Tim Henman both claimed 40. Had I been able to play continuously between 1968 and 72 my final tally would have been very comparable to their figures, which remains a great source of personal frustration.

Not that I was pondering the possibility of all that when the WCT tour resumed in late July. By then the American Marty Riessen had joined us, closely followed by South Africa's Ray Moore. First port of call was Bastad where I beat John Newcombe for third place. We then moved on to Cannes, Newport (Rhode Island), Transvaal, Johannesburg, Durban, Border, Port Elizabeth – where I was champion – Western Province, Kimberley and finally Vienna at the start of November. We played 27 events spread over 11 months with John Newcombe winning seven of them and competing in ten finals, as did Dennis Ralston. I made around $47,000, which was a very tidy sum at the time, but felt I'd worked bloody hard for it.

The planning and organisation of the tour may have been a joke at times but the tennis itself was top quality and I had to deal with more downs than ups amidst such an elite field. I was a much better player for the experience, though, and a more rounded individual having spent so much time with a lively, intelligent group of men who had plenty to say about the game and life in general. It felt life-affirming to be part of the 'revolution' and the next few years on that WCT tour provided some great memories. We saw the introduction of yellow tennis balls, on-tour trainers and full-time PR guys, who capitalised brilliantly on this sudden surge in popularity for the sport. In due course two 32-player tours were staged simultaneously around the world and when NBC TV in the States started to show some of the finals in 1972, viewing figures went through the roof. The end-of-season showdown between Rod Laver and Ken Rosewall that year was watched by a record 23 million Americans and by the mid-70s 85 players were involved, competing for prize money that had been unthinkable just a few years earlier. There were some special moments for me, notably in 1973 when I qualified for the last-eight finals in Dallas only to come face to face with my nemesis Ken Rosewall. Truth be told I played brilliantly that day and led by two sets to one after winning a gripping third-set tie-break. Yet he always seemed to find a way to beat me and so it proved once more.

However, as the game made rapid strides I started to falter. Though still fit and competitive in my early to mid-30s, results tailed off, my ranking fell significantly and, over a period of months, the unthinkable became the unavoidable. There was no getting around it. I needed to find another job. It's a moment every professional athlete has to come to terms with and I, at least, had some wonderful memories to cushion the blow of retirement from the game's top tier.

Before we move on to what came next, here's a look at some of the best of those.

Chapter 16

Rocket to the Moon – Wimbledon 1970

IN ALL honesty, I'm not someone who sits down and thinks too much about the past. Certain events trigger specific memories and it's usually during Wimbledon fortnight that the most vivid ones, and the best matches, of my career swim to the surface. 'Go on,' I hear you say, or at least I hope you do! 'What are the ultimate highlights?'

One match above all others has to stand out from the rest simply because of who it was against.

The Rocket

The man who ruled the world for so long and appeared nigh-on unbeatable at times. Rod Laver's record is remarkable: 198 singles titles, the most won by a player in history; 11 Grand Slam titles including the calendar career slam in 1962 and 69, the one thing Novak Djokovic has failed to accomplish during his extraordinary reign. The Queensland Cowboy also picked up nine slam doubles titles and three mixed doubles. He was superb on every surface and played a big part in five Davis Cup wins for Australia. No wonder the main court at Melbourne Park is named in his honour.

Rod wasn't a big man at 5ft 8in but was considered 'technically faultless' and his speed and strength were quite something. What I really liked was how he'd hit the ball harder and harder if things weren't going to plan. He was brave, hugely respected by his peers and, not surprisingly, a daunting prospect when your name was lined up against his, as mine was at Wimbledon in 1970. The mickey-taking began the moment the draw was made. Laver, seeded one, had been crowned champion at the All England Club in his last four appearances there, in 1961, 62, 68 and 69, missing the intervening years because of his professional status. I was the 16th seed and scheduled to meet him in the fourth round.

Not that you should take anything for granted. Perhaps guilty of looking too far ahead I very nearly lost to Brian Fairlie of New Zealand in the first round. A set down in double-quick time, I was taken the distance before coming through 6-4 in the fifth. That was followed by an unconvincing start against India's Chiradip Mukerjea, but having gone a set down to him, something clicked in the next three, which were comfortable. Charlie Pasarell put up quite a fight in the second set of our third-round clash but an 8-6, 17-15, 6-4 win took me through to a showdown with the main man who, by contrast had dropped just one set and lost only 21 games in his three wins, over Butch Seewagen, John Alexander and Frew McMillan. That run had extended Laver's unbeaten record at Wimbledon to 31 matches. You had to go back to the 1960 final, a decade earlier, for his last defeat, which had been at the hands of fellow Aussie Neale Fraser.

The newspaper boys had already made up their minds. The *Daily Mail*'s Laurie Pignon, and Peter Wilson of the *Mirror* were two of the best in their line of work and the message from both was clear. This was going to be Laver's tournament – nobody else need bother turning up. Thanks, guys!

I'd played Laver in Australia and knew a fair bit about him. He was a joy to see in action with a topspin backhand that nobody else had developed with wooden rackets. He was also a genius when someone tried to lob him. I loved the way he followed the ball back, keeping his eye on it all the time, waiting patiently until it dropped before spinning around and pouncing, usually to deadly effect, with so many different shots at his disposal. I'd watch him whenever I could. Now I had a close-up view.

Walking out alongside him I was tense rather than nervous but, most importantly, felt prepared. My ability to visualise what I wanted to do tactically was a comfort. I knew which patterns of play might work and how a specifically angled serve might be of benefit to me as the match developed. You couldn't rely on aces. The rackets have been transformed since then, of course, but you had to adopt a more subtle approach and keep thinking all the time to try to gain an edge. Essentially, it's mobile chess. As a lefty I'd try to keep the ball on my opponent's backhand and get it as high as possible. Kick serves were a big weapon because nobody stood miles behind their baseline, like Daniil Medvedev, for example, today. They all stepped in and played on or just inside the baseline so the more you could get the ball over their shoulder the better. It's a tactic Rafael Nadal used brilliantly against Roger Federer's backhand on clay and I knew exactly what I had to do. Never mind how well Laver played; it was all about whether I could execute my strategy to a good enough level. Holding serve was essential, with a mix of spins and slice. I had to pull him out of position on a consistent basis, seize the initiative and finish the point as quickly as I could. And, like a spin bowler, I had to be able to disguise the service motion so he wouldn't be able to anticipate the direction easily.

A few years earlier I'd become obsessed with baseball. It was when Roger Maris of the New York Yankees broke Babe Ruth's 34-year-old home run record with Mickey Mantle also in the frame. They were amazing but I was mesmerised by the craftiness of the pitchers. After that, whenever we toured America, I'd be glued to the TV every night in my hotel room trying to learn some tips from those pitchers on the mound with their sliders, forkballs, curveballs and everything else. That attention to detail definitely benefitted my serve.

Not that the serve, or any other part of my game, worked particularly well in the opening set against Laver. I lost it 6-4 but wasn't downhearted. I'd seen enough already to believe my game could frustrate him and have never been one to panic after losing a set. The beauty of the scoring system means you always have a chance. Win the last point and the match is yours. Lose any other and you're still in with a shout. The power of positive thinking is worth its weight in gold on a tennis court.

I decided to give him no power at all. He'd have to generate pace for himself while I dinked the ball here and there, executing as many slow chips as possible to keep it in front of him and force lots of awkward low volleys from under the net, which then allowed me to make the pass.

And the plan worked perfectly! The next three sets went by in a blur and I won them all 6-4, 6-2, 6-1. It was incredible. The best performance of my life against the greatest player in the sport on the biggest stage tennis could provide. It didn't get any better than that and I have never felt prouder. This was the day I was either going to collapse and possibly be humiliated in front of a sell-out Centre Court crowd or come through the strongest test I'd ever faced.

In his autobiography, *The Education of a Tennis Player*, Rod wrote of his regrets about that day but was kind to me.

'Roger deserves full credit. He lost the first set and kept plugging. When he had his chances he made the most of them and got better. He kept the pressure on me so that I couldn't recover.'

The press made a big thing of my win, though I sensed some of the 'experts' secretly thought it was more a case of Rod having a bad day than anything I had done. How often does that tend to be the automatic conclusion when a great like Federer, Nadal or Djokovic loses in surprising fashion? Well, the press could think what they liked. I'd become the first man to beat Laver at Wimbledon for ten years and nobody could take that away from me.

So often a brilliant win is followed by huge disappointment but I was determined that wouldn't happen. In the quarter-finals I faced the imposing American Clark Graebner, a *Superman* lookalike with a power game Clark Kent would be proud of. Clark had beaten

Nastase in the previous round but I raced into a two-set lead for the loss of just three games and although he steadied the ship in set three I romped home in four to secure a place in the semis for the second time. Alas, as was the case three years earlier against Wilhelm Bungert, and would be three later as we all know against Jan Kodes, it wasn't destined to be my day or year. The match-up with Ken Rosewall never really suited me. Muscles had a truly magical backhand and was used to dealing with lefties having played Laver so many times. I was probably guilty of showing him too much respect whenever we locked horns but he was a little genius. Although I won the second set, an all-Australian final brought the curtain down on Wimbledon in 1970 with John Newcombe winning a five-setter against his close friend.

Chapter 17

Double Doubles Glory

A SLAM singles title may have escaped my clutches but I do have two major doubles titles to look back on with more than a degree of pride, captured in back-to back years at the US Open. I loved playing doubles: the constant support of, and for, your partner, the subtleties required in that format, along with a different type of concentration and the dramatic shifts in momentum.

Without wishing to state the obvious, having a good partner tends to be a help! I wasn't part of a regular team upon my arrival in New York in 1971 and, as a result of an injury to Tony Roche, the man with whom he won 12 slam titles in all, John Newcombe had no one to lace up his shoes with either that particular fortnight. Destiny playing its part again. So, we agreed to pair up as the number seven seeds with no great expectations but a fierce determination nonetheless and what a fortnight it turned out to be.

Newk was a wonderful guy and seriously good; you only have to look at his record to see that. He's part of a revered and very exclusive list of men to be ranked number one in singles and doubles and was rated the tenth-best male player between 1965 and 2005 by *Tennis Magazine*. You don't win seven singles titles at slam level without knowing what you're doing. Throw in 17 doubles titles at the majors, two mixed, five Davis Cup triumphs and the WCT finals title in 1974 and you get a full flavour of what the fun-loving Aussie with the famous bristling moustache was all about. As he, like me, had been one of the Handsome Eight, I felt a real affinity towards him, as I did with most of the Australians of that era. He had power, tactical acumen, a heavy and often lethal serve plus one of the strongest and most effective forehand volleys you could ever wish to see. Oh, and he knew how to have fun off court as well, which was an added bonus!

As a pair we clicked from the word go and reached the final without dropping a set, beating the likes of Bob Lutz and Charlie Pasarell and the Bob Hewitt-Frew McMillan combo along the way. Awaiting us in the showpiece event was Erik van Dillen and that man Stan Smith, who keeps cropping up. He'd just beaten Jan Kodes to win his first singles slam so was understandably full of confidence and swagger. We lost the first set in a tie-break but then recovered to win the next two in what I recall were dreary, wet conditions at Forest Hills, which made the grass increasingly awkward to play on. Back came Smith and Van Dillen to win the fourth by six games to four and so set up a nine-point sudden-death tie-break, which was being used for the first time. I hate to admit it but, all these years on, I can't remember the scoring sequence in what was an incredibly tense passage of play but, somehow, we won by five points to three and I was a Grand Slam champion at last. That gives me a legacy of sorts, which means an awful lot. Blurred as the memories are, I will always cherish that achievement and the opportunity to play with such a legend of the game in so prestigious an event.

And, just to prove it was no fluke, I did it again 12 months later, this time against Newcombe!

By 1972 I had formed a long-standing, more-than-useful partnership with Cliff Drysdale. We were sixth seeds and I was close to my prime at the age of 30. One of my biggest strengths during that period was lightning speed around the court. I felt as though I could get to anything, which inspired great confidence in the rest of my game.

During my 20s I'd played a lot of competitive squash and been good enough to qualify for the British Amateur Championships. I also represented Queen's Club, and all that effort and appreciation of a different set of skills really helped my mobility and coordination. In fact, I carried on playing squash for years afterwards against, amongst others, the brilliant actor Leonard Rossiter, who was a regular part of a showbiz team put together by Bill Franklyn. Bill was quite a character and achieved immortality for his 'Schhh … you know who' Schweppes adverts, while Leonard, a perfectionist at work, became a squash addict even though he didn't start playing till his mid-30s. I'd been shown a quote in which he admitted, 'I like to win. I think fooling around in sport is very tedious. It needs a fairly good player to outclass me now,' so knew it wouldn't be a hit-and-giggle whenever he was around and it certainly wasn't. There were stories that he'd taken his milkman on a family holiday just to have someone to play squash with. It was such a shock when an underlying heart condition led to his death at the age of 57 in 1984.

Drysdale and I actually made a slow start at the 1972 US Open and were two sets to one down in our first-round match against Dick Dell and Butch Seewagen before edging it in five. We also dropped a set to Patricio Cornejo and Jaime Fillol but found some momentum to see off Vitas Gerulaitis and Gene Scott in round three and, following another straight-sets win in the quarters over Andres Gimeno and Antonio Munoz, put on a masterclass to thump Nastase and Manuel Orantes 6-4, 6-4, 6-2 in the semi-final.

The all-Australian line-up of Newcombe and Owen Davidson provided the opposition in the final but we were on such a roll by now that nobody could touch us and a 6-4, 7-6, 6-3 win rounded off a near perfect set of performances that I would love to reminisce over with Cliff today and no doubt would but for subsequent events. We shared the princely sum of $3,000, which was actually a big improvement on the year before when Newk and I had $2,000 to split, but those titles mean so much to me. There was a wait of 44 years before another British player laid his hands on that US Open doubles trophy. I cheered on Jamie Murray as loudly as anyone else when he and Bruno Soares beat Pablo Carreno Busta and Guillermo Garcia-Lopez, though I couldn't help but feel winning my titles back in the 70s was one heck of a lot tougher.

Chapter 18

The Art of Beating Arthur

AS I stroll around Wimbledon and the surrounding area, at a rather more sedate pace these days (for medical reasons which I'll enlighten you about in gripping detail later!), I sometimes compile a list in my head of the very best players I took on, plus those who have followed in our footsteps, and assign them a certain position in the Taylor Superleague. It's a moveable feast and so difficult to evaluate precisely. What does 'great' really mean? Does my own personal knowledge of someone subconsciously affect my judgement at the expense of others I've only seen in action from a distance? And how can you accurately compare different generations with all the technical changes that have transformed tennis over the years? I have put together some chart-toppers later in the book that you can either nod appreciatively at or dismiss at your leisure.

Whatever credentials and qualifications you choose to adhere to, one man is assured of his place at the top table, but not just for what he did on court. Arthur Ashe was the first, and so far only, African American male tennis player to win the US Open, Wimbledon and Australian Open as well as being the first black man selected to play in the Davis Cup for the States. He was a trailblazer and a genuine legend of the sport who campaigned on behalf of many different causes during and after his playing career. He didn't relish being the only black star in tennis but never shied away from his beliefs and responsibilities and had a knack for defining whatever message he wanted to spread. 'True heroism,' he once said, 'is remarkably sober, very undramatic. It is not the urge to surpass all others at whatever cost, but the urge to serve others at whatever cost.' That always struck a chord with me as did his assertion that 'one important key to success is self-confidence. An important key to self-confidence is preparation.' Now, that had always been my motto too, so I could certainly see where he was coming from.

Arthur and I met on a number of occasions and, more often than not, he shaded things. The head-to-head was 9-4 in his favour with those matches spread over a seven-year period between 1969 and 76.

Our second-round clash at Queen's in 1973 was, for obvious reasons, quite a highly charged affair, though not as awkward as might have been the case. The potential boycott of Wimbledon was dominating the agenda and Ashe was a visible, and vocal, part of the ATP's demands. A year later he became the union's elected president but, at the time, I didn't realise quite how influential he was proving to be in all the negotiations behind the scenes.

He was a good man but he was also just another player to beat as far as I was concerned, particularly that summer when everything was kicking off. Arthur always seemed very level-headed and gracious but was never afraid to make a point. There was an interesting moment on court after he lost the US Open Final to Nastase in 74 having been up by two sets to one and a break to the good in the fourth. Irritated by some of Nastase's predictable antics, Ashe initially praised his opponent in the post-match presentation before adding, 'And when he brushes up on some of his court manners, he is going to be even better.' He and Nastase had a few bust-ups but actually got on well, even after the 'Bucharest Buffoon' once left a mouse in his locker! But those barbed comments were proof that he'd say what he felt, whenever and wherever, and I respected him for that.

What I didn't agree with was his insistence, after we'd all turned pro in the late 60s, that there shouldn't be first-round loser's prize money. He was quite adamant about that and didn't want this new, Open phase of the game to suggest players were being given money just to turn up. He was shouted down and rightly so but it surprised me he thought that way in the first place. Incidentally, the increase in prize money for the early rounds of slams over the past few years makes perfect sense. You need strength in depth and, for that to happen, players struggling to make an impact outside the top 100 require assistance. Unless you've been directly involved to some degree with professional tennis I don't think anyone can really appreciate just how hard it is to make a living lower down the ranks and the effort and skill that's required to have a ranking at all. It's brutal.

Anyway, I digress. Arthur was an aggressive player and, early in his career, had been guilty of making unnecessary errors in pursuit of the spectacular. One of his Davis Cup captains Donald Dell noted he 'could beat any player on a given day or lose to a bad player if he was mishitting'. He learnt from that, though, became a little more conservative and with an excellent serve and fabulous volleying skills was always likely to be a handful, on grass in particular. I have vivid memories of the day he won Wimbledon against Jimmy Connors in 1975. They were total opposites in terms of personality and did not get on. The problem for Ashe was that the match-up didn't suit him either. Connors had won their three previous encounters and was a red-hot favourite, with some of Arthur's friends worried he might be embarrassed in the final. I was eating in the players' restaurant around 20 minutes or so before the start and Connors was there, laughing and joking, seemingly without a care in the world. Talk about underestimating your opponent!

Arthur was canny, though. He gave Jimmy nothing on his forehand, hit low to his forehand volley and drove him mad. Before anyone knew what was happening, Ashe had the first two sets in his pocket for the loss of two games and then survived a brief fightback by becoming a little more aggressive from the back of the court to win in four. An amazing day and the only time Ashe ever beat Connors.

Having defeated Arthur at Hilton Head the year before, I knew what to do against him that wet afternoon at Queen's when the rain was so persistent we had to play indoors, much to the disappointment of all concerned. It wasn't rocket science. I was a serve and volleyer and a tough match for anyone if both aspects of that strategy were working. Initially, they didn't to the required standard and I lost the first set 6-4. That's alright, though. You know, by now, that a slow start doesn't worry me and, sure enough, I won the next two to cement my place as a player to watch that week and at Wimbledon.

In his book, *Portrait in Motion*, Arthur reflected on the match and was complimentary about my game. 'Roger can be tenacious. He's fast ... and a top counterpuncher. He'll lob you, dink you, run you around, and he's a very steady volleyer.' He also highlighted a weakness on my backhand side, which I can't refute. What I do dismiss as nonsense is his claim that I was 'forever questioning line calls' which, he added, 'makes him aggravating to play against'. Now, that is rubbish, though I think I know where he got the notion from.

We played a big final on the WCT tour in Chicago earlier that year which ended in controversy. I was fighting like crazy to finish the regular season (which concluded in May) in the top eight and so qualify for the end-of-year finals. Come the showdown in Chicago I was guaranteed eighth spot but a win over Ashe would lift me to seventh in the overall standings, and that was significant because first played eighth, second played seventh, etc. and my nemesis Ken Rosewall was number one and the man I most wanted to avoid. Understandably the crowd was very pro Ashe in Chicago, where we played indoors on a fast wooden surface. I won the first set and reached match point in a scintillating second-set tie-break only to fall victim to what was an outrageous call. With so much on the line, if you'll excuse the pun, I did make a big deal about that and felt cheated. But it was an exception, not the norm. I ended up losing the tie-break by 11 points to 9, and the match following another breaker at the end of set three. Sure, I was fuming afterwards, but so would anyone in the circumstances. Nobody wants to get a reputation for being a constant whiner, and he was bang out of order to suggest I was one of those. Arthur tried to justify his comments by adding that nobody ever questioned my honesty. 'He really believes that the out-balls are in and that his luck is all bad. I guess if you aren't as handsome as Roger Taylor, you figure you get all the bad breaks with women. If you are as handsome as Roger Taylor, you take the women for granted and bitch about the line calls.' Umm. Okay, we'll talk about the women later but Arthur's analysis in this instance was way off and unbecoming of an intelligent man with so many interesting things to say.

Chapter 19

Jimmy and the Tie-Break

JIMMY CONNORS had plenty to say over the years, much of which left him in trouble with someone or other. His durability was unbelievable, though, and proof of what an amazing competitor he was. He won 109 titles spread over three decades, and had 1,274 wins from 1,557 matches, which is extraordinary. Though not a big guy, he was tough, a street fighter and full of energy with that brilliant double-handed backhand and the metal racket that made such an impression. As, of course, did his mother. Gloria played a huge role in Jimmy's career and inadvertently grabbed international headlines during her son's first ever match at Wimbledon in 1972 against Bob Hewitt. In his book *The Outsider* Jimmy tells the story of how, during the second set, Gloria merely shouted out, 'Come on Jimmy', and the tennis world went crazy. 'You would have thought she had run on to the court like a streaker and incited a riot such was the reaction,' he wrote. Back then, of course, vocal encouragement was frowned upon, certainly at Wimbledon, and her 'outburst' had the traditionalists spluttering into their early-evening gin and tonics.

Jimmy was forever linked with his mum thereafter. Apparently, a tabloid cartoon appeared a few days later showing him holding hands with a giant gorilla as he walked on to Centre Court with a caption reading, 'Sorry, everyone, Mum couldn't make it today.'

He didn't need anyone to hold his hand, though. Tough as nails, in-your-face and yet instantly charismatic, he brought something unique to every arena he entered. With his mum a positive and stable influence and his manager Bill Riordan guiding him so shrewdly, Jimmy had a tight-knit team to keep things ticking over while he set about his business in relentless fashion.

Bill was a former boxing promoter who had taken over the US Indoor Championships in Baltimore, Maryland. You'd fly into one of the New York airports and then take a little propeller plane a short distance, bouncing all over the place as you landed. Players would arrive at different times and Bill came up with all sorts of clever promotional devices to build interest. I remember that, somewhat bizarrely, he once invented a fictitious player from Finland who emerged from the little airport terminal with horns on his head; it was a small, friendly town and he did what he could to develop local, as well as national, interest. He also arranged a supposed 'winner-takes-all' match worth $100,000 in February 1975 between Connors and Rod Laver, who was in his mid-30s by then. It was shown across the States on national TV and Jimmy won pretty comfortably. Riordan also promoted a number of other 'winner-takes-all' challenge matches, involving Connors against John Newcombe, Manuel Orantes and Ilie Nastase, who was another of Bill's clients. They were said to be worth $250,000 dollars to the winner, which proved to be Connors every time. However, a couple of years later Riordan admitted the prize money never actually existed and that the players had been given guarantees, so taking full blame for the subterfuge.

I'm not surprised Jimmy called his book *The Outsider* because that's exactly what he was. While managed by Riordan he shied away from playing in the Davis Cup and, although you'd see him on a regular basis, I certainly never got to know him. He appeared to be on the periphery, not involving himself in anything directly, while Bill sorted out his deals.

What I do want to emphasise is how difficult he was to play against. Serving at him was a problem because he had so many options. A sliced backhand return was most players' 'go-to' in those days but Jimmy came along with that metal racket, which was like a trampoline, and the ball came flying back at you so explosively. He didn't have a big serve, though. As a lefty he could spin and slide you into awkward positions but it wasn't a huge weapon, so when we met at the Pennsylvania Lawn Tennis Championships at Merion, in the August of 1972, I had a few ideas up my sleeve.

This was a prestigious tournament, first staged in 1894, and had become part of the Grand Prix tennis circuit a couple of years earlier. A little like Queen's before Wimbledon, it was the key event ahead of the US Open and I went into it feeling great. Sure enough, I reached the semis where Jimmy was waiting and, after edging a tight first set, played like a dream to take the second easily. Not that I thought the job was done for one minute against someone like Connors, who was growling at the back of the court, trying to feed off the crowd in an effort to fight back. And that's precisely what he did. Sets three and four went his way and the fifth was nip and tuck. With nothing to separate us at six games all it was tie-break time. Now, that year they had introduced the nine-point, first-to-five, tie-break. This was the brainchild of a remarkable man called Jimmy Van Alen. Jimmy was a poet, musician, publisher and civic leader among other things. He also invented the first tie-breaker and VASSS, the Van Alen Streamlined Scoring System. It meant he had left quite a mark by the time he died in July 1991. A couple of days later Stefan Edberg lost a four-set Wimbledon semi-final to Michael Stich 4-6, 7-6, 7-6, 7-6. Having heard of Van Alen's passing, the graceful Swede noted, 'If he hadn't lived, Michael and I might still be playing out there.'

Van Alen was so ahead of his time and introduced a whole host of new concepts at his own tournament in Newport, Rhode Island, which is now home to the International Tennis Hall of Fame. All the players were housed in luxury accommodation near the club and Jimmy was a constant presence, immaculately dressed with a boater and courteous old-fashioned mannerisms.

Talking of old-fashioned, his mother, who must have been in her 90s, used to arrive each day in a vintage white Rolls-Royce, which was parked by her chauffeur next to the entrance. More often than not she didn't actually get out of the car. Instead, the players were lined up and, one by one, climbed into the back of the vehicle to be introduced by Jimmy before heading off to get ready. The conversation was stilted to say the least, but he ran the show and all of us were more than happy to do whatever was required.

I made the final there one year, losing to New Zealander Ian Crookenden, and although the grass surface left plenty to be desired, it was one of my favourite events.

There was nothing old-fashioned about Van Alen's innovative ideas. He introduced a plate event for those knocked out in the first round, experimented with a 'one serve only rule' which included the server having to stand three metres behind the baseline and also tinkered with a 'three-shot rule' which meant the point didn't start for real until the returner hit his second shot. He was always trying out different scoring methods as well and that is what secured his legacy.

The VASSS stipulated that whoever's turn it was to serve at the conclusion of set four (or two, in a best-of-three-set match) would do so for the first two points and also for points five and six, leaving his or her opponent to serve on points three and four and seven, eight and nine, assuming it went the distance. The start of the tie-break was also accompanied by the introduction of a red flag which the umpire tied to his chair so informing anyone nearby that a significant passage of play was unfolding. This would often lead to scores of spectators rushing over to share in the drama.

That afternoon I served first but failed to build a lead and found myself 4-2 down with three Connors serves to come. Oh dear! Now, Jimmy didn't serve and volley very often and the grass, being totally honest, wasn't great so I decided to chip and charge. It was risky but it worked not once, not twice but three times in a row to secure victory. I recall it being all over in a flash but the manner of the win, under intense pressure, still feels good more than 50 years on. I went on to beat Malcolm Anderson in the final too, so it was quite a week. Funnily enough, that part of the world has been kind to Englishmen. John Lloyd won the title two years after me and Justin Rose triumphed at the 2013 US Open golf tournament just across the road at the amazing course they have there.

I thought that particular scoring system was clever but it never caught on. The International Tennis Federation (ITF) didn't like it. When I returned from the States at the end of the year, I was asked to play an exhibition tie-break at Queen's Club, right by the entrance gates on a court that was knocked down some years later when they extended the car park. We trialled the current format of one serve, followed by two each from then on so I'll happily lay claim to being a pioneer of sorts! In truth, though, I preferred the sudden death way at four-all. Okay, we would never have had those classic McEnroe-Borg 20-18 spectacles but it sped things up and created instant excitement. It certainly worked for me on that occasion, though not, alas, a week or two later, as we're about to find out.

Chapter 20

Him Again

I SUPPOSE it was almost inevitable that one of my most memorable matches would have to be against Mr Nastase. While most of our encounters had incidents and moments of brilliance, the second-round clash at the 1972 US Open built into an absolute classic, having initially looked as though it was going to be a damp squib. I very nearly didn't even make it past round one that year. Drawn to play the South African-born Rhodesian Andrew Pattison I struggled to find any consistency and was relieved to squeeze through in five far from convincing sets. Ilie, by contrast, who was seeded four, lost only two games in his first match to Colombia's Jairo Velasco Sr. Appropriately enough, considering his last name, Jairo went on to be rather more successful when competing in the legends category, winning titles in the over-45, 50, 70 and 75 sections.

When Nastase tapped into his A game for any significant period of time he was terrifying to play against and, after a tight first set, which he won 7-5, I found myself on the receiving end of his 'magic touch' repertoire as he claimed the second 6-2. The beauty of five-setters is that you always have a chance to play your way back into business. Gradually, the momentum shifted and when I took the third set in a tie-break he lost a bit of focus and started showing some of the mental fragility that always made me feel I had a chance to beat him. Sure enough, the fourth set was one-way traffic in my direction, though both of us were playing some seriously good tennis, which the crowd was lapping up.

It was touch and go in the fifth right up to another nine-point breaker at six games all. I was in a zone that day, which enabled me to ignore the occasional outbursts from the other end of the court as the tension rose but, although I served first, he went 3-1 up in the tie-break and, unlike his good friend Connors, managed to secure victory from there.

He went on to become champion at the end of the fortnight by beating Arthur Ashe in the final having found himself in big trouble when down by two sets to one. Though, as mentioned, Ashe publicly berated him for some of his behaviour afterwards, Nastase nonetheless demonstrated a tenacity that fortnight which would have brought him much greater success over the years had it been a constant. He was a magician, though, and that borderline craziness was part of the parcel.

The pain of losing was lessened to a degree when we were both given $2,500 for playing the 'match of the tournament' in the eyes of the United States Tennis Association but it takes a long time to dissect and accept defeats like that. Ilie went on to beat Patrice Dominguez, Bob Hewitt, Fred Stolle and Tom Gorman relatively comfortably to reach the final. All good players, of course, but, inevitably, there was a part of me that wondered, 'What if I had come through that day?' Then again, we all think like that, don't we?

Chapter 21

A Short Chapter but the Longest Match

I'VE BEEN lucky enough to play in front of large, knowledgeable crowds at the best venues in the world. It's fair to say this next match did not feature any of those components. Not by a long chalk. However, it was a record breaker!

Picture the scene. It's the winter of 1966 and I'm part of the Great Britain King's Cup squad in freezing Poland. Captain Bobby Wilson, Mike Sangster and I were a pretty tight-knit group in those days having won the competition in 1964 and 65. The cup was named in honour of the Swedish King, Gustav, who created the event sometime after the Second World War. He was a huge fan of the sport and attended the final each year. It was an indoor spectacle with countries like Hungary, Bulgaria, Poland, Sweden, Austria, Italy, Finland and Czechoslovakia usually involved. For whatever reason, I invariably produced my very best form in this competition and only lost one match in four years, although, in truth, it never captured big headlines and I don't know how many people remember it to this day. I do, though, and in particular an extraordinary tie in Warsaw.

As a player you were on to a winner straightaway in these situations with free accommodation at swanky hotels always thrown in along with some decent food and expenses, which were not something to take for granted back in the 60s. We stayed at the Grand Hotel, which was great ... the venue for the tie was not, though! It was a sports hall and the multi-purpose wooden court surface was covered in all sorts of different coloured lines for basketball and goodness knows what else. You could just about make out where the square was and you also realised, very quickly, that it was lightning fast.

The tie began at 6pm. Now, with the temperature outside minus 12, none of the windows in the main arena were open. Inside, everybody seemed to be smoking and I walked out into this fug that had me coughing before I'd even reached the net. It was unbelievable, as were the subsequent line calls from the locals, who couldn't resist the odd mischievous grin after a particularly bad one. You had to expect that, though and, to be fair to them, calling lines wasn't easy with a surface that resembled a map of the London Underground.

Eventually it did kick off a little bit between their captain, a former middleweight boxer whose name escapes me, and Bobby Wilson. Bobby was very proper with a 'we're British and must do the right thing' sort of attitude, as a general rule. However, he became increasingly irate over what he perceived to be some outrageous skulduggery. He ended up face to face with his opposite number in front of the umpire's chair with a vociferous crowd making their feelings clear while in the process of lighting up more cigarettes. In the midst of all this I was doing my best to stay focused against a good player called Wieslaw Gasiorek, who made the fourth round at the French Open a couple of times and the third round at Wimbledon in the early 60s.

The surface was so fast it was almost impossible to break serve. All you'd see through the fumes was a fuzzy object heading your way and beyond before you had time to move. Loss of concentration was the danger and, finally, he did break me to win the first set 29-27. No tie-breaks back then. It hadn't taken as long as the scoreline might suggest because the points were so short but it seemed like one heck of a way back.

The second set was even longer! I finally won it by 33 games to 31 at which point the restless crowd became extremely agitated. The prospect of a marathon third was unthinkable but, luckily, I'd worn him out by then and won the decider 6-3. In the history of tennis there's only been a handful of top-class matches with a 30 in the set scoreline and only once before had our second set been exceeded in length; former Wimbledon and US Open champion Vic Seixas (who celebrated his 100th birthday in 2023) and Bill Bowrey had played out a 34-32 set earlier in 1966. However, our 129-game clash was the longest overall match on record, something to cherish, not that there was any respite. I played out a 33-31 set the following day too as we won the tie.

Mike Sangster had to go out for his match after mine that first night. He battled through a 26-24 set, so we didn't finish until the early hours of the morning, by which time we must have inhaled enough cigarette smoke to kill a herd of elephants. We got changed and walked upstairs to find the whole place deserted. They'd all disappeared, leaving us stranded outside this sports hall in minus 12 degrees, many years before Ubers had ever been thought of. We finally thumbed a lift from someone who must have thought it rather strange to see the Great Britain team wandering around in the freezing cold at 3am. But experiences like that were great in terms of team bonding and to be in *The Guinness Book of Records* was quite something too. We won the King's Cup again that year with further victories over Finland, Czechoslovakia and then Italy in Milan without losing a rubber.

As the years went by and tie-breaks were introduced I started to think our record would never be beaten but then, lo and behold, John Isner and Nicolas Mahut produced their 11-hour five-minute, 183-game, three-day marathon at Wimbledon in 2010. I live just around the corner from the club and walked past Court 18 every day, and was amazed like everyone else that it was still going on and that my record was destined to be eclipsed. Mind you, those two didn't have to contend with several thousand heavily smoking Poles doing their best to disrupt the equilibrium!

Chapter 22

The Winner Takes It All

SO MANY different factors combine to create the stand-out moments but, ultimately, as a professional athlete it's all about winning. We've covered some of my agonising near misses and there are other painful experiences to come, notably as Davis Cup captain, but every now and then it all goes to plan from start to finish. Only one player can end the week undefeated, clutching a trophy and cheque in his or her sweaty palms and, on 18 occasions as a pro, nine times a singles champion and nine with a partner, that was me. Those moments of great satisfaction came from a wide variety of different places all over the world. Port Elizabeth, Auckland, Leicester, Palermo, Haverford (Pennsylvania), Copenhagen, Newport (Rhode Island), Fairfield in Connecticut and Roanoke in North Carolina were the scenes of my singles successes. On the doubles front we can tack on New York twice, Hobart, Gstaad, Monte Carlo, Newport again, Cleveland, Vancouver and Kitzbuhel, which was my last ever pro title, alongside Buster Mottram in 1977. Add to that all those special Davis Cup and King's Cup triumphs and the not-inconsiderable success I enjoyed as an amateur and there are more than enough warm memories to keep those painful blows at bay.

I thought about, and have eventually decided to include, a momentous Davis Cup tie against Spain in this series of highlights, which – and do feel free to call me big-headed – has been rather fun to write! In May 1975 we travelled to Barcelona for a huge test on clay against a team consisting of Manuel Orantes, Jose Higueras and Juan Gisbert. They were masters of the surface and hot favourites but Buster Mottram and I genuinely believed we had a chance to cause an upset. Paul Hutchins was captain and had also selected John Lloyd and John Feaver.

Buster played the opening rubber against Orantes and was distinctly second best throughout. He lost 6-4, 6-1, 6-2 to leave our backs firmly against the wall. I then split the opening two sets with Higueras before coming through in four to level the match after day one. Then, in the early hours of Saturday morning, I woke up feeling horrendous. Without wishing to go into too much detail, regular visits to the loo were required and I later discovered Paul Hutchins had gone down with the same bug. Buster and I did what we could in the doubles that afternoon but lost 6-4, 6-4, 4-6, 6-0 to Orantes and Gisbert at which point I retreated to my room, or more specifically bathroom, and concluded I'd never felt more unwell in my life.

At 2-1 down in the tie, we now faced a selection dilemma. Buster was raring to go against Higueras in the fourth rubber but, assuming he won that, who should play in the decider? Normally I'd have been chomping at the bit but with my stomach still spinning out of control we agreed it would have to be John Lloyd. Paul and I staggered out of our rooms to have a word with him but the response was not what we'd anticipated. John, forever taping his fingers and re-gripping a racket, looked agitated and clearly wasn't up for it. That's understandable to a degree. A deciding rubber away from home on clay against one of the best players in the world is a demanding test but it's a challenge that should be relished. Paul looked at me, I looked at Paul and, before haring back to our respective bathrooms, decided I'd somehow have to find a way to get on court.

Sure enough, Buster beat Higueras with a brilliant display on the Sunday, which saw him lose only four games. Still feeling far from normal and dosed up with an assortment of medicines to steady my insides, I duly commenced battle with Orantes. And what a battle it proved to be. In slow, heavy conditions he won the first set 6-3, after which I won the second by the same margin. The pattern continued as he took the third 7-5 before I levelled again, also 7-5. I was serve-volleying whenever possible in this battle of left-handers but some of the rallies seemed to be never-ending. Maybe it was because I felt so under the weather but, as the match developed, I went into 'the zone'. I could see this tunnel in front of me. At the end of it was a glowing red light tinged with clay and a figure I never fully comprehended as being Orantes. That may sound distracting but it had a positive effect on the way I played.

We'd already been on court for more than four hours come the start of the final set and, by now, the crowd of around 8,000, sensing the possibility of a Spanish defeat, had become animated and angry. I questioned a call early in the decider, which prompted a ferocious reaction from the stands. They all started whistling their disapproval and didn't stop! Orantes, a lovely guy, came up to me at the net and suggested I apologise to calm the situation. Well, there was no way I was going to do that so we continued in the most ridiculous fashion. Every time the ball travelled towards me 8,000 people whistled like mad before becoming totally silent as I sent it back down the other end. This went on for ages with the umpire unable, or unwilling, to calm things down.

As we headed deep into the final set the atmosphere became dangerously hostile. I was increasingly aware of this fellow in the front row who'd been giving me death stares and constantly going 'psst' every time I went near him or was about to serve. Without putting too fine a point on it, he really started to piss me off and I decided to confront him after the match whatever the outcome. Eventually, after a monumental effort, I reached match point on my serve at 5-4 amidst a crescendo of noise. What an opportunity to record one of the great Davis Cup wins. Still very much in the zone I missed my first serve but sent the second swinging away to his backhand before coming in to punch a volley into his backhand corner. It was a good volley too. Orantes ran across and conjured a shot he later admitted could have gone anywhere. It was one of those 'shut your eyes and hope' moments, similar to a couple we saw from Novak Djokovic against Roger Federer when match points down at the US Open. I turned and watched as the ball fizzed over the net and flew down the line, catching the outside edge. Unbelievable, and terminal. I couldn't recover from that and went on to lose the fifth set 7-5, which meant Spain won the tie 3-2.

By the end I was close to being broken both physically and mentally but walking up to shake hands with Manuel at the net there was only one thought in my mind. I was determined to go and grab that little so-and-so in the crowd who'd been such a pain. As I turned in his direction he looked at me with sudden alarm and ran up the stairs towards the exit. I started to chase him but, not realising just how tired I was, couldn't find the energy to climb over the hoardings. Instead, I ended up with one leg over the wall with the other still on court as some other rather unfriendly locals raced across to have their say. One of them tried to lunge at me but instead hit poor old John Feaver who'd come over to try to help calm the situation. It was chaos but, in hindsight, I'm glad I didn't have the energy to run after that clown or I might still be serving a ban to this day! It was the most unpleasant atmosphere I ever experienced but I'd be lying if I didn't admit to enjoying those confrontations, even if that one did go over the top.

Reflecting on my successes, it's so difficult to place one title above the rest. Clearly, the two US Open doubles crowns are hard to better, but receiving what at the time was my biggest pay-day of $10,000 from Princess Benedikte of Denmark in 1973, after winning the WCT title in Copenhagen, has to be up there. That was some week, with big wins over Tom Okker and Mark Cox the stand-out memories along with the final itself against Marty Riessen, which required a final-set tie-break. The Danes nick-named me 'the husky left-hander', which was perfectly acceptable, and the princess was most gracious when handing over the cheque. Shaking hands with royalty was a far cry from those cold nights at Weston Park and I know how proud Mum and Dad were of me that weekend.

I also beat Okker to win the Auckland title in 1970 when another Brit, Ann Jones, triumphed in the women's event. Great though the feeling was, as Tom, with his speed and strong heavily top-spun forehand, was a very awkward man to play against, there was no opportunity to celebrate that success over the 'flying Dutchman' as I had to be in Philadelphia two days later! Such was the nature of the schedule in those early days of Open tennis. It's an 18-hour flight now and was a lot longer back then. Frances was with me and the jet lag for both of us was incredibly debilitating. Night after night that following week, staying as guests at someone's house, we lay there trying to adjust our body clocks, to no avail. You had to put up with that sort of thing, though. Pierre Barthes once had to fly from France to Australia at the drop of a hat when someone pulled out of an event at late notice and more or less run straight on to court. There was no point complaining, it was a case of have racket and go wherever. The accommodation itself could be hit and miss too. It wasn't a succession of five-star hotels and 24 hours a day room service. Some of the 'host' hospitality on offer was limited and occasionally dangerous. We had to pack our bags within an hour of arriving at one house when it became clear the family was experiencing a chicken-pox outbreak.

Barthes, who I liked a lot, was the man I beat in the Palermo final. That was an important stepping stone for me on clay and included wins over Adriano Panatta and Ion Tiriac along the way. Winning is a habit and is addictive. That's why I carried on playing through my 40s, 50s, 60s and 70s; you never lose that competitive juice and thrill of the fight. Sure, you start losing more than you win, but coming out on top is priceless and unforgettable.

Now, talking about something unforgettable …

Chapter 23

The Name's Bond, James Bond. (Or At Least It Nearly Was)

AS YOU know, and was demonstrated by that King's Cup marathon, I prided myself on being fit, focused and professional whenever possible. To my way of thinking, every extra bit of effort away from the court, be it in the gym or running on Wimbledon Common, might prove the difference come a tight match in a big event. Don't leave anything to chance; what can be more important for a professional athlete?

Rarely did I lose focus, especially come the grass-court season. For me the tournament at Queen's was almost as important as Wimbledon. Having been a runner-up there twice I was made an honorary member for life, which is more than the All England Club decided my efforts merited despite three semi-finals and a pretty decent Davis Cup record. I'll focus more on that issue later.

There was one bizarre interlude in the summer of 1967 that did threaten to derail my efforts during the grass campaign but could have led to a whole new chapter in my life. I was in great shape that year and genuinely believed I could win both Queen's and Wimbledon. Sure enough, I saw off Ray Keldie, Nick Kalogeropoulos, Cliff Drysdale, Tom Okker and then Owen Davidson in the semi-finals at Queen's to force a showdown with John Newcombe. As mentioned earlier that match-up never worked well for me but I wasn't unduly disheartened.

Reaching the final brought a lot of headlines and, unbeknown to me, interest from the world of Hollywood. Wimbledon began and, on the first Tuesday, I was watching a match in the stands with Frances when Noel Berryman, the vice-chairman of Queen's Club, came up to us and sat down. I'd become friendly with Noel having spent so much time at Queen's, training there and getting to know a lot of people behind the scenes.

'You're not going to believe this,' he said, 'but you know everyone's looking for a new James Bond to succeed Sean Connery?' And I nodded because it had been an ongoing story in the papers with plenty of speculation as to who would be given the role.

'Well,' he went on, 'I've brought some guests today, the scriptwriter Richard Maybourne, and his wife, who are very close to the Bond franchise. During Saturday's final she turned to Richard while watching you against Newcombe and proclaimed, "There's your new James Bond."

'She meant you, Roger,' he added with a big smile.

Of course, I immediately assumed this was some kind of a wind-up but Noel insisted he was deadly serious and asked if I'd be interested in meeting some of the money men at their offices in Park Lane to talk about the project. Frances started laughing, saying the whole thing was ridiculous and to stop being so silly, but I was keen to explore the options despite never having set foot on a stage before or done any acting.

Noel was very excited and said they wanted me to go to their offices the following Sunday. Now, that was bang in the middle of Wimbledon, which was an obvious concern. It was now or never, though, and I agreed. So, in between winning a few matches that first week against Chauncey Steele and Martin Mulligan amongst others I stared menacingly into mirrors trying to capture the essence of 007: 'The name's Bond, James Bond,' eyebrows up, a glint in the eye (or was it a nervous tick), while painfully aware that an unmistakeable South Yorkshire accent was definitely not what Ian

Fleming envisioned when writing the books and certainly not what the Broccoli clan had placed at the top of their wish list when the search to replace Connery began.

Sunday came around and we headed into town. I was in a state of conflict: excited, nervous and also worried that my attention was being taken away from Wimbledon. A little voice kept telling me I should be in the gym, or halfway around the common for a fifth time, not decked out in a smart suit pretending to be the world's most famous spy.

We arrived and I was shepherded into a room full of men, none of whom I knew. Two of these moguls had huge cigars on the go and they all stared at me without saying a word … not one word. They kept on staring, making me feel incredibly self-conscious! And that was it. I never even had a chance to tell them 'I'm Bond, James Bond, don't you know' before the meeting ended and I headed back to Wimbledon.

By now I'd reached the last 32 in which I beat the Finnish player Pekka Saila very comfortably to set up a round-of-16 clash with Cliff Drysdale. Meanwhile, negotiations continued off-stage and, despite the fact nobody had spoken to me, or asked me to speak, Noel re-appeared and announced they'd like me to go to Pinewood Studios, oh, and could I bring my swimsuit! At which point Frances became very irate, saying the whole thing was absolute madness. She's a Scottish Baptist and clearly didn't fancy becoming a Bond girl. In hindsight, the fact that she was having none of it proved a key factor in me not being more pro-active. I didn't directly say no to the offer and, strange as it may sound, wouldn't have been too concerned wandering around in my trunks at Pinewood Studios. I was in pretty good shape and not the least bit body-conscious but through an apparent lack of interest on my behalf nothing more came of it. These days you'd have an agent and a publicist and God knows who else making sure something got sorted, running down the road to the studio, if necessary, but life was different back then.

I'm often asked how much I regret not making more of the opportunity and still laugh at some of the reports from those days which referred to me as the James Bond of tennis. It would have been fun, of course it would. I reckon I could have jogged down the beach resembling a lethal assassin, jumping in the air with gun at the ready before walking into the sunset with a mystery blonde on my arm. Whether I could have matched the smouldering intensity Connery brought to the table or Roger Moore's more humorous approach is open to debate. Actually, it isn't. The answer is a resounding 'no' but it wouldn't have been for a lack of effort!

The man they actually chose to replace Connery, before Moore came along, was George Lazenby, which maintains the tennis theme. He went on to marry the hugely successful American player-turned-broadcaster Pam Shriver, who will re-appear later in the book. And there's a curious final chapter to the tale. A few years on, I was in California for a tournament, sitting quietly at a bar. Next to me was a guy who looked like a broken man. He was swaying in his chair, very much the worse for wear. And it was Lazenby! He'd made *On Her Majesty's Secret Service* and fallen out with his co-star Diana Rigg. I remember a subsequent quote from the producer Cubby Broccoli who said casting Lazenby was 'his biggest mistake in 16 years. He was so arrogant and couldn't deal with the success.'

There were all sorts of stories as to why he only did one film but as I sat there, looking across at this figure slumped on his stool, I wondered if maybe I'd had a lucky escape after all. That said, every time I watch a Bond movie there's a little bit of me that wonders what if? And I did perfect the 'Bond, James Bond' line, you know.

Chapter 24

We Are Superstars

I WAS a superstar for two memorable days in a non-tennis capacity.

Back in the 60s and 70s, commercial opportunities, a very tidy source of income for today's top sporting stars, were few and far between. I did what I could to capitalise on my success and, in 1972, signed a contract with IMG, unquestionably the leading sports agency at the time and one that continues to be a huge player in so many different markets today. Founded by Mark McCormack in 1960, three of golf's all-time greats, Arnold Palmer, Gary Player and Jack Nicklaus, were the company's first clients. The rest is history.

Prize money was my main source of income but the amounts paid out were modest, to say the least. Commercial deals were pretty much limited to what I needed to ply my trade. Agreements for shoes, clothing and rackets were available but little else and, with so few leading manufacturers in those days, it wasn't easy to get cute and trade one off against another. Dunlop and Slazenger were the only serious players in the tennis world, and the UK market was not big.

Arnold Palmer was the man who swung the dial. At one point he was said to have had 167 different deals, ranging from dry-clothing companies to taxi firms and restaurants, etc. Modern-day A-listers owe much to him but it took a long time for those types of endorsements to become more obtainable for lesser mortals.

There was, however, one very popular television programme that paid well and was certain to raise your profile. *Superstars* was the brainchild of former figure skater and two-time Olympic champion Dick Button, who sold the idea to ABC Sports. A two-hour American special was broadcast in the winter of 1973 with ten top athletes from ten different sports competing in a variety of challenges. Olympic pole vault gold-medallist Bob Seagren was the first winner though heavyweight boxing champion Joe Frazier grabbed the headlines by nearly drowning in the 50-metre swimming heats. Having been pulled out of the water he admitted he didn't know how to swim. When asked why he still entered the race, Frazier responded, 'How was I to know I couldn't swim unless I tried it!' The incident left him in awe of pro swimmers and in particular the star of the 1972 Olympics; 'That Mark Spitz is a tough muthafucker!' was his candid assessment of the American who won seven golds in Munich, each in world-record time.

The programme was a hit in the States throughout the 70s and continued to be shown on and off by various broadcasters until 2003 with a revival edition in 2009 that Jennifer Capriati was due to take part in before an injury forced her to withdraw.

The series was also sold to the UK, becoming an instant ratings winner, and between 1973 and 2012 there were 17 editions, with the first one, officially called *Britain's Sporting Superstars*, staged at the Crystal Palace National Sports Centre with yours truly one of the super seven chosen for the line-up!

Top athletics coach and BBC sports commentator Ron Pickering was a principal figure in the planning and production of the event and other consultants were hired to ensure there were no mishaps. They included a guy called Mark Barker who was loaned out by the army to help with the shooting. He did his best to ensure sensible precautions were followed on the range at all times, though I gather the following year QPR legend Stan Bowles came very close to shooting his own foot off!

The most famous casualty was another footballer, Kevin Keegan. During the 1976 event, the Liverpool and England hero fell off his bike at high speed after clipping the wheel of his opponent, a Belgian soccer player called Gilbert Van Binst. Keegan tumbled on to the cinder track and sustained nasty cuts and bruises to his shoulders, back and arms before dusting himself down and winning the re-run race. Not surprisingly, Liverpool FC were furious when they discovered what had happened. Can you imagine Mo Salah being allowed to take part in something similar today! That incident has never been forgotten. Years later Keegan was quoted as saying, 'It is a source of constant amazement to me that after all these years and the many things I have done, there is still a section of the public for whom my lifetime's achievements consist of my hairstyle, my performance in the European Cup against Saint-Etienne, and falling off a bike in *Superstars*.'

Boosting my profile was clearly going to be advantageous so when my agent, Gordon Lazenbury, suggested taking part, I jumped at the opportunity. Here was a chance to demonstrate to a national audience that there was a little more to me than just hitting a tennis ball with skill and precision. Initially, I expected the whole thing to be fairly relaxed but it soon became clear that wasn't going to be the case. With seven very competitive professional sportsmen all keen to shine, the desire to succeed became intense. And a fabulous cast had been assembled.

Bobby Moore was top of the billing. He had lifted the World Cup for England seven years earlier and was still in tip-top shape, playing for West Ham. Tony Jacklin was perhaps the least fit among us but had won the Open and the US Open to put golf firmly on the map in this country and was very strong mentally. As an athlete David Hemery was expected to win. A quiet man, he'd won the 400m hurdles at the 1968 Olympics in Mexico as well as silver and bronze medals at Munich in 72. From the world of rugby came Welsh fly-half Barry John who had starred on a number of memorable occasions for his country and the British and Irish Lions. He had supreme confidence in his own ability and an impressive mental approach to everything he undertook. Three-time world champion Jackie Stewart was still driving professionally in 1973 and the Flying Scot was ultra-determined to make as big an impact as possible having kept himself in excellent shape throughout his motor-racing career. He was also an excellent shot and surprised me a little by being the loudest and most in-your-face of the group. But the man I was most excited to meet that week was Joe Bugner. I've always been a big boxing fan. There are so many similarities between boxing and tennis, and Bugner, who actually has triple citizenship having been born in Hungary and become a naturalised citizen in both Australia and the UK, had captured my attention with some of his big fights, notably against Muhammad Ali, Joe Frazier and Henry Cooper. I went to the controversial fight at the Empire Pool in March 71 which he won against 'Our 'Enery', much to the annoyance of the British public who I don't think ever really forgave him. I also went to Earl's Court to see him fight Joe Frazier just a few months before *Superstars*. He had a great defence but lacked the firepower to match Frazier and lost on points in a gruelling contest.

It was a genuine thrill to meet them all, though. Back then television coverage of big sporting events was very limited compared to today. You'd see bits and pieces but to actually come face to face with these guys and have a chance to see how they ticked was a real treat. Bobby Moore was a bit special. It doesn't get any bigger than captaining your country to World Cup glory, particularly on home soil, but he was so normal and easy to talk to. I just wish we'd had longer to get to know one another. The whole thing was recorded in a couple of days so there was precious little time to hang around and forge any meaningful relationships.

And there was plenty to think about with ten events and each contestant taking part in eight of them. You weren't allowed to compete in your own sport and the points were awarded on a 7-4-2-1 scale for the top-four finishers. There was also a handicapping system, which wasn't used in the American version. This allowed Hemery to compete in one of the track and field events with a distance penalty, which was considered a fairer option than for him not to race at all.

The schedule began with the 100m dash, followed by shooting, swimming, a three-hole golf event, a four-part fitness test, tennis, football penalties, a bike race, weightlifting and, finally, a 600m steeplechase.

I clearly remember the sense of excitement and trepidation ahead of the sprint. Moving outside your comfort zone is a good thing for body and soul but the possibility of making a fool of myself in front of some legends and a huge BBC audience lurked uneasily in the back of my mind. Fortunately, I managed to avoid any serious banana skins and finished second behind Barry John in the 100m. The surprise in that event was Jackie Stewart's performance. He powered past Joe Bugner for third place to prove he wasn't only a Flying Scot when helped by a turbo-powered engine.

Jackie was expected to win the clay-pigeon shooting as he'd been a competitive skeet shooter with a rifle. Everyone was given 20 shots to break five clay discs from a distance of ten metres with an air rifle. You picked up 20 points for each broken disc with three points deducted for every extra shot required to break all five discs. Perhaps still smarting after being pipped for third place in the sprint, Joe Bugner hit all the discs with just 11 shots, one fewer than Jackie, who was not happy. I was just relieved not to have to compete in that event having never picked up a gun in my life.

And the challenges kept on coming! There was a big crowd for the swimming. Hemery won that with Bobby Moore second. I surprised myself in the golf. Thank God we only had to play three holes because I was by no means a regular or consistent player. A third-place finish behind Stewart and Barry John was satisfying, though it would be stretching the truth to suggest we tore the course up. I took 18 shots and Jackie beat Barry in a play-off after they'd both carded 15.

The worst part of the whole thing was the four-part fitness test which Ron Pickering, who clearly had a slightly sadistic side to him, had devised. It consisted of a shuttle run, standing long jump, squat thrusts and the parallel-bar dips. Inevitably, Hemery was head and shoulders above the rest of us in this one. I remember being rather proud of myself for managing 27 dips but it wasn't long before regular contestants, like the judo supremo Brian Jacks, were managing around 100 in just 60 seconds. He also managed 118 squat thrusts one year. That hurts just thinking about it!

I didn't compete in the tennis event, which Barry John won, and he led the field after then coming first in the football penalties competition. We had six attempts at beating the brilliant Pat Jennings who was in his pomp as a Tottenham player and Northern Ireland international. I got one past him but Barry beat Bugner in a shoot-off after each scored three times. Hemery then won the bike race in which I managed a creditable joint third before Bugner, a giant of a man, came out on top in the weightlifting. I was fourth, which was a decent effort.

It meant that Barry, Joe and David all had a chance to become the inaugural champion going into the last event, the 600m steeplechase, which provided one of my most vivid memories of those two exhausting mid-summer days. Hemery had to start a further 100m behind the field as a result of the handicapping system but didn't take long to close the gap. There was a very unpleasant water jump halfway round. I'd made a good start but turned to look behind me as I clambered over the jump to see Hemery flying towards us all and Bugner coming to a grinding halt as he completely misjudged the jump and failed to get over it. Purple-faced and indignant at this critical error, poor old Joe eventually heaved himself up in unseemly fashion. I shouldn't have laughed but it did look very funny. To be fair to him, it's worth reiterating there had been no training whatsoever ahead of our attempts to master these specialist skills. I'm just amazed we all battled on gamely with no obvious complaints, misgivings or injuries.

In truth, the whole thing was set up for David Hemery who eased past Barry and Bobby with 60m remaining to take the first of what would be three *Superstars* titles. In his nine appearances on the programme he was also runner-up three times and he went on to be recognised as Britain's best *Superstar* from 1973 to 1977.

I finished third in the steeplechase and fifth overall, which was okay though rather frustrating because only the top four picked up extra prize money on top of our appearance fee. Hemery's bonus was £4,000, Barry John earned an extra £2,500 for coming second while Joe Bugner and Jackie Stewart each took home the princely sum of £750 for joint third. It was a fun experience but I drove away wishing I'd done better and been more prepared. There weren't many regrets, though, and, at least for those two sunny days in the August of 73, I can always say I was, officially, a superstar!

Chapter 25

Uncovering a Very Private Life

I'VE DONE plenty of soul-searching before committing this chapter to print. Expressing my emotions is not something that comes naturally and talking in detail about the people closest to me feels strangely uncomfortable. I'm sure everyone looks back at aspects of their life with an acceptance they could have done this or that better. I'm no exception. But there's no rehearsal. You do what you think is right at the time and try to learn from the mistakes you inevitably make.

The day-to-day routine of a professional tennis player is not exactly compatible with a conventional domestic set-up. The travelling is constant and the very nature of an individual sport invariably leads to a blinkered mindset where the needs of you, the player, often outweigh all other considerations.

Let me be totally honest and admit that, as a young man, all I cared about was tennis and becoming as good a player as possible. The need to compete and improve consumed me then, and never really went away. It's addictive and makes you feel truly alive. The relentless need to prove yourself day after day on court is incredibly demanding, even if you don't realise it at the time. The constant highs and lows affect your psyche, leaving you in a parallel world to normal everyday existence. And that can be very tough for those nearest and dearest to you.

I first met Frances Maclennan during my trip to the South of France with Barry in the early 60s. She was a talented player in her own right who competed on the UK circuit in places such as Hurlingham, Sutton, Connaught and Surbiton and went on to perform with distinction at Wimbledon as a doubles player for eight years, reaching the semi-finals with Robin Lloyd in 1968.

Frances came from a wealthy background. Her father was a successful businessman who did particularly well in the whisky trade. She was one of a number of tennis-playing Brits staying at a lovely hotel in the Antibes peninsula and we started chatting on a regular basis during that special spring. It wasn't exactly love at first sight but we grew increasingly close as our paths continued to cross over the next few years. A mixed doubles team at Wimbledon one summer, we eventually married in 1969 when I was in my late 20s.

It's easy to say with the benefit of hindsight but Frances and I were different and to all intents and purposes unsuited in so many ways. She's a very clever, incredibly efficient woman but not one to show a great deal of emotion. Long periods on her own with young children while I was on tour were a real challenge; so too the responsibility of all the planning when, as a young family, we lived for a time in the States while I played team tennis, and again during the early years of the time we lived in Portugal. We did, and still do, share two key attributes that kept us together as a married couple for 13 years and helped maintain a bond as responsible parents living separate lives since then. Both of us are loyal and determined and that has proved invaluable during the dark days.

The darkest day of all came as recently as November 2024 when I received a chilling phone call from Portugal. My son Greig, I was told, had been found dead aged just 46. I can't begin to describe the shock that paralysed me as I listened in disbelief. A few weeks on I'm still unable to come to terms with it. The complexities of the legal system in Portugal means a lengthy wait between the autopsy and official news regarding the cause of death. As I write we don't yet know all the details. Greig was found in bed by his distraught Russian wife Anastasia with no obvious explanation as to what had happened. A number of us, including Frances and my second wife Alison, flew out the next day to be with her and did what we could to find some comfort amongst ourselves.

His life hadn't been easy. A gifted tennis player, he found out to his cost just how hard it is to break through at even the lowest level on the professional tour. There are so many talented individuals around the world and you need time, money and resilience, plus an awful lot of ability, to have any chance of making an impact. It didn't happen for him and he fought some personal battles thereafter. That said, through the help of my close friend and doctor Bob Murphy, he had been in a much better place mentally of late and appeared a long way down the road to recovery. He was swimming regularly and considering taking up tennis again. We'd already made plans for him and Anastasia to come over to Wimbledon for the 2025 Championships and he was looking forward to that. I can't for the life of me comprehend the fact that I'll never see him again.

With only six years separating the three of them, Greig's sisters, Zoe and Katriona, were understandably devasted as well. They shared an awful lot while growing up together and nothing can prepare you for something like this.

Zoe was born in 1970. With two tennis pros as parents it was no surprise to witness her growing passion for the sport and appreciate the natural talent she demonstrated on court. She was also very bright and I was so proud when she gained a place at the prestigious London School of Economics, which is consistently ranked amongst the top three universities in the country. After her studies she worked for a decade as a management accountant and financial analyst for a number of blue-chip companies. Blessed with a strong creative side she eventually decided to retrain in fashion at Istituto Marangoni before focusing on architectural interior design in New York and London.

Using those skills to great effect she re-designed and then ran the pro shop at Queen's, achieving the highest turnover for the club during the financial crisis. She also designed and decorated our kitchen at home along with the spacious extension from where much of this book has been written. Tennis has always played a big part in her life. As a youngster she interned at the Canadian Open, and worked at the Aussie Open, Queen's and Wimbledon. Tennis captain at university she was Queen's Club captain for many years in the premier division of the national league. Club champion in singles, doubles and mixed she definitely had the ability to play at an even higher level and there's a part of me that will always feel a degree of guilt for not being around enough at a key stage in her development to make that happen. Had we not divorced when she was 12, I might have been able to play a much bigger role. Frances didn't encourage Zoe to take up the sport seriously, though, and, although I played with her whenever I could, those opportunities were limited. Education, not sport, was the priority for the children as far as Frances was concerned and I'm not going to criticise her for that.

Greig, our youngest and born in 1978, missed out as well in that regard with me mainly based in Portugal during his formative years. I remember taking him to see Michael Stich at the French Open one spring after which he tried to mould his game on the German. Yet, as with Zoe, I don't think Frances really pushed him, so he had to rely on the rare occasions I was around, which was never going to be enough. And that hurts because he had a lot of talent and won a trophy for being the player 'most likely to succeed' in Surrey when he was a teenager. Jeremy Bates had won that a few years earlier so Greig understandably had dreams of following in my footsteps.

I took him on a trip around Europe when he was seeking his first pro point on the tour but there was too much going on for me to dedicate enough time to help him reach the next level. At that stage I was also coaching Claire Taylor (no relation), a left-hander from Oxfordshire, who was making an impression on the ITF tour. She went on to reach a top ranking of 184 in 1996, a couple of years after playing Martina Navratilova at Wimbledon. During our time together we travelled to the States where she won a prestigious tournament in Woodlands Texas, a major achievement for a British youngster. We developed a close bond but when I then told her I needed to go away with Greig for three weeks she went straight to Alan Jones who was a respected coach in his own right. That was a blow because, although I wasn't specifically looking for a top player, Claire was really good. She used to beat the then British number one Sam Smith regularly, could hit the ball hard and had a double-handed backhand that made opponents sit up and take notice. On the downside she wasn't a good trainer, something I found hard to tolerate, but I would like to have carried on with her for a while longer.

My other daughter, Katriona, was born in 1972. She was an adorable little girl who has faced a series of challenges in her life. Come year two at Wimbledon High School, a teacher pointed out that she wasn't able to read the board at the front of the class, an obvious concern. We arranged to have Katriona's eyes tested and discovered she had Stargardt disease, a rare form of macular dystrophy, which resulted in visual deterioration to the point at which she was registered blind..

Yet throughout her early years Katriona never let on that she couldn't see properly, an indication of the incredible resolve and independence that has characterised her remarkable life. Since then, she has used her strong competitive spirit, resilience and single-mindedness to achieve great things and find fulfilment in other areas. That includes battling breast cancer twice, which she has spoken about publicly, and becoming a loving mother to my two gorgeous grandchildren Toby and Ruby.

Career-wise Katriona started out as an intellectual property solicitor in the City of London, a huge achievement given the scale of the practical obstacles she faced throughout school and university. She made a great success of that, working all hours in a top law firm, while remaining thoroughly independent.

As the years went by so her passion for music developed, and that eventually led to a big change in direction. She swapped law to train as a singer at London's prestigious Royal School of Speech and Drama and is now a professional jazz and Latin singer as well as being a talented songwriter and vocal coach. I am incredibly proud of the way she decided to follow her dreams and reinvent herself, starting again in a rewarding but seriously competitive industry. Her musical journey has seen her record six albums, pen copious songs, headline at a packed Ronnie Scott's Jazz Club, open for Grammy award-winning singer George Benson and perform for the likes of Princess Anne, Elaine Paige and Novak Djokovic.

Her love of music originates from old records I used to listen to. The likes of Oscar Peterson and Ray Charles were favourites of mine and I never missed an opportunity to go to a jazz club, particularly in places like New York, during my playing days. One of my contemporaries (I say that though he was actually 12 years older) Torben Ulrich, father of Metallica star Lars Ulrich, secured legendary status as both a player who never seemed to train but always looked in pristine condition and through his musical skills. He used to tell us where to go for a good gig and more often than not we'd stay out far too late, having an absolute blast. Torben lived life to the full before passing away at the age of 95 in late 2023. He really was an incredible guy, who also made films, wrote books on poetry and painted to an advanced level.

Now is a good time to mention another top-class musician, composer and lyricist with whom I have developed a long-lasting friendship and who kindly lent support to Katriona. Jeff Wayne is best known for his musical version of *The War of the Worlds* but has been prolific when it comes to television themes and advertising jingles. He's also mad keen about tennis and captained the Hertfordshire men's team for 35 years. Jeff's dad, Jerry, was an actor, singer and producer as well as being a national-standard tennis player who competed at the Forest Hills Championships before it became the US Open. The family moved to England when Jeff was young and he soon developed a love for the sport, which meant so much to his father. A consummate host, he has his own court called Waynebledon, the venue for some magnificent matches and social events, and his enthusiasm remains undimmed after all these years. Jeff and I actually played together at the European Over-45s in East Germany where we reached the semi-finals without dropping a set. That week I beat Alex Metreveli in the singles and, according to Jeff, jumped over the net afterwards in exuberant fashion celebrating victory against the man I would have (should have) come face to face with in the 1973 Wimbledon final. I did tell you I never lost my competitive edge!

That win-at-all costs attitude extended to playing Jeff in the quarter-finals of the National Grass Court Championships. A BBC television crew turned up to film this battle of the musician and former British number one. It should, of course, have been staged on grass, which is what Jeff had diligently prepared for but, and I can't recall the reason why, the match was switched to clay. I won love and love before mumbling some words of apology at the net. It's not a result I'm proud of but, to be fair, he did send down the only ace of the contest. Jeff was hugely supportive of Katriona, for whom he has an enormous amount of respect. He's described her as a 'wonderfully talented musician and singer blessed with a rare talent', and that means a lot.

After we separated in 1982 Frances took the children back to England while I stayed in Portugal. A single man once more there's no point in pretending that I started to live the life of a monk. Involved in a few relationships I had no intention of getting married again or having any more children, something I made very clear. You never quite know what's coming next, though, and I became very close to a charming lady called Michelle Kay who lived nearby. One thing led to another and she became pregnant in 1989. It was a bolt out of the blue but Alex turned out to be the most delightful little boy and we have always had a fantastic relationship. He lives in north London having graduated from Plymouth University with a degree in media arts. Focusing on film-making and photography, he's involved in a wide range of creative media projects for companies and organisations in the hospitality business.

As well as having a good relationship with his half-siblings, Alex is also close to my sister Vivian's three children, Matthew, Clare and Vanessa. They come to Wimbledon as my guests on the first Monday of the Championships, which is a highlight of the year, and he fits in superbly. Vivian's love and support, as mentioned earlier, is striking and the younger members of her immediate family will do absolutely anything to help her out, regularly driving up to where she lives just outside Sheffield to bring her straight back for Christmas, Easter or whatever event is being celebrated before taking her home again. I'm so full of admiration for the way she's fostered those relationships. The pure love of a mother can be incredibly powerful and rewarding.

Chapter 26

A Headline Waiting to Happen

YOU CAN'T choose family but there's one former member of our clan I was happy to avoid whenever possible.

Before going any further, I want to make it clear that the purpose of this book is not to pick fights in public without reason or settle old scores for the sake of it. I've mentioned before that I don't seek confrontation and, by nature, am a private person with an open mind and inclination to try to see the best in everyone. But, as you've probably gathered by now, I also tend to say what I think and if that ruffles a few feathers, then so be it.

On more than one occasion my feathers have been ruffled by one of the best-known names in British tennis. A decent player who went on to captain the Great Britain Davis Cup team and make a fortune from his business empire. A prominent figure in the sport for decades who was also my brother-in-law; though it's fair to say we were never brothers-in-arms.

David Lloyd

Our link has a degree of synchronicity to it. There are three Lloyd brothers, David, Tony and John, and three Maclennan sisters, Frances, Lindsey and Veronica, along with a brother called Keith. Lindsey was incredibly clever and became a professor of medicine. She played a huge role in developing the ultrasound process by which heart problems can be detected in unborn children. Veronica was the youngest of the three girls and a very useful tennis player, though not in Frances's class. She had been seeded at Junior Wimbledon in 1965 but focused more on her studies and secured a top-class degree in psychology and politics at Glasgow University. The psychology part probably came in handy on a day-to day basis when she fell in love and tied the knot with the unpredictable David in 1972. The fact we were married to sisters and both had a passion for tennis suggests we'd inevitably become great mates. It was never like that, though, and there was hardly any social interaction. We'd see each other at tournaments all the time but there was no warmth between us.

The absence of any camaraderie can partly be explained by the fact we were competitors though, to be perfectly honest, I never considered him to be one of my rivals. People often ask me how good such and such a person was as a player. My definition of a 'good' player is someone who breaks through at major tournaments. David never did so there's my answer as far as he's concerned. He had ability, of course he did. If you weren't focused, or properly prepared, he could beat you. But I never considered him a threat.

For whatever reason, we just didn't see eye to eye. There was something contentious about our relationship but, from what I could see, that summed up his dealings in general. He was always embroiled in a dispute with someone or other. I remember the time he threatened to take legal action against Mark Cox over an innocuous piece he'd written in the *Leicester Times* about a Davis Cup selection snub for Lloyd. The two of them actually got on well and formed a very useful doubles partnership. Their games gelled on court but David could take umbrage very quickly.

He has always been an incredibly competitive individual. Brought up in a tennis family he loved the limelight and never shied away from being controversial. The press used to say he was a headline waiting to happen and they weren't wrong. One headline in particular, which we will come on to later, caused major friction between us.

In Lloyd's biography *How to Succeed in Business*, legendary writer Richard Evans, for whom I have much respect and who has an unrivalled knowledge of tennis following his decades covering the sport, tells the story of a row David had with a representative of Barnet Council regarding an issue at his new club in the area. The argument took place in one of the BBC Radio commentary boxes at Wimbledon where Richard and David were covering a match. During a break in play David reached for his mobile and began a very loud and increasingly ill-tempered conversation regarding a complaint issued by a woman who lived across the road from the club. She was unhappy about some lights continually being left on past closing time in contravention of the lease. The council representative was siding with her and issuing various threats that triggered the famous Lloyd temper.

'Right, you want to fight?' he said. 'So, we'll fight. But I want to warn you of one thing first. I NEVER LOSE.'

And that little tale says a lot about a man who left school at the age of 15 and went on to become a hugely successful self-made business giant but one ruthless in pursuit of his goals.

Along with his clubs in the UK, David also conducted business in Europe and after Frances and I divorced, he employed her to help run a venture in La Manga. Something went wrong there and, guess what, they ended up falling out. Greg Rusedski, for so long close to him, was another who became embroiled in legal wrangles with David, over a land deal that went spectacularly awry. It appeared to be part and parcel of the way he went about things.

Which is not to say he was all bad. There's no doubt he was a popular personality around the circuit during our playing days, on a superficial level at least. He liked to have a laugh and a joke and demonstrated plenty of heart and spirit on court while lacking sufficient talent to be really successful. And he was very hard-working and visionary when it came to setting up his clubs in the UK. That chain changed the tennis landscape in this country which is quite a legacy and something to be very proud of.

Yet for those of us who knew him, there was too much nonsense that went hand-in-hand with his achievements. I was standing next to David one day at Wimbledon when he said the club should dig up all the grass courts and put down concrete! That was back in the mid to late 90s when they were having trouble with the surface, and one-dimensional tennis, ruled by big servers with little else in the way of subtlety, was making for a pretty poor spectacle. Sure, something had to be done but ripping up the grass was an extreme suggestion and an example of David looking for a quick headline.

What he really wanted, above all else, was to run British tennis and be top dog at the LTA. Partly in pursuit of that goal he set up the Slater squad with financier Jim Slater, nick-named the godfather of asset-stripping, who had already invested money in British chess. Though not a tennis player himself, Slater was a big fan of the sport and had become disillusioned by the lack of home-grown players making any real impact at pro level. His cut-throat approach to business life was akin to David's own philosophy so the partnership made sense. The Slater scheme sponsored a number of young players, who had their fees at Reeds School in Surrey paid for and, while continuing their education, made tennis the priority and included some very good one-to-one coaching. Tim Henman was among the original batch of players to be signed up, followed soon afterwards by Jamie Delgado, who became the first British player to win the prestigious Under-14 Orange Bowl title in Miami and more recently enjoyed a successful coaching career with Andy Murray and Grigor Dimitrov.

David had high hopes for Delgado but he lacked height and was never able to transfer his brilliance as a youngster on to the pro tour. It is incredibly difficult to know for sure who will and won't make it. So many things can happen between the ages of 13 and 18, and indeed well beyond. One example of that is a now long-forgotten contemporary of Henman and Delgado. James Baily from Hampshire caused a minor sensation by winning the boys' junior title at the Australian Open in Melbourne in 1993. Less than two years later he walked away from the game never to return and he's by no means the only one. It's an unforgiving sport that demands so much and often gives so little back. You have to be tough as nails mentally; able to cope with the daily ups and downs while dedicating yourself to becoming as fit as possible, always aware one bad injury could spell the end at any moment.

Another brilliant British junior, Annabel Croft, quickly decided that being a tennis pro wasn't for her. Annabel won the Wimbledon and Australia junior titles and quickly hit the heights on tour before concluding there were other things in her life she'd rather do. And, my word she's done them well. Annabel said that playing tennis was like having an argument in public every day and became so gruelling mentally. I can see that. It takes a very specific type of person to keep going, often with a minimal amount of financial or emotional assistance.

Lloyd, via the feedback of the Slater squad's head coach, Nick Brown, eventually decided Henman wasn't going to make it as a singles player. That was obviously a crushing blow for him at the time but Tim rebounded by joining forces with David Felgate, lucky man, and the rest is history. I don't blame David Lloyd for not persevering with Henman. Identifying top talent isn't a precise science and, in those days, juniors weren't developing physically as quickly as they tend to today with the help of better rackets and more emphasis placed on strength and conditioning along with improved nutrition. There are so many stumbling blocks. Delgado came from a Spanish background and had lovely flowing groundstrokes but he didn't serve and volley at all and was restricted by that lack of height. Mark Petchey had some ability but tended to unravel under pressure; the list is endless. British players are fortunate in some ways. They're given extra opportunities through wild cards for the grass events and I don't have a problem with that but good players don't go backwards. Far too many of our youngsters have been given chance after chance when it's become clear they don't have what it takes. Alex Bogdanovic is a classic example. He was awarded a Wimbledon wild card eight years in a row and lost in the first round every time. Bogo was a lovely lad and so talented. He was able to do anything with a ball and used to beat all the other British guys. However, he wasn't great on the practice court and could be very hard to motivate. I worked with him at Sutton for a while and found it to be such a frustrating experience.

Julie Pullin went one 'better' with nine wild cards and not one victory. We desperately want our players to succeed and a run at Wimbledon can be the start of something special but, sometimes, it just doesn't happen and that's the same in every sport and business. How often do we hear about music promoters who turned down the Beatles, that sort of thing? Everything's easy in hindsight. There's also some politics attached to the wild-card situation. If a coach has a player in the main draw at Wimbledon, it's a feather in his or her cap. They probably won't bother to mention their player only got in as a result of a wild card. That honesty doesn't exist and I'm sure it never will.

I've thought long and hard about the merits of wild cards. The short-term benefits to young players are obvious. They provide a great source of funding and an opportunity to make a big impression very quickly. There has to be more to it than that though. Wimbledon in particular can be such an overwhelming experience for inexperienced Brits. I believe it's essential to ensure those given one of these golden tickets are properly managed ahead of the fortnight. We should do everything possible to make them feel at home and also strive to ensure the money they make, (appearing in the first round was worth £60,000 in 2024) is sensibly invested to maximise their chances of benefitting fully in tennis terms from the experience. And when it comes to choosing the recipients of those wild cards you have to look so closely at who has the personality, constant high standards and elite fitness levels required at the top of the sport. Can they go on and shine as individuals in far-flung parts of the world where they will effectively be on their own for long periods? What you can't do is keep giving them to the same people year after year if they haven't demonstrated significant improvement as a result of the opportunity.

Squad systems had been tried before. John Barrett once had a group based at the YMCA and I ran a similar scheme in the mid-80s when Paul Hutchins was in charge. This was around the time Andrew Castle made his breakthrough with a wonderful performance against Mats Wilander at Wimbledon. I'd known Andy for a while and, when he returned from university in America where he shared a room with the Swede Mikael Pernfors who'd just reached the French Open Final, I was asked to look after him and another promising youngster, Mike Walker, during the grass-court season of 1986. Mike was a left-hander from Wales and both had been given wild cards for Wimbledon.

Andy also played at Queen's that year and picked up a couple of wins over a fellow Brit Stuart Bale and then Russell Simpson before losing to Paul Annacone. Come Wimbledon they were understandably twitchy and didn't even know where the changing rooms were so it was a thrilling but daunting new experience for both. Mike drew an Italian, Claudio Mezzadri. The one thing I stressed to him was that he couldn't afford to stay back and play into the hands of his opponent. So, what did he do? Stayed back, and allowed Claudio to dictate the pattern before coming in with a chip and charge routine that saw him recover from two sets to one down and win the last two sets for the loss of just three games. Painful viewing!

Andy was better and came through his first-round match against Australia's Broderick Dyke who was inside the world's top 40 at the time and enjoyed a fair amount of success as a doubles player over the years. I was impressed by the way he handled the pressure to win a couple of tie-breaks in that match, which took him through to a clash with the second seed Mats Wilander. Now, back then, Mats, at the age of 22, was already a mighty force. On his way to number one in the world he had a couple of Australian and French Open titles under his belt and went on to finish his glittering playing days with seven slams, three Davis Cups and a host of other titles. I'd become a fan of the Swede following his semi-final victory over Jose Luis Clerk at the French in 1982. Mats asked to replay the final point because he didn't want to win courtesy of a questionable umpiring decision. Now, who does that remind you of? He was awarded the Pierre de Coubertin World Fair Play Trophy for that gesture and has subsequently gone on to demonstrate his wisdom and expertise with a distinguished career in broadcasting.

But for a few hours in the high summer of 86 he went into a cold sweat as Castle pushed him hard to lead by two sets to one. Nobody had given this unheralded Englishman a chance but he looked the part, cheered on by his American girlfriend, Shelley, who had a big influence on him … dare I say, too big an influence. They eventually fell out in spectacular fashion and she certainly wasn't the most relaxing person to sit next to during a match. I tend not to get carried away when watching, preferring the Kipling approach emblazoned by the entrance to Centre Court, 'If you can meet with triumph and disaster and treat those two imposters just the same', but Shelley was a live wire and couldn't keep still. My ears are still ringing to this day!

The crowd was going crazy by now as well but I just wanted Andy to stay focused and remember the key components we'd discussed come the pressure moments. Get that first serve in, make the first volley into your opponent's more vulnerable side and avoid such traps as volleying into the open space until it's absolutely clear you're on top in the point. It's little things like that which are essential to control the nerves and allow you to thrive under pressure which, as Billie Jean King so rightly said, should be viewed as a privilege.

There had been an interesting moment just before the match. We were sitting in the changing rooms when John Barrett wandered through. Members were allowed to do that in those days before the club finally put a stop to it in case somebody noticed an injured player and passed on the information. I have the utmost respect for John, who has done it all as a player, commentator, author, administrator and businessman, but our approach to the game differs. He turned to Andy and said, 'Good luck, old chap, go out, enjoy it and have fun.' As soon as he walked out of the room I said, 'Forget all that. You'll only enjoy this if you beat him. Just think about getting to three games all. Then you only need 12 more points to win the set and you're going to count those down in your mind. That's what you have to focus on.' It's imperative to keep thinking strategically about how you can win. I didn't say he could beat him. Just have a plan plus a quiet belief and take it from there was the message.

He did everything he could. The crowd loved his approach, all arms and legs with a touch of swagger, but Wilander won a tight fourth set and Andy was burned out come the fifth, which proved one-sided. He walked off court with his head held high, though,h and, inevitably, discussions followed as to whether we should link up on a more permanent basis. He wanted to and so did I but Shelley didn't like the idea and that was that. There's no point wondering what might have been had we teamed up. The decision was made and he's gone on to be very successful as a broadcaster but I do feel he had the ability to be quite special had he decided to take full responsibility for his career back then.

Castle's performance that day did reap dividends. Amidst the excitement and hullabaloo of a young Brit making a mark at Wimbledon, wealthy businessman and tennis lover Max Lewinsohn invested around £100,000 in the British game and set up the Dominium squad, which allowed me, along with Patrick Hughesman, who I hired as general manager, free rein to build up a group of hopefuls. We organised a sifting process and invited players from all over the country to try out. Making it open to everyone was really important as far as I was concerned. Knowing only too well the disadvantages of coming from a less than fashionable background, I was keen to see if we could unearth a rough diamond from somewhere like Cumbria.

That was home to a lad called Philip Gainford, who'd managed to reach the final of the Under-16 Nationals. He had an immense amount of talent but was something of a loose cannon. Who knows what he might have gone on to achieve had his circumstances been different. There was also a guy called Andy York who stood out. He was around 6ft 3in and totally bald as a result of suffering from alopecia. But what an athlete! All the players underwent vigorous tests with the latest fitness equipment and Andy's report stated he had the physique of an elite middle-distance runner. Some of the things he could do on court were incredible. He possessed a brilliant smash, hitting winners when it didn't even look as though he could reach the ball, and he was also an excellent badminton player. But he didn't really want it. I'm sure he thought he did, but, deep down, he didn't.

Two others who came through that process were Robert Collins from London and Bournemouth's Alan Orchard. There were no guarantees for any of the players we selected but I like to think that, although none went on to become world-beaters, their lives all changed for the better as a result of the experience. We drilled a work ethic into them and, in most cases, a love for the game that has kept them in the tennis world, one way or another, ever since.

Coaching promising young players with a good attitude is one of the most rewarding things to do. At the end of 86 I travelled to Australia and New Zealand with eight guys who, at different times, had shown real ability without being able to find the consistency which is so important if you are to climb inside the world's top 100. That squad consisted of Jeremy Bates, Jason Goodall, Nick Fulwood, David Felgate, Stuart Bale, Stephen Botfield, Mike Walker and Andrew Castle. It proved to be a pretty demoralising experience as we went from qualifier to qualifier with precious few wins to celebrate. Bates was the best of that bunch and, had his serve been more of a weapon, could have gone a long way up the rankings. He also had a problem controlling his temper. A number of line judges came up to me during the trip and complained about him complaining all the time! That negative mindset got in his way on a regular basis but with a better serve he could have been really good. Stuart Bale had a massive serve and was often called upon to practise with Boris Becker but, in truth, there wasn't a great deal more than that to his game. Stuart also had a very pale complexion which made it hard for him to play in hot conditions without causing serious damage to his skin.

I do have regrets on the coaching front. Certain opportunities passed me by but I was still playing on the over-35 circuit and was part of the Legends tour with the likes of Rosewall and Laver, which was great fun to be involved in. I loved being able to tell people I was a legend! But if I could do it all again, then a concerted one-on-one relationship with an Andy Castle, a Tim Henman or even an Andy Murray is something I would court much more proactively. I was operating off my own back then, juggling too many things at once and should have had an agent, because pushing myself forward did not come naturally. I look at some of the high-performance coaches these days and wonder how on earth they've got where they are. Too many of the current crop are nice guys and girls who won't cause any trouble and that's what the LTA want: lots of 'yes' men and women who will do what they are told with no questions asked.

When I worked with some of the top junior girls alongside Mike Walker, a mother walked in one day, picked up a chair and hurled it across the room. Now, I'm not advocating that kind of behaviour on a regular basis but a bit of passion, and enough honesty to get your point across if you don't agree with something, is a positive as far as I'm concerned. And that's why I've always been regarded with suspicion.

Heated discussions. An ATP meeting at the height of the row in 1973.

Niki Pilic, Cliff Drysdale, Arthur Ashe and Jack Kramer outside the High Court in June 1973.

Growing concerns. With Roy Emerson as the possibility of a boycott increased. 20 June 1973.

Herman David, chairman of the All-England Club, caught in the maelstrom.

Bjorn and I in the '73 quarter-final. Something caught our attention.

It was out ... and Bjorn knew it. Wimbledon '73.

That match. Taylor versus Kodes in 1973

Jan Kodes. Wimbledon Final 1973. Still hurts to see that picture.

Ilie Nastase. He wasn't always a model citizen.

Bob Hewitt. An angry man most of the time.

Jack Solomon's never misses a promotional trick. Here Roger Taylor is being presented with a special tray commemorating Wimbledon '70 by guest chairman Fred Perry at a World Sporting Club dinner-boxing evening at Grosvenor House.

My silverware – not Fred's! 1973.

Royal approval. Princess Benedicte of Denmark presents the biggest cheque of my career at the time, around £10,000. A pretty tidy sum in the early 70s. Copyright Nordisk Pressfoto

The name could have been Bond, James Bond. London 1967.

Eat your heart out Daniel Craig! Rome 1973.

A day at the Palace. An MBE for me, JPR Williams and Liverpool legend Tommy Smith in 1977.

On court again with Bjorn. Spain 1979.

David Lloyd and I shared the same principles of hard work and I genuinely believe we could have teamed up together effectively had he been less outspoken (he'd describe it as being honest.) He toned down his criticism of the way the game was being governed when appointed Davis Cup captain in the mid-90s but his disregard for much of what had been done in the preceding years was there for all to see. He was very critical of the standard of coaching around the country and the decision to use Bisham Abbey as a centre of excellence, to the exclusion of all else. Some of what he said made sense but it was the way he said it that caused ripples. The Lloyd clan was a huge presence in the British game throughout the 70s, 80s and 90s and still is. John Lloyd had the looks and the game to become a big star and was someone I warmed to. He had a likeable demeanour and very famous wife in Chrissie Evert but lacked his brother's ruthlessness on court. David's son Scott secured the job his father always wanted when he became the LTA's chief executive in 2018. Scott has always been rather cool towards me and no attempt has ever been made to tap into my experience and knowledge for the good of the game in this country. That comes as no surprise to me, though. You're either with David or you're not and, when I succeeded him as Davis Cup captain, I realised just how far apart we were.

Chapter 27

Even the Blind School Could Have Beaten Them

THAT OPPORTUNITY came at the start of the new millennium and was a rather welcome surprise.

Despite my best efforts as a Davis Cup player, and the drama and success of captaining the British Wightman Cup team which I will tell you about in the next chapter, the LTA appeared to studiously avoid my name whenever the subject of Davis Cup captain cropped up. Since retiring I'd seen Paul Hutchins eventually replaced by Warren Jacques, with Tony Pickard, Bill Knight and then David Lloyd assuming the mantle. Lloyd's era coincided with the emergence of Tim Henman and Greg Rusedski, two world-class players who provided the backbone to a very strong line-up. Under Lloyd the team was promoted to the Europe/Africa Zone 1 league, one step below the world group that comprised the best nations, before eventually regaining its place amongst the elite; the highlight, a thrilling tie against the Americans in Birmingham during the spring of 1998 that ended in a 3-2 defeat.

Great Britain had been crowned Davis Cup champions nine times but the most recent of those triumphs, in 1936, was remembered by next to no one. Two years after my last rubber as a player we did reach the final, under Hutchins, beating Australia in the semis before losing 4-1 to the United States. Another semi-final run followed in 1981, after which a major decline set in.

As you know Lloyd and I couldn't have been more different. His brash, assertive style clearly worked to his advantage in the business world and, initially, despite past battles, he looked to be a good fit for the LTA in terms of his captaincy. However, a man not adverse to confrontation was never going to toe the party line for long and, sure enough, his reign ended in ugly fashion.

A 4-1 defeat away to the Czech Republic in February of 2000 led to his sacking, with the LTA claiming they'd 'lost confidence' in his abilities. Lloyd had lashed out at Arvind Parmar and Jamie Delgado following the tie and, in a sustained attack, said a number of the country's top players weren't fit enough to compete at the highest level. His relationship with the LTA had always been stormy and continued in a similar fashion over the following few years. In 2009 he said, 'The current LTA rules and regulations are impossible to work in. It's like having a communist state in a capital world. No business in the world I've come across works the way the LTA does.' Hardly a ringing endorsement from a former Davis Cup captain. David was furious at the way he'd been treated. He also claimed he'd intended to resign after the next tie anyway and 'if the LTA had any brains, and waited, we wouldn't have had to have any shouting matches.'

Come on, David. You relish those!

Now, at the time John Crowther was chief executive of the LTA. Without beating about the bush, it's fair to say he knew next to nothing about performance tennis. Not the first appointment along those lines by our governing body and there have been plenty more since. The performance director was Patrice Hagelauer, a Frenchman who'd achieved success in his homeland but was already struggling to make headway amidst the bureaucracy and inconsistency that has long been a hallmark of the Lawn Tennis Association.

Out of the blue I received a call late in February 2000 asking me to come down to the offices at Queen's Club for a meeting with Crowther. Lloyd's sacking hadn't been made public at that stage and

I had no real clue as to what they wanted to talk to me about. So, I arrived with my business partner at the time, Mike Walker, to be left in an office for ages while, behind the scenes, something significant was clearly happening.

Eventually a very flustered Crowther appeared. Wearing a smart silvery-grey summer suit drenched in sweat he was visibly dripping under the arms. What immediately became clear was that he had just sacked David Lloyd after a lengthy phone call and the former captain was now threatening to sue him and the whole of the LTA!

Having somewhat breathlessly brought me up to speed with these nuggets, he then shuffled around awkwardly and enquired, rather nervously, as to whether I'd be interested in taking over! I honestly hadn't been expecting any of this and can't say I was filled with confidence by the way things were being handled. But Crowther was desperate to get an agreement sorted straightaway and I could think of no obvious reason to turn the chance down. I was working with Mike at the Sutton Academy, which was fine, but hardly a deal-breaker so, after some rapid negotiations, I said yes.

And within minutes of that, I was being presented to the newspaper boys and girls and the TV and radio crews; it was a miracle my suit didn't suffer the same sorry, soggy fate as Crowther's. I realised straightaway that the LTA were desperate to appoint someone who could stand up to Lloyd and be able to deal with everything he planned to unleash in the aftermath of his sacking and I seemed to fit the bill.

Almost before I knew what was happening the press bombarded me with questions, some of them having already been briefed by David. Barry Flatman, a top writer who knew what he was doing, and had a long association with the Lloyds, piped up straightaway, asking what I knew about the men's game in this country. Now, at the time, my work in Sutton was with the girls' team but that didn't mean I'd forgotten, or was ignoring everything else! I answered (but stored it away, Barry!) and went on to talk about a need to instil new team spirit in the team, saying I hoped to emulate the achievements of one of my contemporaries and doubles partners John Newcombe, who'd been a very successful captain for Australia. And that was it. Hello, captain! Good luck, captain! And goodness knows what to expect next!

Lloyd didn't disappoint and quickly sued the LTA over my use of the words 'team spirit' among other things. The dispute was eventually resolved without the need for legal action but I heard a variety of different stories about the ill-fated tie in Ostrava which, along with his rant, had made the board's decision to sack him nigh-on inevitable.

My first official role as captain was to attend the draw for our next tie in the world group qualifying round. Defeat against the Czechs meant we had to win to retain our place in the top 16. A home tie against Ecuador on grass a week after Wimbledon looked, on the face of things, to be a reasonably straightforward prospect. They had one outstanding player in Nicolas Lapentti, who'd been as high as number six in the world and made the semi-finals of the Australian Open a year before. His very inexperienced 6ft 4in 17-year-old brother Giovanni was also in the team along with Luis Morejon, who'd never broken the world's top 100 or qualified for the main draw of a slam.

It was a tie we couldn't lose. Could we?

David Lloyd couldn't resist a pop. 'Even the blind school could beat Ecuador,' he said, fully aware through his close connections with my family that Katriona is blind. Now, whether he meant that as a deliberate slight to her and the rest of us I don't know to this day. But, in the circumstances, it was an incredibly insensitive thing to say and a comment I've never forgotten, or forgiven. It was a dagger to my heart.

During his tenure Lloyd had developed a close relationship with one of the star players I'd inherited, which did little to build morale as I settled into the job.

Greg Rusedski had been at the centre of British tennis from the moment he controversially switched allegiance from Canada to Great Britain in 1995. A wonderful talent, he was a left-hander with a lethal serve who reached the US Open Final in 1997, enough to make him BBC Sports Personality of the Year, and climb to number four in the world. Greg finished 1997 and 1999 as British number one and his rivalry with Tim Henman pushed both men in a positive way on court. Unfortunately, there was zero chemistry between the two of them off it.

You have to be selfish in an individual sport. Everybody in tennis knows and accepts that to a degree. Yet, on those few occasions when you come together as a team, it's vitally important to respect each other and see things as a collective. Greg struggled in that department.

He came into the tie on the back of an awful first-round defeat to Vince Spadea at Wimbledon. The maverick American had lost 22 matches in a row, the worst losing streak on the ATP tour, but somehow managed to beat Greg 9-7 in the fifth set. It was, without doubt, one of the lowest points in his career.

Nonetheless, with Henman and Rusedski leading the way, backed up by Arvind Parmar and big-serving lefty Barry Cowan, there didn't appear to be much to worry about.

There soon was, though.

Greg played Lapentti in the first rubber on No.1 Court and, against expectation, lost the first set 6-3. Being captain is an awkward job in many ways, not least during the matches when you are sitting courtside, next to the player at each change of ends, wondering how best to communicate. I didn't know Greg well but was aware of his close alliance with David Lloyd, which meant our relationship already had a frosty edge to it. In a titanic struggle he fought back and came within a few points of winning but eventually lost 6-3, 6-7, 7-5, 4-6, 7-5. Oh dear. That's the honeymoon period over then.

Another issue with the captaincy arose from the timing of the matches. There were two singles rubbers on the Friday with only a

20-minute gap between them, followed by the doubles on Saturday and the reverse singles on the Sunday, again with just a 20-minute gap in between. After the Rusedski loss I barely had time to return to the locker room and freshen up before heading back to No.1 Court for Henman's match against Morejon. Little did I know that, backstage, Greg was now complaining about a bad foot, or ankle and telling everyone who'd listen that he couldn't play again that weekend. The news gradually filtered through to me as I started to wonder what else could go wrong.

I'd known Tim for a long time and had a soft spot for him. He was far from being an outstanding junior but always had a fabulous work ethic and an intelligence that set him apart from the rest, in my eye. I remember meeting him for the first time when I lived and worked in Portugal. He was only ten or 11 and came down to the club with his parents. He always reminds me that, initially, I never hit with him. There were better players and I was incredibly busy anyway. He always joked about that but we kept in touch; even when he was being ruled pretty firmly by his long-term coach David Felgate. I'd offer him little tips every now and then and like to think I played a small part in his success.

Just after his split with Felgate I remember talking to him in Monte Carlo when he played Alex Corretja; it was just a line about 'hitting up the curve' on his backhand side rather than staying on the baseline and slicing all the time. He won that match comfortably, came up to me afterwards and said, 'If you've got anything else to tell me, then let me know!'

In many ways I wish we'd had the chance to work together on a more regular basis. But the main thing about Tim was that he'd always been a terrific competitor and that, allied to plenty of natural talent, took him a long way.

Back to the story. Tim cruised through for the loss of just seven games, which eased the stress to a degree and left the score level at one-all going into the weekend.

My dilemma now was who to partner him with in the doubles once it had been confirmed Greg was crocked. At that time there were a number of players desperate to be given a chance to secure their position in the team alongside the big two. We had Jamie Delgado, Martin Lee and Miles Maclagan along with Arvind and Barry who'd been given the nod for this particular tie. I decided that Arvind would play the reverse rubber so selected him for the doubles as preparation for that, hoping Tim could guide him along on the Saturday. It was immediately clear just how nervous Arv was, complaining that various parts of his body were starting to hurt. Not a good sign.

Barry, meanwhile, who is a lovely guy but quite stubborn at times, was in my ear, clearly disappointed not to be selected for the doubles. It was one thing after another but, as captain, you have to do what you think is best for the team and stick to your guns.

Of course, the Lapentti brothers knew each other's game inside out and had been preparing beautifully for this match over a three-week period. And, lo and behold, they won in straight sets, 6-3, 7-5, 6-3.

At 2-1 down everybody assumed Tim would win the first of the reverse singles which meant it would all come down to Arvind in the last rubber. Needless to say, I didn't sleep well that night in our hotel, the Cannizaro House. Incidentally, I went on to be chided for choosing that venue a few days later. Someone let the press know how much the rooms cost and what a waste of money it had been in the circumstances. The fact it was more or less within walking distance of Wimbledon, that the Davis Cup budget doesn't come directly from the LTA's coffers and that there were no other suitable alternatives nearby was conveniently overlooked. One of the perks when I played Davis Cup was staying in a good hotel to ensure maximum preparation. The Grand in Eastbourne was a particular favourite of mine and nobody ever said a word. But here was another example of outside forces attempting to undermine me from the word go.

On the Sunday Tim did the business in clinical fashion against Nicholas Lapentti, winning one, four and four. So, on to the final rubber between Arv and Lapentti junior.

In tactical terms our plan was pretty straightforward. Giovanni had one way of playing. He crushed his serve and came in behind it just about every time. He may have been 6ft-plus-a-lot but was still a pretty easy target, be it with a passing shot or even a lob. Arvind stuck to the plan, playing beautifully to go up by two sets to love in next to no time.

And then, for no apparent reason, he fell apart. Completely. I've never seen anything like it in all my years as a player or coach. It was as if he went into a daze, looking straight through me, in a total fug. His coach Dave Sammel was there, passing notes, telling him to believe, but nothing worked. In horrible slow motion a 6-4, 6-3 lead turned into a 4-6, 3-6, 6-1, 6-3, 6-3 defeat and we'd lost the tie 3-2.

The Ecuadorians started running around No.1 Court like lunatics, diving on top of each other as I went back to the locker room where the atmosphere was, as you'd expect, funereal. There I receive a message that Sue Barker, who was covering the tie for television, wanted to interview me. And the very first thing she asked, live on TV, was whether I was going to resign. Bloody hell. I'd only been in the job a few weeks but that's how hard-nosed she was. The third Lloyd brother, Tony, was there for each day of the tie and at one point was told to take a banner down by security. I honestly don't know what it said but am pretty sure it didn't include anything complimentary about me!

The press loved it!

I escaped most of the scathing criticism that followed, with Richard Lewis, at that point head of men's tennis, the primary scapegoat. The internal goings-on at the LTA could fill five lengthy volumes but I decided to keep my head down and plan for a smoother run in the Europe/Africa Zone Group 1 which we'd been relegated to as a result of the Ecuador defeat.

While coming to terms with that morale-sapping loss, I then had to finalise plans for September's Sydney Olympics. Most of the arrangements had already been made. The men's team consisted of Tim, Greg, Barry Cowan and Kyle Spencer, an American-born British doubles expert, based in the States, who made the quartet at a time when our options were limited, to say the least – a far cry from the current state of affairs as far as men's doubles in this country is concerned. In the absence of anyone high enough to qualify for the women's singles, Julie Pullin and Lorna Woodroffe completed the line-up in doubles. We flew out, in business class, minus Greg who was seeking ranking points at a tournament in some far-flung destination, with Tim also delayed.

In truth, I felt a little uncomfortable about the whole thing from the word go. Our budget was generous to the extent we could have travelled first class. I thought that wouldn't look good and, with some very well-known athletes at the back of our plane, settled a little uneasily into my very comfortable seat. Sitting next to me was the minister for sport Kate Hoey who, unlike some politicians to hold that office, was very experienced in the sports world and had been Northern Ireland's high-jump champion in 1966. We immediately bonded as she looked ahead to a much more successful games following the failures of the British team in Atlanta.

I've always loved the Olympics and greatly admire those who dedicate their lives in pursuit of a gold medal. For most of them the Olympic Games represented their Wimbledon and I couldn't quite reconcile that with the attitude of many within tennis, especially in the UK, who prioritised the four slams ahead of winning a medal every four years. There had been some British success. Tim and Neil Broad won silver together at Atlanta in 1996 but was that the pinnacle of Henman's career and is that what he will be remembered for 100 years from now? I don't think so. That said, it was very exciting to be part of Team GB at such an incredible event and, staying in excellent accommodation in the heart of the athlete's village, we made full use of the terrific practice facilities on offer.

Everything was running smoothly until I received a message from the LTA asking me to nominate Henman as the man to carry the British flag at the opening ceremony. Now, Tim was a big star by then but, amidst so many decorated athletes, it struck me as being a rather strange request. Nonetheless I dutifully contacted the British Olympic Association and made the suggestion. Their response was curt. To be honest, they almost laughed at me and, no wonder, with so many multiple gold-medal winners to choose from. No disrespect to Tim but it betrayed some pretty skewed and arrogant thinking from the LTA. The vote eventually went to triple-gold-medal rower Matthew Pinsent, a decision nobody could quibble over.

Greg was nowhere to be seen at this point, still attempting to pick up some cheap ranking points, with most of the world's top players at the Games. When he finally arrived in Sydney my problems multiplied. Greg asked if his coach could be part of the GB team at the opening ceremony, walking around the stadium behind the flag. I'd received endless emails confirming the closing date for handing over the list of names of those who would be part of the ceremony and there was no way anybody could be added at the last minute.

These were distractions I could have done without but they were put to one side as we continued our preparations while also taking the opportunity to watch as much of the sporting action as possible. Each country had a ticket office for all the events. Ours was identified by a red phone box, which I visited on numerous occasions to see what was available. The atmosphere inside the village was fabulous, not least when the swimmers started to party once their events had been completed. To make it even better Team GB was starring all over the place with a regular supply of medals adding to the feel-good factor. In fact, just about everyone exceeded their expectations, except us.

The singles draw paired Tim with Karol Kucera of Slovakia, who had caused him plenty of trouble in the past and did so again here, winning three and two. Greg faced the awkward Arnaud Clement of France and also went down in straight sets.

Barry Cowan, a late replacement in the singles following a withdrawal, did at least take a set off the experienced Canadian Daniel Nestor but lost 6-4 in the third and that was that as far as our singles hopes were concerned.

It proved no better with the doubles either. Barry and Kyle Spencer faced an awkward obstacle in the shape of Marat Safin and Yevgeny Kafelnikov and gave them a real scare early on. Kyle's forehand was limited but he knew how to put away a backhand. In the Russian pair's opening service game Kyle conjured two magnificent returns on the deuce court with his double-hander to secure an early break. He told us later that during the warm-up he'd deliberately hit a number of backhands into the bottom of the net to suggest that was his weaker wing but the Russians quickly cottoned on and eventually won 7-6, 6-4. Despite his limitations as a player Kyle proved a delight to work with and I was touched to receive a message from him recently. He spoke fondly about our time together and how much he appreciated the efforts I made and the interest I had shown in his career. That sort of feedback means so much to me but, alas, is all too rare in the British game. I also enjoy Barry's company whenever we bump into each other at the All England Club and consider him one of the best commentators in the business.

Defeat for the boys in the doubles meant there was a huge amount of pressure on Julie Pullin and Lorna Woodroffe come their turn. A medal of any sort in the tennis would be the icing on the cake for a British team that had enjoyed so much success elsewhere, while a win of any sort would be a relief to me after what had gone before.

Everyone turned up to watch their first-round match against Kristie Boogert and Miriam Oremans of the Netherlands, including Kate Hoey, but we were destined to go home with a 100 per cent losing record. Both girls were in floods of tears at the end of a straight-sets defeat to a pair who went on to reach the final where they lost out on a gold medal to the Williams sisters. It meant the trip ended on a depressingly low note and made those comfortable business-class seats even more uncomfortable to sit on as we headed home.

The following year we were favoured with an excellent draw against Portugal in the Davis Cup. The tie took place in Birmingham and, playing indoors on carpet, we cruised through 5-0. That put us into the hat for a world group qualifier and, shock horror, we drew Ecuador again, this time away! I will never forget sitting there as captain at the draw ceremony realising all too quickly that, as a succession of other nations were read out, we were destined to go head-to-head once more. The press pack were falling about the place and I was tempted to start laughing like a maniac too but, naturally, put on a straight face and insisted I was delighted we had a chance to put things right.

On clay in Guayaquil of all places! Where Nicolas Lapentti hadn't lost for years!

The tie was to be staged between 21 and 23 September 2001. Ten days on, as it turned out, from the horror of 9/11.

Planning for Davis Cup ties is never straightforward, especially when you have two top-ten players in the team. I'd quickly discovered it was nigh-on impossible to persuade Tim and Greg to turn up more than a few days before the start of the contest. For some reason, though, Greg wanted to get there early this time, which was almost unheard of. So, we met in Miami and spent several days there, which I looked upon as a chance to bond with him. Although the weather was pretty awful, we played golf at Fred Stolle's club, Aventura, where I'd been head coach many years before and enjoyed some excellent facilities that included covered courts and big television screens in a shaded area near the pool.

I never did bond with Greg, though, and found him to be a real Jekyll and Hyde character. He could be charming but, partly I suspect because of the David Lloyd link, we couldn't find common ground. He'd never listen to anybody and kept winding me up. 'Why are you so nervous, Roger? What's wrong with you?' And yet he was the one who seemed to be especially anxious!

I began to find his antics incredibly annoying, told him not to be so silly and reminded him I'd been here before as a player, coach and captain. I tried to reason with him that we were all a bit tense and desperately wanted to put the record straight against Ecuador. But it went in one ear and out the other. I couldn't really speak to him.

Three of the other players, Martin Lee, Lee Childs and Barry Cowan, eventually joined us, along with the coaching and fitness team but Tim was still in the air.

I then received a rather chilling message from the LTA telling me to put on a TV and, like the rest of the world, was mesmerised by the horrific scenes from New York as first one plane and then another crashed into the twin towers. At which point, of course, America shut down completely. You couldn't get in or out, and we had no idea what was going on or what was going to happen.

We finally discovered that Tim's BA flight had been diverted to Bermuda. He had to stay there for a day or two and then, somehow, found a way to join us, which was an amazing effort in the circumstances. Living in lockdown I phoned the ITF to cancel the tie which, I assumed, would be a formality. Their governing body was meeting in Mexico and the message came back that, no, you can't cancel, the tie has to go ahead – even though we didn't have any of our players in Ecuador and no apparent way of getting them there! I was basically told to sort something out. Thanks very much.

Gradually, the US started to open up a bit. I was able to find two seats here and two seats there on flights from Miami to Ecuador and we finally arrived in Guayaquil, trying to focus on the job in hand.

It wasn't long, though, before I started to experience a horrendous sense of déjà vu. Greg, whose record on clay was modest to say the least, lost the first set of the first rubber to Nicolas Lapentti by six games to two. Here we go again! As Oscar Wilde almost said, 'To lose one match against Ecuador may be regarded as a misfortune; to lose two would be downright carelessness.'

And, almost certainly signal the end of my tenure.

At which point I turned to Greg and said, 'I'm a left-hander like you. If you want to win this match, listen to me now. I can tell you how to do it.'

It was a righty against a lefty with Greg hitting topspin forehands while always slicing on his backhand, invariably across court. A very normal approach back then. Lapentti had a big forehand. So, when you directed the ball to that stronger side he was able to whip it back across court to Greg's weaker wing, the backhand, enabling him to dominate play. And that's precisely what was happening.

So, what was the answer?

I told Greg he needed to play his backhand cross-court shorter, to just behind the service line, which is a bit under the grip. That wouldn't work these days with the rackets being so light but it was an effective weapon then. Greg had to bring Lapentti up the court and then be brave enough to come forward himself at the right moment and exploit the space.

To be fair, he did precisely that and it worked a treat! He won 2-6, 6-2, 7-5, 6-3. A huge victory in the circumstances.

Tim then completed a near perfect first day by easing past Luis Morejon in straight sets and a morale-boosting victory was within touching distance. The next day Tim and Greg teamed up to beat the Lapentti brothers two, three and four and victory was ours. The crowd, volatile, to say the least, during the tie, decided to hurl whatever they could on the court at the conclusion of it: seats, bottles, cushions, anything portable flew in our general direction. I don't mind admitting to being pretty pumped-up at this point but the team, perhaps wisely, resisted my suggestion of an over-elaborate victory lap of honour; best to hasten back to the relative sanctuary of the locker room. There was still time to unfurl a large Union flag and wave it all over the place, which merely heightened the tension, but was most satisfying.

I brought in Martin and Barry for the reverse singles, which were dead rubbers of course. Martin was victorious and a 4-1 win was some response to the woes of the Wimbledon clash just over a year before. Not that we were ever given much credit for it. For obvious reasons, none of the journalists, radio or TV people, most of whom thought we'd get beaten anyway, were able to make the trip and with the world understandably preoccupied by the devastation of the terrorist attack in New York, it was a low-impact result.

We were then faced with the issue of trying to get home. Greg didn't want to go back through America despite the fact we were booked via Miami with open-ended tickets and plenty of room with nobody else venturing far from their front door. So, he went home via Madrid on his own while the rest of us headed back as a team.

Victory meant a return to the world group and, the following February, we faced Sweden in Birmingham. They were a very strong team with Thomas Enqvist, Thomas Johansson and Jonas Bjorkman at or near the peak of their powers. Tim won the first rubber against Bjorkman in four sets but Greg lost two tie-breaks and eventually went down 7-6, 7-6, 6-2 to Enqvist.

Hope was rekindled after a gripping battle in the doubles which our top two eventually won 6-3 in the fifth against Bjorkman and Johansson. However, Enqvist then beat Tim in the first of the reverse singles on Sunday morning. That meant it all came down to Rusedski v Johansson in the last rubber.

Without wishing to state the obvious, home advantage allows you to try and maximise your strengths. Greg had one of the most explosive serves in the game so, naturally, we laid the quickest possible surface and used the fastest balls available. Throughout the week, I'd tried to build up team spirit with videos of other British sporting success, notably some of the Lions' famous rugby union wins in South Africa. Our song for the week had been the Oasis hit 'Wonderwall' with the line 'maybe you're going to be the one that saves me'. We'd sung it to death and, ahead of the decider, everybody started belting this tune out in front of Greg in the locker room. There was clearly a lot of adrenalin flowing through his veins. Suddenly, he stood up, ran out of the door and raced on to court without his bags! Somewhat sheepishly I had to follow with his gear as if that had always been our intention.

It was all set up in terms of the result but, after a bright start which saw him take the first set 6-4, Greg didn't serve well enough and lost in four. Which meant, of course, that we lost 3-2. Another gut-wrencher.

In truth, I didn't enjoy the experience one little bit whenever Greg was on court. He didn't welcome me as captain and the whole dynamic was so far removed from my playing days in that environment when I built up such a special bond with the likes of Bill Knight, Mike Sangster, Bobby Wilson, Roger Becker, Alan Mills and Mark Cox. Davis Cup meant everything and the togetherness was a constant. I never had that with Greg.

Which brings us to another tension-strewn encounter. Defeat to Sweden led to a world group qualifying tie seven months later, again in Birmingham, this time against Thailand.

Now, at that point Tim had a bad shoulder, which everyone had known about for a while. He joined the squad but was really struggling and it looked very much as though he would not be able to play. That said, he was being as positive as possible and very helpful in typical Tim fashion as we started our preparations at Wimbledon. Greg was playing with Jeremy Bates while I slipped away to the LTA for a press briefing ahead of the tie. Most of the questions were about Tim's injury concerns and I made it pretty clear he was unlikely to compete. The focus then shifted to Greg who I confirmed was ready and looking forward to it.

That was all fine and I headed back to the covered courts at Wimbledon in relatively good spirits only to discover Greg had done something to his foot and wasn't going to be able to play after all. You have to be kidding! So, we have no Tim Henman and no

Greg Rusedski. Don't panic, Captain Mainwaring, but what do we do now?

Martin Lee, a brilliant junior player in his day but incredibly volatile, was also in the squad and I had earmarked him to replace Tim. The trouble with Martin was that, all too often, he would be his own worst enemy, forever blowing his top, so the situation was fragile, to say the least.

I called Tim and asked if he was sitting down before telling him the breaking news that Greg had withdrawn. There was a pause before he memorably responded in unprintable fashion, his feelings about that all too clear.

Not a man to be downhearted for long he quickly pulled himself together, told me not to worry, we'd get it done and that he'd come to Birmingham and do everything possible to be fit in time. So, we travelled north in his Porsche while Greg went home.

Everybody and his wife from the LTA made the trip. Gavin Fletcher was in charge of the court, Heidi Cohu was there to run the PR side of things and it all felt a bit of a circus.

A javelin coach from the British Olympic Association who had a special harness designed to ease shoulder pain started working closely with Tim. I instructed Heidi to inform the media Greg was out through injury but, to my astonishment, she said we couldn't do that.

'But he's not playing.'

Apparently, that was irrelevant, though, which really annoyed me. I went straight back to Heidi and told her, in no uncertain terms, I had a job to do; Greg was out and that was that. I then found myself on the receiving end of all sorts of grief from Greg's publicity agent for what I was about to reveal, which baffled me. I was simply passing on the facts. Madness!

Tim, meanwhile, kept working on his shoulder and skipping like crazy at the side of the court. He still couldn't hit a ball, though, and the time to make a definitive decision on the line-up was fast approaching. Arvind Parmar was also there along with Miles

Maclagan but I was committed to selecting Martin Lee in the singles even though he'd looked awful on the practice court and was banging balls here, there and everywhere.

Come Thursday morning Tim was fit enough to start hitting and had a session with Martin, who was still completely out of sorts. Tim eventually went up to him: 'Martin, what's going on, mate? This is your big chance to show everyone what you can do.'

'Don't worry, I can turn it on.'

To which Tim replied, 'Why would you ever turn it off?'

Great line! And he had no answer to that. There's too much false bravado in the game and that was a classic example.

It was now clear that, whether or not he should, Tim had to play. He'd worked so hard with the harness and got stronger and stronger during the week. Late on Thursday he declared himself fit. Brave lad.

He duly went on court for the first rubber against Danai Udomchoke who was a small but gifted player. As mentioned, I've always had a really good relationship with Tim and once more he was prepared to listen to me. I'd been a serve and volleyer so knew exactly what his game was about. 'Keep coming in,' I said from the sidelines. 'Make another metre before you stop.'

The danger for a serve and volley player is fractional hesitation as you wait for the return. If you slow down by the smallest of margins, you're in trouble. It's not an easy way to play with all the side steps and different movements and, of course, a clever opponent will drop the ball in front and put you in some really awkward positions. But Tim was so charged up, and recovered from a set down to win convincingly in four.

We were up and running!

Then it was Martin's turn, and he had a shocker, barely winning a point in the first set against the very talented Paradorn Srichaphan. He lost 6-0, 7-6, 6-2 to leave the tie level at the end of day one. The less said about that match the better.

And so to the doubles. Now, I'd considered bringing in two Yorkshire players, Johnny Marray, who went on to win Wimbledon a few years later, and David Sherwood. I'd spoken to Tim about them but his preference was to play with Miles Maclagan and I didn't have any problem with that. The press wasn't too sure, though, and wanted to know if they'd played together before.

'Sure,' said Tim, 'a load of times … at under-12 level!' Everyone was laughing about that, including me, though I think I might have been crying at the same time! But it worked out well and, despite losing a first-set tie-break, they hit back to win 6-7, 6-4, 7-5, 6-2.

Buoyed by that, Tim, whose shoulder was holding up really well, then produced a terrific performance to see off Srichaphan three, two and three and the tie was won. Our roller-coaster ride continued as we returned to the world group for 2003.

This time we were given a horrendous draw away to Australia. They had the reigning Wimbledon champion Lleyton Hewitt, big-serving Mark Philippoussis and one of the greatest doubles players of all time, Todd Woodbridge, in their ranks.

Oh, and Tim and Greg were both missing for us through injury. Great!

The tie was going to be played on clay so I brought in Alan Mackin and Alex Bogdanovic for the singles with Arvind and Miles paired for the doubles. We had a good practice week in La Manga and were as fit as possible but the Aussies clearly weren't impressed and showed us scant respect. The first rubber featured Mackin, a Scotsman who never climbed higher than 213 in the world rankings, and the Scud, as Philippoussis was affectionately labelled. The Aussie of Greek and Italian descent romped through a one-sided encounter 6-3, 6-3, 6-3 and went on to reach the Wimbledon final later that year.

Having fed one sacrificial lamb to the crowd at the Sydney International Tennis Centre, it was the turn of Bogo. Now, I did have a theory as to how a left-hander could trouble Lleyton Hewitt.

Hook it up to his backhand, capitalise on the fact that he's quite short, and when he pulled it back across court, attack his forehand. And, for a while, that worked. Alex opened up a promising lead in the first set but lost it 7-5 and won only three more games thereafter.

There was no comeback from that. Miles and Arvind lost in four to Hewitt and Woodbridge and the only ray of sunshine was a victory for Bogo over Woody in the dead fifth rubber. An inevitable defeat shoved us back down to another world group play-off tie the following September, this time away to Morocco in Casablanca.

And that is when it became really awkward!

In the build-up to the tie, a rumour started to circulate. A big-name player had, apparently, tested positive for a banned substance but no one was sure who. The story bubbled away behind the scenes.

As touched upon earlier in the book, I wanted to include a very young Andy Murray in the squad just a few months before he went on to win the boys' junior title at the US Open. Andy was only 16 and, while already very highly regarded, was obviously still a work in progress. I called and said I'd like him to join us for the experience and, in hindsight, really should have been more persuasive. The thing was I hadn't actually seen him play. Andy didn't have any world ranking points, which was his priority at the time, so he politely declined my offer, which was a real pity.

We arrived in Casablanca with all hopes resting on the shoulders of Rusedski and Henman, as usual. There was something wrong with Greg, though, and I couldn't for the life of me work out what it was. He was acting strangely, and constantly seeing the medical team to use the saline drip and have ice bath after ice bath. Then, out of the blue, he changed all his rackets. I had to go to the post office in town to collect a batch of new ones, which was very out of the ordinary, but none of us knew him well enough to have a proper chat and find out what was going on.

Now, of course, we know it was a massive build-up of stress.

Shortly after the tie Greg was named as the player at the centre of the drug rumour. It was reported that he'd tested positive for the steroid nandrolone in July and that signalled the start of a nightmare period for him that dragged into 2004. It's vitally important to stress he was eventually cleared of any wrongdoing by an independent anti-doping tribunal, which ruled he had taken the drug inadvertently through pills handed out via trainers employed by the ATP. A number of other players were also cleared for the same reason and I totally agreed with what Tim said at the conclusion of the case: 'I'm so glad he's been able to prove his innocence. I've said all along that he just wasn't the type of person that would take something.'

Greg had his issues but, at heart, I believe him to be a good man with a clear sense of right and wrong and am so glad for him, and his family, that the cloud was lifted.

But back to the crisis on the clay in Casablanca. Tim opened up against Hicham Arazi, dubbed the Moroccan magician, who reached 22 in the world and played with incredible touch. Tim's touch deserted him that day. It was one of his most disappointing performances at Davis Cup level but that can happen to anyone. It put even more pressure on an already distracted Rusedski who, to be fair, fought like a tiger on his least favourite surface before losing 3-6, 6-3, 6-4, 3-6, 6-1 and was the victim of outrageous gamesmanship from his opponent Younes El Aynaoui. At various intervals towards the end of the match he complained about the court being too dry, the condition of the balls, the number of British flags in the stadium and anything else he could think of, having summoned the match referee. Ironically, a readers' poll in a leading Moroccan newspaper had just voted El Aynaoui their favourite role model in society ahead of the prime minister! He'd also received a gold medal, the nation's highest sporting honour, from King Mohammed VI. Perhaps there wasn't too much competition.

Two down after day one, our boys then demonstrated what a fine doubles team they were by beating Arazi and Mounir El

Aarej in straight sets on the Saturday. And when Tim bounced back to beat El Aynaoui in the first of the reverse singles it was game on.

Yet again it came down to Greg in the final rubber and what a match it proved to be. He battled back from losing the first set to win the second. A thrilling third-set tie-break then went to Arazi by nine points to seven. Prior to the tie it had been agreed that, once the floodlights came on, a new set wouldn't start, so play was then suspended till Monday morning. That was a blessing for Greg who had been suffering from what looked to be heat exhaustion, leaving him with precious little left in the tank.

When play resumed, there was, again, hardly anything to separate them but another tie-break went the way of Arazi, this time by seven points to five, and Morocco had crossed the line as 3-2 winners. The familiar sense of anguish, of coming so close, was overpowering.

Greg and I never discussed what went on behind the scenes during the trip and haven't to this day. As a captain it's your duty to bring out the best in your players and I tried my hardest. You can't gel with everyone, though.

And that proved to be the end of my time in charge. I'd sum up those years as bitter-sweet. Tim said some lovely things afterwards, not least that Casablanca had been one of the best trips he'd experienced in terms of preparation and fitness, etc. But others were less complimentary. I can only wonder how critical of me Greg was behind the scenes. Arvind had a little pop too, which was all music to the ears of David Felgate, formerly Tim's coach, but no friend of mine. He was, unbeknown to be, preparing to take over as head of men's tennis and, with my contract up, there was never any chance I'd be part of the new-look team.

My last official duty was as part of the British delegation involved in a networking convention ahead of the vote for the 2012 Olympics which London duly won. A message came through during that visit requesting me to attend a meeting with John Crowther at some unearthly hour the next day.

The first person I saw upon arrival at the LTA was Sarah Sayers from human resources, always present at hirings ... and firings! I knew then what was coming next.

So, I walked into the main office to find David Felgate sitting next to Crowther, grinning like a Cheshire cat. His legs were tucked underneath him in schoolboy fashion and he was clearly in his element.

I decided not to prolong the misery and asked straight out if this was a fait accompli? Was my time up? Did they feel I had nothing left to offer British tennis? And, after a pause, Crowther, who looked as though he was starting to sweat up in the paddock again, nodded. With Felgate giving a pretty good impression of someone who'd just won the lottery, there was nothing more to say.

Nobody then, or subsequently, ever properly thanked me for my efforts. Nobody at all. But that's tennis, and tennis players. All for one and one for one. I wasn't surprised but it still hurt.

A few of the press guys suggested I make a story out of everything that had gone on but I resisted the temptation, even when Felgate rang a few days later to gleefully tell me he'd secured the top job in the men's game and was going to appoint Jeremy Bates as my successor. A move that proved to be unsuccessful as it turned out.

Don't get me wrong. I was by no means a perfect captain. Maybe there was a little bit of a generational gap and perhaps I could have done more to get the best out of players, particularly Greg. I know some of the players felt I wasn't decisive enough with team selections before and during certain ties but that's still an excuse. You have to be ready. Whenever and wherever. Just take your chance if and when it comes.

My chance had come. Now it had gone. It was time to move on.

Chapter 28

No Whitewash at This Wightman Cup

SEVERAL DECADES earlier I had taken on a similar role that led to one of the most satisfying non-playing achievements of my career. In late summer 1978, for reasons unclear to me at the time, I was asked to coach the Great Britain Wightman Cup team. It was for the 50th edition of the event, sponsored by Carnation, at the Royal Albert Hall in November of that year.

The competition, featuring the best women from GB and the United States, had become a depressingly one-sided spectacle and plans were afoot to call time on it at the end of the year. Great Britain had only won five editions since 1930 and had been hammered 7-0 in Oakland, California 12 months earlier.

Not surprisingly, there hadn't been a stampede to take over the role. I'm pretty sure a few more obvious candidates rejected the opportunity before I was approached by Paul Hutchins. After a bit of soul-searching I thought, why not? We had some very good players in Virginia Wade and Sue Barker (long before she re-appeared as a member of the Spanish Inquisition at the Ecuador Davis Cup tie!) but the American team was an all-star cast comprising Chris Evert, Tracy Austin, Billie Jean King and Pam Shriver. Admittedly Austin and Shriver were still teenagers but they'd already demonstrated their might at professional level with Austin having beaten Betty Stove to claim a title in Stuttgart a few weeks earlier so it was akin to bringing over the armada. There were seven matches: three singles, one doubles, then two more singles prior to the second doubles encounter.

Having accepted the challenge, I then broke out in a cold sweat trying to work out how we could possibly claim four of those rubbers. Virginia and Sue were capable of winning a couple of the singles and one of the doubles, though that was by no means a given, but where was the other point going to come from?

I was still as fit as a fiddle back then and really enjoyed the on-court coaching as we prepared for the match. Michelle Tyler, Anne Hobbs and Sue Mappin made up the team. Michelle had won the French Open Girls' event a couple of years earlier but had shown no real sign of developing her skills at tour level. She never did, in truth, and retired from the sport a year later to start work at a department store in Bromley, so it's fair to say she wasn't in the same league as your Everts and Billie-Jeans.

Anne Hobbs went on to have a really good career, winning two titles, making the fourth round at all the slams and reaching 33 in the world as a singles player. She was even better in doubles and made the final at the Australian and US Opens and the semis at the French and Wimbledon in the 80s. She was still a teenager in 78, though, and desperately short of experience.

Sue Mappin was a Sheffield girl and only six or seven years younger than me so we had plenty in common. British under-21 champion in 1966, she had been part of the team that won the Wightman Cup in 1974. That was staged at the Deeside Leisure centre in Queensferry, Wales and saw the hosts cruise to a 6-1 victory. As impressive as it sounds, and as well as Virginia, Sue (on debut), Glynis Coles, Lesley Charles and Sue played, it was against below-par opposition. The American team consisted of Julie Heldman, Janet Newberry, Jeanne Evert, Betsy Nagelsen and Mona Schallau who were all fine players but a long way short of their class of 78.

I'd known Sue Mappin for most of my life. Our mothers were friends who went to Wimbledon together, and Roger Taylor and

Dickie Dillon was a pair of names that stood out for her as she started to climb the local ladder. We were considered a formidable pairing and she was a big fan of Dickie's, telling me years later she initially thought he had a better chance of making it in the game before realising his work ethic didn't quite match up to mine. Sue and I had a lot in common. Yorkshire people tend to stick together and we shared a lingering suspicion that our faces never really fitted with those in positions of power. Sue couldn't believe it when she was finally made a member of the All England Club and has always been supportive of my decision regarding the boycott in 73, puzzled that Wimbledon and the LTA haven't shown more appreciation for my stance that year.

I was delighted to have her in the team, though it was always going to be a brutal assignment against Austin, Evert, King and co. Yet, despite the gulf in class between the two squads, this was destined to be a remarkable triumph.

The great British tennis writer of that era, Laurie Pignon, was on hand to record the drama and compiled a superb report for the 1979 *BP World of Tennis Yearbook*. In it he recounted a 'victory that was as dramatic as it was unexpected, neither Agatha Christie nor Alfred Hitchcock could have contrived such an atmosphere of suspense. If ever there was a marriage between sport and theatre, it was at the Royal Albert Hall in November when summer came to England rather late.'

Dramatic it was, alright. Pignon went on: 'The script speaks for itself: after three days, six rubbers, two sets and eight games, everything was even. This great hall, which has so often echoed to the sounds of Elgar, produced a new sort of melody that night which was music to British ears.'

What a wonderfully evocative description and absolutely spot on. So, how did it reach such an astonishing conclusion? Silly question. It was all down to my brilliant tactical acumen and shrewd selection policy! Okay, partly down to my brilliant tactical acumen and shrewd selection policy. A succession of gritty and at times inspired performances from the home team, with young Miss Tyler leading the way, had quite an influence as well!

It's fair to say we did not make a flying start. The first rubber lasted less than an hour and saw Sue Barker win just three games against Chrissie Evert who was playing her 13th Wightman Cup singles and had yet to taste defeat. At times it can be rather uncomfortable to sit courtside, attempting to offer relevant advice as your player succumbs to the inevitable. This was most certainly one of those occasions.

That left the stage clear, a little earlier than they'd perhaps anticipated, for Michelle Tyler and Pam Shriver. I'd given the nod to Michelle after hearing how well she'd played against Rosie Casals in her debut appearance the previous year, a match she finally lost 6-4 in the third. I didn't know Michelle well and decided to let Virginia sit with her courtside. Whatever worked best for the team was the way to go and Virginia and I knew each other well enough to avoid any potential clashes. She is charming, one of the best players ever to have represented Great Britain, but she can be a very imposing figure too. I've heard tales about her being a law unto herself at some Fed Cup ties but there were no problems here, and what a match it proved to be amidst a unique setting. The crowd is so close to the action at the Royal Albert Hall, with Sue Mappin later describing it as 'like being in a goldfish bowl with the eyes of so many spectators at the same level as the players'.

Amidst the popping of champagne corks and sound of knives and forks making short work of whatever dinner consisted of up in the luxury boxes, our great underdog showed remarkable levels of concentration and a terrific fighting spirit against Shriver, who was only 16 and, to be fair to her, had barely played for a few weeks. Despite losing a 3-1 lead and then the first set, Tyler stormed back, to the audible delight of the crowd, and won 5-7, 6-3, 6-3. I'd been wondering where that extra point was going to come from and there it was, on day one.

The following evening began with an eagerly anticipated showdown between Virginia Wade, the Wimbledon champion 16 months earlier, and 15-year-old Tracy Austin who'd recently come out on top when the pair met in Phoenix. It was a typical Wade match. Some highs, some lows and plenty of nerves for her adoring public as she lost the first set 6-3, finally won the second 7-5 having led 4-1, before moving through the gears to take the decider 6-3 and put us 2-1 up.

The lead was short-lived. Billie Jean King, who was player-coach that week, decided not to compete in the singles but teamed up with Austin to see off Sue Mappin and Anne Hobbs in three sets. So, all square heading into the final day.

I remember a bright, sunny, autumn afternoon that fateful Saturday and I'll never forget Chris Evert's brutal demolition of Virginia Wade to put the Americans back on top. Evert won the first set to love in about 20 minutes, losing just eight points, and it was a similar story in the second. Wade got her name on the board in the ninth game but that was as good as it got. Evert was incredible and, in that sort of form, would have wiped the floor with anyone.

I did my best to stay positive ahead of Sue Barker's must-win battle with Tracy Austin who'd comfortably beaten her at the US Open the year before, but the reality of the situation was all too apparent and when Tracy won the first set 6-3 our dream of a major upset was fading fast. That said, the way Barker had stretched her formidable young opponent to the limit in the early stages suggested there was still some hope.

And so it proved.

In set two Sue started to serve in almost super-human fashion. Her forehand came to the boil as well and, cheered to the rafters by the sell-out crowd, she lost only three more games to record one of the best wins of her career and leave the score at three apiece with the final doubles rubber to come. A truly wonderful performance.

I was vaguely aware of some uncertainty in the American ranks as to who they should play in the last match. JoAnne Russell had shone while partnering Billie Jean King during the 1977 clash in California and was part of their squad. In the end, though, they decided to pair Evert with the under-cooked Shriver. Pam went on to win more than 20 doubles title at slam level and 112 in all, 79 of those with Martina Navratilova, but had played only one junior event since reaching the final of the US Open in September prior to arriving in London and had struggled to get up to speed in the singles.

It was a no-brainer for us to go with our two most experienced performers, Barker and Wade, who promptly went on to take the first set 6-0. Too good to be true? Well, yes, it was.

The US team, oblivious to the hysteria that had gripped the Royal Albert Hall, wrestled back the initiative by taking the second set 7-5 and, at four-all in the decider, we headed into the climactic finale few had dared consider possible at the start of the week. Back to Laurie Pignon, as caught up in the excitement as everyone else come the denouement.

'At the winning of a point, the unsolicited choir which filled the seats even into the darkness above the lights, thundered its patriotic approval. Then, as they waited for the next ball to be served, it was as if an invisible conductor had rapped his baton as the place was engulfed in expectant silence. So the *cantata-allegro molto* and *pianissimo* continued until Wade and Barker won the last two games to win the cup for only the tenth time in 50 attempts.'

What a night, though I can't remember too much about the dinner that followed. Having heard all those champagne corks popping for the past few days it was our turn to let some bubbly smooth away the tension and celebrate in fitting fashion one of the great upsets of recent times. The men's team reached the final of the Davis Cup that year as well and, together, we won the BBC Sports Team of the Year Award, a reflection of just how big a story and triumph it was. More than 45 years on I still treasure being part of that adventure and place it in my top-ten list of achievements. The Americans were gracious in defeat but it really hurt them. The picture of a distraught Tracy Austin, Chrissie Evert and Pam Shriver attempting to make sense of it all in front of a couple of microphones speaks a thousand words. Their captain, Vicki Berner, was generous in defeat but did end the night by muttering, somewhat ominously, 'Just you wait till next year!'

And she duly gained revenge. The 1979 edition, staged at West Palm Beach, Florida was a rout that the home team won 7-0. Indeed, Great Britain never won the Wightman Cup again, managing to claim only eight rubbers of the 77 played in the following 11 years before we were finally put out of our misery when the curtain came down on the event in 1989.

Not that I was around for any of those. There continued to be a great deal of uncertainty over the future of the fixture immediately after our triumph. Sue Mappin later confirmed how delighted all the players had been when I was appointed and spoke about my 'inspirational' leadership and ability to make the team relaxed and play to their best. I would have relished an opportunity to defend the title in America but with everything left in limbo and no concrete offer coming my way, it was time for something new and exciting in sunny Portugal.

Chapter 29

Bjorn Again in Spain and Portugal

STRANGE AS it may sound, Bjorn Borg had a part to play as I transitioned into the world of tennis holidays and a life in Portugal that, while full of hard work, was incredibly rewarding as well. Bjorn and I developed a bond of sorts after our match at Wimbledon. I still laugh at the memory of a frenzied group of girls climbing over the little wall at the side of the court and rushing up to him by the umpire's chair as he packed his bags at the end. Totally surrounded by them, all I could see was his blond hair as they screamed hysterically and created a most un-Wimbledon-like scene! I'd never witnessed anything like it before. The match itself had obviously been played in good spirit throughout. He did break a racket but that wasn't a result of any aggression on Bjorn's behalf, rather his desire to take apart one of my 'donkey drop' serves! So, we'd parted on good terms and bumped into each other every now and then.

Long before my playing career started to wind down I'd harboured thoughts of setting up a tennis centre of some sort in Portugal and selling holidays at the same time. The Algarve was slowly starting to open up and is obviously a beautiful part of the world. The more we travelled there the more Frances and I fell in love with the place and began to seriously consider our options. In the mid to late 70s one of the villa companies that had tapped into the market and ran their business from an office in Knightsbridge approached us. George Felner de Costa, also known as 'gorgeous

George', was a charismatic individual with plenty of charm and powers of persuasion that made him a natural when it came to selling luxury villas. We started to dip our toe in the water. Frances, who has always been extremely organised and efficient, worked at their Brompton Road office, which she really enjoyed, while I began in earnest to put plans in place for my own coaching business.

My first experience of working at a luxury country club had come in the late 60s when tennis started to boom in the United States. Long-established golf clubs were expanding their facilities and I was offered the job of head pro at Aventura in Miami. The role was designed to fit in around my commitments as a newly established member of the Handsome Eight and I was keen to accept it. Frances wasn't sold on the idea of living in the States, though, and worried in particular about the children's education, so we didn't stay for long before coming home. Fred Stolle was given the job instead and remained for years, having a wonderful time by all accounts.

Back in London there were precious few job opportunities as the 60s came to an end. The LTA claimed to have no money and, with taxation levels at an all-time high, few others did either. It was then that I started looking in earnest for a club of my own, possibly in England but preferably overseas where the tax situation could be managed. That search took me to the Channel Islands, La Manga and Monte Carlo, which all had their attractions but, for whatever reason, didn't suit our particular needs. In truth, the tennis facilities weren't great either. Most of the places we saw were pretty run-down with poorly maintained clay and hard courts and wooden clubhouses that had next to nobody in them.

The more we looked elsewhere the more we realised Portugal was the venue ticking most boxes and our timing was to prove opportune. The Vale do Lobo was part of the Algarve's golden triangle that also includes Vilamoura and Quinta do Lago. It was a natural, unspoilt region built within the hills and pine trees of the Portuguese countryside. The beach was a short walk away and, in truth, the place had everything you could wish for as a sun-lover in need of rest, relaxation and some leisurely sports activity. Plans had been drawn up for the Vale do Lobo Resort, a 750-acre villa development with a whole host of facilities, including golf and tennis. We settled there for part of each year and I took charge of the design of the tennis club which was inspired by the very famous one in Monte Carlo. Once completed, there was a clubhouse and terrace overlooking 12 all-weather championship courts, six of which were floodlit, plus a swimming pool and bar.

I was being financially advised by IMG at the time. A young fellow called Martin Sorrell was part of the company and has gone on to do rather well since then, first with Saatchi and Saatchi and then the world's largest advertising and PR group WPP. It all led to him being valued at £368 million in the *Sunday Times* Rich List in 2019. Martin helped set up a tax-saving system for me which meant I could only stay in the UK for 63 days a year, presenting a serious logistical challenge. A decent run at Queen's and Wimbledon took up a sizeable chunk of that allowance so I had to be very careful. I loved those early days in Portugal, though, so it wasn't a major problem and the environment was great for Frances and the children. My only regret was not having enough money to buy a substantial plot of land right at the start of our adventure. That was how the real money could be made and I sensed the opportunity without being able to fully capitalise on it personally.

The 1974 Carnival Revolution in Portugal, which resulted in the overthrow of the authoritarian government and a slow transition to democracy, led to a period of financial instability within the country. The resort, owned by Trusthouse Forte and the McAlpine group, started to struggle and a liquidator, John Margetts, was eventually called in. Now, John and I knew each other quite well. A tennis lover, he'd been a guest of mine at Wimbledon more than once and, based on his advice, we decided the time was right to buy one of the villas, which were being auctioned off, and so make permanent what had become a regular commute between the Algarve and Wimbledon, where I have always had a home.

The resort was eventually bought by a Dutch diamond merchant, Sander van Gelder, who was a shrewd businessman but had zero interest in sport. The golf course that had been painstakingly designed was beautiful and snaked along the coast but Sander only had eyes for the cash prize and that meant building as many holiday homes as possible. At one board meeting he presented some plans to the directors who quickly realised several new buildings were being earmarked for precisely where the magnificent seventh green was positioned near the sea.

'But Mr Van Gelder, that means there will only be 17 holes on the course.'

'So what?!' he famously replied. 'Can't they make do with 17?'

Sander, who passed away in 2023 at the age of 85, was that sort of guy. I will say no more!

Life was frantic but a lot of fun and one excursion to Spain in 1979 made it clear to me this was the direction I wanted to continue travelling in. Through some of 'gorgeous' George Felner de Costa's contacts I heard Bjorn Borg was being paid a small fortune to star in a big publicity launch for a brand-spanking-new tennis club at the Hotel Puente Romana in Marbella. The wife of one of the Lebanese owners was a massive Borg fan and very keen to meet him, as were so many others following his extraordinary run of success at Wimbledon and Roland-Garros.

Money wasn't an issue. The Lebanese owned a Vanderbilt super-yacht which was too big to enter the marina so a cutter was sent out, operated by a number of sailors, all in Japanese uniforms with caps, to bring the official party on to dry land. It was quite a sight!

On a whim I invited around 30 clients, who had been regular visitors to Portugal, to come over, with the possibility of seeing Borg. I didn't make any promises about meeting or playing a few points with the great man but there was no shortage of interest nonetheless.

And it worked out perfectly as I was the only person there who really knew him. Everybody else stood around in awe so, although he had a busy itinerary, we chatted and I mentioned my travelling entourage. If he had a spare moment, I casually mentioned, would it be possible to take a picture or two with them? Bjorn is such a lovely, calm guy to speak to and promised not just a photo but a hit with a couple of the better ones as well. I was really touched because he was being pulled here, there and everywhere. In between the meeting and greeting he was photographed with an assortment of different rackets: Donnay for one territory, another brand for Asia and so on. In actual fact they were all the same wooden rackets painted in various ways depending on the manufacturer.

Borgy had this aura which captivated everyone who met him and the tales circulating about him at that time built up the legend. It was said he'd just broken the strings on 28 rackets during the French Open. He had them strung so tight they'd 'ping' at night in his bedroom. Everybody was eating out of his hand as he told us some of his stories. And he was so generous with his time on court. There were a couple of very promising juniors with me on that trip, both of whom I have stayed in touch with to this day: Tony Mitchell and Steve Rowe. Tony first made a name for himself as the Yorkshire under-12 champion when coached by Colin Graham. He started travelling up and down the country after that and was introduced to me by Sue Mappin. Derek Bone, head of the LTA junior section in those days, developed an interest in him after a notable set of wins during a tournament at Queen's.

'Where have you been all my life?' Derek asked Tony. Well, Yorkshire isn't exactly halfway round the world but at times it may as well have been. Tony was only 5ft 8in but had so much potential and a wonderful work ethic. I genuinely think he could have gone on to enjoy a really successful pro career but he was blighted by a wrist injury that required seven operations in six years during his late teens and early 20s. I really felt for him because he was fantastic to coach and seemed to revel in the tough, disciplined approach I insisted upon.

Through another contact of mine, entrepreneur and film producer David Haring who had a dream to develop a British Wimbledon champion, Tony went to the States and teamed up with the great Pancho Segura. He was one of the game's great professionals during the 1950s and a legendary coach later in life. Segura became the teaching pro at Beverly Hills Tennis Club in the early 1960s and worked on the forehands of Doris Day, Charlton Heston, Gene Hackman, Kirk Douglas and Lauren Bacall to name but a few of his A-list clientele. He also teamed up with Jimmy Connors, Tracy Austin and my old friend Stan Smith when he moved to La Costa resort in Carlsbad, California. That's where Tony decided to go despite being warned in no uncertain terms not to. Paul Hutchins, who at that time was head of men's tennis in the UK, said going there would be 'the biggest mistake of his life'. What absolute nonsense. These days aspiring young Brits think nothing of honing their skills in the States but the LTA was paranoid at the prospect of anyone flying the nest back then.

Tony loved it. Bobby Riggs was one of his regular playing partners, so too John Wayne's daughter Marisa, but the wrist never healed and he finally had to call time on his career at the age of 24. We still speak on a regular basis and I know he's never found anything to fully replace the satisfaction tennis gave him, both mentally and physically. What he learnt on court has taken him a very long way in the business world, though. Using the 'hold serve and get the ball back' mantra, Tony stayed in the States and made a lot of money in speciality finance, energy and real estate. I know he thinks I can be bloody-minded and stubborn – and, let's be honest, I can – but Tony once told me I taught him to be a man and I have all the time in the world for him.

The other talented youngster, Steve Rowe, enjoyed a great little session with Bjorn, who then said there was enough time to hit with the rest of the group, some of whom weren't quite so gifted. They couldn't believe it but I lined them up and off they went to cross swords with the world's greatest player at the time for five magical minutes each before having their photograph taken alongside him. Everybody relished the opportunity except for one guy, David Sellar, who was actually very good but kept slipping back in the queue as it got near to being his turn. He was overwhelmed by the experience and didn't hit with Bjorn at all in the end, which was a real shame.

That night there were parties everywhere and one VIP discotheque where we hung out and had a few drinks. Eventually, a few of us were invited, via the cutter, on to the yacht, which was lit up in the most dazzling manner with glamorous people lining the deck. Bjorn, his usual laid-back self in jeans and T-shirt, was immediately introduced to the lady who'd organised the whole thing. She may have been a multi-millionaire but you could tell what a big moment it was for her as she stepped forward and presented him with a necklace that had BJORN BORG in gold with two diamonds, one nestled in the O of Bjorn and the other in the O of Borg. It had been specially designed by her jeweller in Paris and he gracefully accepted it as though it was the sort of thing he was given every day; come to think of it he probably was! I patiently waited for the ROGER TAYLOR double-diamond delight … and am still waiting to this day!

He was charming, though, and such good company once you got to know him. There was a close-knit group of Spanish coaches who he tended to stick with and Adriano Panatta was there that week as well. Panatta had won the French Open three years earlier and was the only man to beat Borg at Roland-Garros, actually managing it twice. Those boys knew how to party so we had a great night to round off two very special days. It cemented our friendship and although our paths don't cross very often it's always a delight to catch up with him. We bumped into each other on the tea lawn at Wimbledon a year or two back. He came up and gave me a big hug.

I feel privileged to have played a high-profile match with him and be able to call him a friend.

The trip was a huge success and fuelled my desire to make the academy in Portugal as big and bold as possible. As I was still competing in the over-35 category and on the Legends tour, I had to do plenty of travelling and there was seldom any time to put my feet up back at the resort. The demand for places at what was officially named the Roger Taylor Tennis Centre in the early 80s was strong between April and October but we stayed open all year round. One of the best ways to promote the business was through the World Travel Market which continues to provide some of the best networking in the travel industry all over the world. I met a lady called June Pod at one of those events. She ran Wimbledon Travel, loved her tennis, and very kindly offered to let me have an office at the back of her shop in the village. I put in an answerphone and ran the operation 'virtually' with great success. Every time the machine bleeped with a new message confirming the arrival of four more people I'd get a little buzz of excitement. Nobody had catered for tennis holidays before so this was always going to be a risky business but there was traction from the word go and demand continued to grow.

We were helped enormously when the BBC programme *Wish You Were Here* turned up to film us. That show had an audience of 15 million in those days of, at most, three or four channels. A number of influential tennis writers including Richard Evans, Penny Shock and Peter Jessup were also generous enough to spread the message in print and, in all honesty, it wasn't a hard sell. There were in excess of 700 villas and apartments to choose from and, more often than not during the summer months, they were all booked out.

It was nonstop from my point of view and I learnt a lot very quickly. At the start, my assumption was that everyone wanted to be a performance player. That's what I was after all. When the first batch of guests arrived I sent them out for a run on an arduous course of my own design which began at the tennis centre and went through the pine trees, over sand dunes and along the beach before finally bringing them back. It nearly killed them! I soon realised that wasn't what the majority were expecting, or looking for. They were on holiday after all and wanted good value social tennis with a bit of structure plus plenty of time to visit the bars and unwind.

So, I designed two rather more gentle running courses, one for the adults and a shorter one for children who could just beat their mum and dad if they put in a bit of effort. That immediately created a friendly competitive spirit that continued on to the court. Identifying the different standards of players as quickly as possible at the start of each week was the biggest challenge. There could be as many as 70 or 80 people all expecting to face opposition of a similar standard and it was up to us to be as professional as possible on that first morning and establish the right groups. To help with the coaching, I brought in seven or eight guys, some of them from Yorkshire, who weren't official 'pros' but knew what to do and, most importantly, the way I wanted things to be structured. It was really important to have a uniform approach to any technical coaching and a constantly vibrant atmosphere.

I was aware that most of the players wanted to hit with me for at least part of the week so I would change court every day. That meant the other coaches had to keep up the level of intensity and follow my example. I'd do a demo each morning and throw in a few trick shots to keep the atmosphere light. Spin serves that bounced before flying over the fence always went down well as did the backspin drop-shot I enjoyed perfecting, but all the coaches shared the same principles when it came to groundstrokes and footwork and we kept an eye out for the weakest players to ensure they maximised what ability they had while not disrupting the experience for others. The worst player in the world can volley because they only have to stand at the net and watch the ball. There turned out to be a fair few like that but the mix worked and lots of friendships were forged, some life-changing. A good example of that relates to David Hirst and his partner Beverley Lockwood. A young, good-standard tennis couple from Huddersfield, the two of them had a natural talent for coaching and became an important part of my team. After a while they became friendly with a German family staying at the resort and developed a good rapport on court while putting their talented young son through his paces. To cut a long story short, David and Beverley were then invited over to Germany to continue that coaching relationship and remain there to this day.

We had three apartments in the tennis centre where the coaches could stay plus space for a few more in my villa. The lads were packed in, two to a room but knew what to expect. The sun shone and there was a feeling of fun and freedom as they enjoyed the time of their lives. I made them so fit and enthusiastic to the extent they'd have press-up competitions in the bar! I was in great shape and it was an idyllic setting to hone and maintain high levels of fitness, particularly during the summer. Inevitably, the number of clients dropped off considerably between November and the end of April but I thought it right to keep the place open 12 months a year so, if one person turned up, they were guaranteed a wonderfully bespoke few days. It might be a single fellow or a gorgeous lady on her own. Whoever booked, and in whatever week, they were treated with great care and courtesy by the pro on duty.

It was by no means just about the tennis. There was a lovely beach bar, run by an Angolan family with a couple of really sweet kids who would bring out this amazing food. It was just a wooden shack on the beach in those early days and was magical. Now, of course, you'll find lots of expensive restaurants in the area, and there's nothing wrong with that, but I do sometimes yearn for the simpler days of the late 60s and 70s.

A lot of credit has to go to Nick Walden, who is in his early 70s now and still coaching at one of the David Lloyd clubs. He was instrumental in developing the courts and looking after all the day-to-day business. We met by chance one afternoon when I was shopping at Harrods. Their sports area was called Olympic Way and Nick was working as a temp. I was on the lookout for a manager/head coach and after chatting to him for a few minutes thought he might be the perfect pick. Sure enough, after an interview and practice session at Queen's, I offered him the job, which proved to be one of the wisest decisions of my business life. Nick drove my red BMW down to Portugal with another coach, Yorkshire lass Julie Hancock, who I knew from the Hallamshire club in Sheffield. They took down boxes of balls, nets, rackets and everything else required to get things ticking over. Nick was really good at developing a set routine. With him in charge I could relax while off playing somewhere or back in England drumming up business. He was there full-time for five years and worked with some other terrific coaches and ex-players. He and Graham Stillwell had a whale of a time together. Adrian Simcox from Lancashire and another Yorkshireman, Simon Ickringill, who went on to be head pro at the wonderful Ilkley club for 39 years also played a big role in those early days. So too did John Howarth who still played for Yorkshire in the men's over-70 team not that long ago and John Howey who subsequently made his mark at Goring Tennis Club in Oxfordshire among other places.

Another mainstay of the operation was a Portuguese coach, Eurico Correia. He introduced me to a local player, Marco Seruca, a lovely lad who reached the final of the Portuguese National Championships, played Davis Cup for his country and went on to run the Estoril Tennis Club.

It didn't take long to fine-tune the weekly schedule. We had T-shirts made with all the details printed on them. Monday would be groundstrokes; Tuesday, serve and volley; Wednesday, smashes and lobs, etc. and everything would lead to a series of finals at the end of the week with prizes for all sorts of things to keep even the least talented player interested. During the summer our Friday afternoon mixed doubles tournament became the talk of the town. It was quite an operation with four teams on each of the 12 courts. They played through their boxes and, eventually, the top four teams would compete on what we called centre court, nearest to the clubhouse, for the top prize, with all their friends and family shouting and cheering. The atmosphere was amazing.

Every now and then a very good player would appear and try to beat me. I may have been in my 40s by then but still hated to finish second best and remained determined not to let anyone get the better of me. You never lose that competitive instinct. There were in particular a few quite loud, aggressive young Americans who fancied their chances and one week a German heptathlete wanted to drill with me for hours and hours. He was a big strapping guy but moved around the court like a ballet dancer and had so much energy.

I loved those challenges which helped keep me in pristine condition. That was just as well as I'd be on court from nine-11 every morning and for another two or three hours in the afternoon while also arranging extra-curricular activities and dealing with any issues that arose. In the evening we'd have a couple of drinks and plenty of dinners with more prizes for anything from the best foot fault to the best serve, forehand and even the worst-dressed player, which would invariably be someone decked out with a kipper tie and check jacket. Fashion sense was open to question back in the 70s and early 80s but it was great fun and business was booming. I started advertising in the *Sunday Times* with the paper's very first ad in the special interest section and we could not have been busier. Yet there were a lot of bills to pay, with court costs, lighting and other hidden expenses that Mr Van Gelder was reluctant to help out with so, while the model was working to perfection, it was never the cash cow many took it to be.

Plenty of celebrities came down to see what it was all about. Ilie Nastase visited, so too Victor Pecci, Adriano Panatta, Maria Bueno and Dan Maskell, who was getting on a bit but loved the environment. A number of soap stars appeared as did one of my favourite actors, Albert Finney, though I don't remember him being a particularly enthusiastic player. The former Wolves, Aston Villa and Scotland striker Andy Gray loved his tennis and could jump 10ft in the air with a frying-pan grip that brought mixed results. Mary Berry had the ingredients to be a half-decent player. Sebastian Coe and I became quite friendly and a lot of jockeys, including John Francome, were often in town. Squash champion Jonah Barrington had his own club just up the road so we became well acquainted.

Our value to Portuguese tourism was recognised when we had a bust-up with Van Gelder over costs and threatened to decamp to Spain. To be honest, that was never going to happen but the powers that be in the tourist office wrote to him saying they couldn't do without our business and that we were opening up the Algarve so look after us or else! It was certainly gratifying to be appreciated. I travelled the world for the Portuguese tourist office promoting the Algarve and my own business at the same time and loved every minute of it.

Behind the scenes, though, there were problems. Big problems.

Frances and I had grown increasingly far apart and finally decided to split up in 1982. The consequences of that were significant. A fiercely intelligent and industrious person, she had been an integral part of the business, and life was very different once she left. It wasn't all doom and gloom, though, as a bubbly blonde from Canada with a tennis pedigree to match her very engaging personality started to become an increasingly important part of my life.

Chapter 30

Being a Double Act Is More Fun!

CONSIDERING WE'D known one another 18 years before finally tying the knot, I think it's fair to say my relationship with Alison Hannah can hardly be construed as a whirlwind romance. Patience is a virtue, though, and, goodness me, it was worth the wait.

A keen university tennis player in her native Canada, and part of a team that included Carling Bassett's sister Vicki, Alison never scaled the heights in performance terms. A good standard county player is her own verdict. Much more importantly, though, she has always been very positive and determined in anything she's turned her hand to. From a young age she was, and remains, best friends with Stacey Allaster who has gone on to enjoy a wonderful career in tennis administration as CEO of the WTA and more recently US Open tournament director. They proved to be a dynamic duo as students, running junior tennis programmes during the summer, securing a big sponsorship deal from Pepsi and signing up hundreds of youngsters to the course. That gave Alison a taste for the coaching role she was born to fulfil and paved the way for Stacey to embark on her own great adventure.

We first met in Portugal in the summer of 1987. Alison was working in a coaching capacity for Jonathan Markson who'd just opened a tennis camp in Praia da Luz. Shortly after arriving she heard about my academy via a local travel agent who was rather keen to meet me – my eyebrows apparently held a special appeal for her! She duly arranged a visit for the two of them and they turned up one sunny afternoon with nothing specific in mind. Blissfully unaware of the whirring cogs inside her constantly active mind, I showed her around. We then had a chat followed by a hit, and that, for then, was that.

Looking back, I remember feeling very relaxed in her company from the word go and handing out some grief about a 'forehand that must clearly have been left at home in Canada'. To be fair, I don't think she was even expecting to play that day. It was short and sweet, though. We said goodbye and didn't bump into each other again for around a year. Alison went back to Canada at the end of that summer to become head pro at the Richmond Hill Country Club, which was an exciting step up for her.

It wasn't until the autumn of 88 that we bumped into each other again. She came back to the Algarve for a short holiday, this time with a Norwegian-based boyfriend in tow. Once again it was nothing more than a hello-and-goodbye encounter before we went our separate ways.

Then, in the summer of 89 things finally started to happen. Single again and re-evaluating her life, Alison was living in Oslo and in need of something completely different. She called me out of the blue during Wimbledon on the off-chance that I might be able to offer up some work. Well aware of her coaching ability and engaging personality despite only having met a couple of times, I had no hesitation in inviting her down to the Algarve as part of the team, at which point our friendship started to blossom. Nothing serious I hasten to add.

I was flitting between London and Portugal with plenty on my mind both personally and professionally and had no desire to become embroiled in anything long term. Her infectious enthusiasm and refreshing approach to life was a real tonic, though this was at a time when I was too preoccupied to fully appreciate everything she brought to the table.

It came as no surprise to see her fit in brilliantly. The other coaches loved having such an easy-going colleague, and between them all created a really special atmosphere within the academy. I genuinely liked her but also had a tendency to be (in Alison's words) 'a little mysterious at times'. To be totally honest, I'm quite shy by nature and tend to keep myself to myself. Being the life and soul of the party didn't come naturally and, although it was important to be the smiling face of the operation, I found the role quite stressful. I did what was necessary without (I hoped) being too stand-offish.

Our relationship continued to develop over the next few years and when, in 1994, the Portuguese side of the business finally came to an end in the face of mounting financial pressure, most of it instigated by Sander Van Gelder, we joined forces on other ventures. We went to Lew Hoad's club in Fuengirola, to La Heredia on the Ronda Road in Spain and also organised holiday trips to Morocco and Vilamoura, which is just up the coast from Vale do Lobo. Alison moved into my villa and as the 90s went by we started to become inseparable, despite her inability to turn off lights or ever lock the front door!

I've mentioned her bubbly personality, which complemented my more reserved approach so well. I can be stubborn and a little negative with my thought process to certain things in life, which she counterbalances like a perfect doubles partner. And I'm proud of everything she's achieved as a player, coach and wife. Her record for Canada at over 40s, 50s and 60s is fantastic – far beyond anything she thought possible in her 20s and 30s. I'd like to think a little guidance and one-on-one coaching from yours truly has helped a bit but she deserves everything that's come her way at county, national and international level.

She's always on the road, either in a playing or coaching capacity, and is so amenable, while being sufficiently tough on court when required. There's never been a problem between her and Frances even when, to my great consternation, both had to spend a few days together at the villa in Portugal one year for a variety of reasons. They got on brilliantly in the circumstances. Frances did change her name back to Maclennan when we finally married but that was understandable and probably just as well. With both being members of the All England Club, it would have been a touch awkward to have two Mrs Taylors roaming the place.

Having stated quite categorically some years earlier that I never wanted to marry for a second time, the option became more and more appealing as we moved into a new millennium, though the catalyst for the about-turn was unexpected. Alison, as a Canadian, constantly had issues with her passport and was required to leave the country every so often to renew it. On one occasion we were both flying back to London from Faro. Only as I was about to hand over my papers at immigration did it become clear I had my son Greig's passport rather than my own. I was taken aside for questioning and so too, because of her Canadian roots, was Alison. She claims I then pretended not to know her at all (an outrageous accusation that may have an element of truth to it) while busily trying to explain I wasn't deliberately attempting to pass myself off as a 14-year-old. The whole episode panned out like a comedy sketch before we eventually managed to board in time. That episode left me thinking how much easier life would be if we were officially together. The age gap of 22 years was a worry but, certain it was the right thing to do, I duly proposed for the second time in my life.

There were several obstacles to overcome before we finally tied the knot. A new law was on the verge of being passed that had significant consequences for foreign passport holders and threatened major complications for Alison. We headed down to Morden Park House registry office keen to secure a date as quickly as possible only to discover they were fully booked for months to come. Shocked, we stood in a corner to discuss our options, at which point I noticed another couple nearby who had clearly picked up on our dilemma. After a while they wandered towards us in rather uncertain fashion.

What did they want?

'You can have our slot if you like,' they said.

We looked at them in disbelief.

'Really?'

'Yes,' was the reply, and they meant it. Certainly not what we were expecting but a sign perhaps that it was meant to be. I still wonder what was going on in their relationship that day and whether they did finally get married themselves. In fact, if either of you happens to be reading this, please get in touch or tell us your story. We'd love to know!

The wedding itself in February 2005 went from being a small, private affair to a lavish production with many of Alison's family coming over from Canada. We stayed at Cannizaro Park and, following the ceremony at Morden Hall, went to San Lorenzo in Wimbledon for a big celebration before returning to Cannizaro. Alison comes from a great family who accepted me from the word go despite our difference in age. Her dad, Bob, was an amazing man who flew countless missions in a Lancaster bomber during the Second World War. He was assigned to the 115 squadron of the RAF which lost a lot of planes between 1939 and 45. Bob first flew on the Short Stirling, a four-engined heavy bomber, then Wellingtons and survived a crash in a field, which killed one of his crew and badly burned two others. Back in Canada they show a great deal of respect to veterans, who have their own number plates and are given preferential treatment wherever they go.

I went to Big Bob's funeral in the summer of 2011, which was quite a spectacle. There are only two airworthy Lancaster bombers still in operation and one of his closest friends, Leon Evans, flew down to Miami to hire one of them for his send-off. There we were at St Catharine's Golf Club in Ontario following the funeral, looking across the 18th fairway when suddenly, out of the clouds, this magnificent plane appeared and flew, ever so slowly, between the avenue of trees up the fairway towards the clubhouse. It was spine-tingling stuff and a reflection of the high esteem that Bob, who trained to become a dentist after the war, was held in. He had three brothers who, like him, were all around 6ft 5in. A wonderful family that Alison goes back to visit every year and one that certainly brought her up the right way.

I know I'm a lucky man ... even if she still fails to turn off the lights and lock the door at night with alarming regularity.

Chapter 31

Roger Taylor at Queen's as Opposed to Roger Taylor of Queen

SHARING A name with one of the world's most famous drummers has occasionally led to a spot of confusion. But while Roger Taylor and Queen ruled the musical world in the 70s and 80s, this Roger Taylor spent as much time as possible at Queen's Club when not playing, coaching or expanding operations in Portugal. Let me state for the record that I have never played the drums nor met my namesake. I do like their songs though, and might occasionally have muttered 'another one bites the dust' after a satisfying win on court.

I'll talk about the All England Club in the next chapter but, for a variety of reasons, am tempted to put Queen's, situated close to Barons Court tube station in West London, as my favourite tennis destination. It boasts a wonderfully varied history; it was built in 1886 as the first multi-sports club anywhere in the world, a great innovation at the time. Since then, it has hosted ice skating, baseball, athletics and rugby tournaments. Come the 1920s Oxford and Cambridge universities staged rugby, football and athletics varsity fixtures there while in more recent years it has become famous for lawn tennis, real tennis, rackets, squash and now padel.

While it's fair to say Queen's will always be in the shadow of Wimbledon, the club is known and respected throughout the world. It hosts the World Rackets Championships, the Real Tennis World Championships and the British Open along with a large number of other events. From 2025 it will have an even higher profile in the tennis world with a WTA event now preceding the ATP week, which has been a fixture on the calendar for so long. Some of the club's members may be put out by that but I'm all for it. Queen's, with its 28 outdoor courts and ten indoor, used to stage a women's event and is a vibrant place with fantastic grass courts that, for some, are even better than down the road at Wimbledon.

The fact I enjoyed so much success there as a player inevitably plays a part in my love for the surroundings. The two finals I reached in 1967 and 1973 against John Newcombe and Ilie Nastase may have ended in defeat but they resulted in me being given honorary membership and are indelible memories. Stan Smith's threat that I would never play tennis again if I didn't join the boycott kick-started an extraordinary week there in 73. Beating two of the key ATP committee members, Arthur Ashe and Cliff Drysdale, on my way to the final fired me up more than I realised as I fought that battle of the boycott and I retain other strong memories from matches played there. As a 14-year-old I lost to Mike Sangster in the British Junior Championships. Then, as a 21-year-old, I made the final of the British Covered Court Championships in 1963. On a super-fast wooden surface Bobby Wilson beat me 16-14, 6-2, 9-7. He was an indoor specialist who won that event four times and racked up several other titles on very similar surfaces in Germany, France and Scandinavia.

These days Lee Childs, part of that Davis Cup trip to Ecuador in 2001, is the head tennis pro there. Lee had so much talent as a youngster but was, if anything, over-coached. The LTA hired Tito Vazquez of Argentina to iron out some of the rough edges in his game and add a touch of South American guile as well. Unfortunately, it didn't make him a better player. If anything, he lost some of his natural strengths without gaining anything tangible from the new approach. It can be so hard when you're being told different things by different coaches and it's a real shame in my view that the UK has never really invested sufficiently in our home-grown talent. There are a lot of good coaches, with Jack Draper's right-hand man James Trotman an obvious example. But, as with Premier League football managers, there seems a natural inclination to believe overseas coaches can provide all the answers and that is wrong. Lee is doing a great job, though, and with former Irish pro Ross Niland managing the club most impressively, Queen's is going from strength to strength. Long may that continue.

Chapter 32

Not Always Cosy, but Always Special

I DON'T think it's an exaggeration to say Wimbledon is, for most people, the be-all and end-all of British tennis. It's the big beast everybody has heard of, even if they've not so much as picked up a racket in their lives or could explain to you with any confidence the scoring system. The Championships continue to attract worldwide attention and make a staggering amount of money, much of which is then diverted to the LTA and various other bodies. Just down the road from the All England Club is the National Tennis Centre in Roehampton, known as the NTC. At times, during the summer in particular, it's a hive of activity, but there's an elitist feel with those big gates keeping everyone out and a speaker-phone system invariably demanding to know what you want before you can even set foot inside. I think it's a real shame those facilities are not made full use of and that so much money was spent on one exclusive set-up.

I don't suppose we will ever mirror the way of life in Germany and France where tennis clubs have long been the centre of social interaction but it wouldn't take a great deal of money to brush up some of the antiquated venues crying out for a little bit of tender loving care, particularly with playing numbers on the rise since Covid. And, to be fair to the LTA, progress is being made in that direction with a nationwide campaign, supported by the government, benefitting thousands of park tennis courts by making them fit for purpose and a key part of the local community.

Of course, there's nothing more elitist than the All England Club itself, with its 565 full members, life members and honorary members combined. I have to be honest and say it's now a fantastic club to be part of, which certainly wasn't always the case. When I first joined in the 70s it was a pretty dark, uninspiring venue with little on offer. Gradually, though, major changes began to take place. Australia led the way. Way back in 1987 they built a retractable roof at their Open venue, which was then called Flinders Park, and were progressive in a number of other areas, not least in terms of looking after the players. Until relatively recently, the impression given at Wimbledon was that the sacred Centre Court mattered as much as, if not more than, the players. It's very different now.

One thing hasn't changed, though. Despite my playing career, coaching skills and longevity, I have never been invited on to the committee or come close to it. Now, let me be the first to say, I'm not your usual committee man and that has tended to be my default answer whenever anyone has questioned me on the subject. I wouldn't go so far as to say it's kept me awake at night but I would like to know why I wasn't considered. And if that wasn't a viable option, it would be nice to at least have my photo on a wall somewhere around the club, alongside various croquet players from many moons ago who have been allocated some space. That would mean a lot and surely isn't too much to ask for, bearing in mind my record there?

Above all I remain mystified, and hugely disappointed, that my son, Greig, was never made a member despite being a regular at the club as a child (members' children can play there as often as they like until the age of 21). By the time he reached his late teens, Greig was as good a player as anyone there aside from the former pros. Tim Henman was one of those to support his application in 2000 along with two vice-chairmen and another prominent member but the offer never came. I don't want to come across as bitter, and appreciate it's a private club perfectly entitled to choose who can and can't join the ranks. But we didn't even receive a letter of acknowledgement or any indication as to why he was constantly overlooked. I don't think it's a case of the club itself disrespecting me but someone in a position of influence most certainly did. I'm not one to go around harping on about my three semi-finals but few other British players have matched, or bettered, that record, and I don't think I'm being unreasonable to expect a degree of respect for what I achieved. The snub affected Greig. He'd been part of the place as a youngster and could have offered a lot as an active tennis-playing member.

As the years have gone by it's gnawed away at me. Who made the decision, and why? There were two people on the committee who were eventually asked to resign having been a part of it for 24 years, way longer than the usual term of office. Ken Weatherley, a former player and founder of the Tennis First charity that helps fund promising young players, was thought to have the final say when it came to membership decisions for all those years. Ann Jones, one of my contemporaries, was also on the committee for 24 years as the only female representative. I always got on well with her, which led me to the conclusion I'd done something to upset Ken. Only he knows if that's the case and, if so, what it was.

I think it's fair to say the club used to be a lot tougher on kids. The white clothing rule was strictly enforced at all times, which is not the case today. The attitude of some of the older members in particular was rather superior as well and that made life uncomfortable for Greig when he came to play. He was often the only youngster down there and it was easy to fall foul of people, perhaps without even realising it. Maybe that's what happened. A place like Wimbledon will always have certain individuals with a considerable say in key matters. Dan Bloxham is head coach at the club now and also master of ceremonies for the Championships. He's very popular and approachable but extremely influential when it comes to inviting prospective members to the 'play-in'. He wasn't around when Greig was trying to become a member; in fact, there wasn't a 'play-in' system back then. But that's how it works and it doesn't pay to question the process. There are far too many perks as a member to ever consider biting the hand that feeds.

I have long had a philosophy that you have to be lucky in life. Everyone, I believe, has a destiny. On court you can play the match of your career and still not win. For whatever reason, it's simply not meant to be. I was destined not to make the Wimbledon final despite coming so close, likewise Tim Henman. Ivan Lendl was desperate to become champion there but it never happened. Yet it worked out for Tim in other ways. When Phil Brook was chairman of the club there were growing concerns about a possible players' boycott over prize money, or a perceived lack of it. This rumbled on for a while. Phil had to attend a number of meetings with the players and brought Henman on to the committee to help facilitate those potentially awkward exchanges. It was a clever move because Tim gets on with just about everybody and had an excellent relationship with most of the players. But the idea that Tim was voted on to the board is completely wrong. He's not the only person to have been co-opted in that manner but was in the right place at the right time which brings me back to destiny. I wouldn't be the least bit surprised to see him become chairman one day.

In terms of key decisions by the committee, it's always easy to criticise in hindsight but I think it would have made sense to put a roof on No.1 Court at the same time as Centre. Not that having those two courts covered has solved all the issues associated with bad weather. The whole business of when to close the roofs and, more importantly, open them again needs to be properly addressed. The Championships really should be played as an outdoor event whenever possible and that doesn't always seem to be the case. Thank goodness we have them, though. I only wish one had been operational back in 1973 and I'm sure Tim feels the same way with regards to his rain-delayed semi-final in 2001.

I supported the ban on Russian and Belarusian players in 2022 and was incredibly surprised none of the sport's other governing bodies followed suit. As sympathetic as I was to individual athletes suffering as a result of their government's actions, war is war with consequences and I believe Wimbledon sent out the right message at that time.

I want to end this section of the chapter with a positive message too. I will always feel let down by my son not being made a member and it would, of course, be gratifying to receive some form of official recognition from the club for my contribution to British tennis. Perhaps my background and character held me back a little. The fact I would not, and never, will be a 'yes' man almost certainly played a part in keeping me side-lined. Yet it remains a privilege to be part of something special that has kept up so spectacularly and impressively with the times. We used to have to go up to Pall Mall in our dinner jackets for the annual general meeting with precious little female involvement. Now the AGM is at Wimbledon (with a free meal afterwards) and there's a much more relaxed feel to the place with two women, the chair Debbie Jevans and chief executive Sally Bolton, leading the way. 'Always like never before' is a brilliant catchphrase that sums up the subtle manner in which the club operates today; tradition with modernity is not always easy to reconcile but it's a balancing act that has successfully managed to keep those two wonderful weeks at the forefront of an ever-changing sporting world.

The history of the club is fascinating too. Many are surprised about, or not even aware of, the croquet element. As far as I know, that was the first sport which allowed men and women to play together. It began in 1868, before the tennis side of things was up and running. I'm guessing in those days it wasn't 'respectable' for women to involve themselves in anything that might lead to a spot of perspiration so playing croquet was the cut-off point in terms of permitted levels of exertion!

Lawn tennis was patented in 1874 as a new sport by retired army major Walter Wingfield. There is a café named after him at the club which is worth visiting should you come to the Championships or visit during the year. The first Wimbledon tennis tournament was held in 1877 on one of the croquet lawns, apparently to pay for the club's pony-drawn lawn roller.

I've lived nearby for most of my life and can't imagine whiling away my time anywhere else. There are two main parts – the village and the town – both of which became popular places to set up home once the railway station opened in 1838. At that time there was a clamour to move away from the cramped, unhygienic living conditions in the centre of London. Just seven miles away Wimbledon was an attractive alternative destination. Not far from the club is Tibbets Corner, which was on the old stagecoach route from London to the south coast. Infamous highwayman Jerry Abershawe was hanged there and his body left to rot as a very public deterrent. A sign remains to this day, depicting a skulking highwayman with a wide-brimmed hat and pistol.

One of the most notorious highwaymen, Dick Turpin, is rumoured to have hidden his guns in an upstairs room at the Green Man pub, which is very close to both Tibbets Corner and my favourite drinking establishment in the area, the Telegraph pub. On many an evening in the summer I have relaxed with a pint of Yorkshire Pride (what else?) at the Telegraph, named after Admiralty Telegraph, a shutter station that stood at the site in 1796 to convey messages between London and Portsmouth during the Napoleonic Wars. There are so many good pubs in the area including the Green Man in Putney Heath, which was the go-to area for those intent on duelling in the 17th century. In 1667 the Duke of Buckingham killed the Earl of Shrewsbury with a single stroke of his sword, so enabling the Duke to continue his 'affectionate relationship' with Lady Shrewsbury. And in 1798 the prime minister, William Pitt the Younger, and William Tierney MP tried to resolve a disagreement over a parliamentary bill by facing each other with pistols on the heath. Both missed their targets. I've no idea what happened to the bill but it's clear SW19 and the surrounding area has long attracted cut-throat competition, albeit of a slightly more sedate nature in recent times!

Chapter 33

Acting the GOAT

WIMBLEDON HAS to go down as the greatest venue of all time but for any tennis fan of the past 20 years a much more nuanced GOAT chat has become de rigueur. During that golden period between 2004 and 2024 we were treated to some extraordinary matches, sensational rivalries and, of course, very welcome British success. It's easy to say the Djokovic-Nadal-Federer-Murray era was the **G**reatest **O**f **A**ll **T**ime and that one of Novak, Rafa and Roger should go down as the greatest ever player but I'm not so sure. Yes, if you go strictly by numbers then, on the men's side, Djokovic tops the list and I have no hesitation in saying he's the best of his generation. The super-Serb's extraordinary success from 2007 up to the Olympic gold-medal triumph in Paris 17 years later is testament to his fitness and dedication. The same can be said of Roger and Rafa in that regard and all three pushed one another to incredible heights.

There are other nominations. Bjorn Borg's five successive Wimbledon crowns and six French titles in eight years left a remarkable legacy. He also made the US Open Final four times while only ever playing at the Australian Open once. Bjorn told me at the peak of his powers that, should he become US champion, he would then focus all his attention on Melbourne in pursuit of the career Grand Slam. Remember, in those days the Aussie Open did not attract the field and prestige it enjoys now.

I loved Boris Becker. Remembering he became Wimbledon champion at the age of 17 and followed that up by doing it again 12 months later still has me shaking my head in disbelief. There was a really special aura that surrounded Boris. His booming serve and acrobatic lunges at the net are, for me, one of the most abiding images in the game's history.

Becker's rise to the top coincided with another special era that saw the likes of Stefan Edberg, Mats Wilander and Ivan Lendl all hit peak form. A little after that, Andre Agassi's swashbuckling style complemented the regimented approach of Pete Sampras beautifully. How American tennis would love to have them back in tandem again. Sampras had the best second serve of all time and his tally of 14 slam titles looked unsurpassable until the brilliant new brigade came along.

All of those listed above are bona fide greats but none of them secure the Taylor vote for the GOAT. Maybe it's my age and the fact I played against him several times but, for me, the accolade has to go to Rod Laver, the only man to win the calendar Grand Slam twice, in 1962 and 69. In total he won 198 singles titles, more than anyone else in history. Eleven of those were at slam level, three in Australia, two at the French, four on the grass at Wimbledon and two more in the States. Just for good measure he also helped himself to nine major doubles titles, three mixed doubles, not forgetting five Davis Cup triumphs with Australia. On top of all that he claimed eight professional major titles. Had his pro status not seen him banned for most of the 60s, one can only imagine how many more big titles would have come along. It wasn't as if he had things all his own way either. Fellow Aussie Ken Rosewall was a ferociously talented opponent. Men like Pancho Gonzales, Roy Emerson and Lew Hoad kept him honest on a regular basis and there were plenty more able to trouble him on their day, including a lefty from Sheffield.

Everyone knows comparing eras is a thankless task. Equipment, modes of transport, the size of those back-up teams at the beck and call of today's superstars and, of course, the money up for grabs now make it a totally different world but refuel the Rocket in the modern era and I'd still expect him to fly higher than the rest.

As I write, it's the turn of Jannik Sinner and Carlos Alcaraz. Who knows what they will go on to achieve. That's the beauty of tennis, though. As one era draws to a close and fears abound that the sport is destined to lose its glamour and appeal, someone else appears, and these two have everything it takes to keep us coming back for more. I did love the rivalry of the Swiss maestro, the Spanish bull and the Serbian warrior, though. The contrast between them added to the spectacle and made for riveting tennis whenever they locked horns. Given the opportunity to watch one of those three in prime condition again I'd choose Federer. His presence and grace on court was a level above the rest. He never seemed rushed or out of breath and spoke superbly whenever interviewed. The men's event is called the 'Gentlemen's' Singles' in the Wimbledon programme and Federer is the epitome of that description.

My caveat against him is that single-handed backhand; glorious to behold but increasingly outdated as the game moves on. The development of the double-hander on that wing is one of the most significant changes we have witnessed. Okay, it's not a new phenomenon. John Bromwich was one of the first to make full use of it in the 1930s along with another great Aussie of that period, Vivian McGrath. Nowadays, though, a single-hander is a rarity. Mini tennis has a big part to play in that. Youngsters begin their journey using soft rackets and balls with little nets and naturally use both hands to scoop the ball up. That makes the double-hander a natural progression. And it's a deadly weapon that I wish more than anything else had been at my disposal. The top ten in the world all had double-handers at one point in 2023, which is no real surprise. I realise a lot of people love to drool over a Gasquet or Dimitrov single-hander and Federer's was a joy to watch but is it sad to see them disappear from the game? Well, definitely if you're a player that still has one! But I'm all for change and if better tennis is the end product, then so be it.

Rafa's exuberant style and work ethic struck a chord with me. He was the man who chased every ball and set new standards of fitness, both of which attributes were the bedrock to my game. That 'pirate look' with cut-off sleeves to highlight his muscles and the longer shorts made him different and attracted a new audience. His serve was vulnerable early on but he worked so hard to improve it and also perfected the inside-out forehand, adding another significant layer to his game. The fact he won Wimbledon a couple of times shows what a good volleyer he was too, even if many tend to overlook that part of his skill-set.

I have a degree of sympathy for Djokovic. His brilliance was overshadowed for so long by having to share the stage with Roger and Rafa. He seemed caught between the need to be as popular as them while realising deep down he could never win that battle, and actually didn't need to. Djoko had those blow-ups which rarely affected his performance but inevitably alienated some spectators. But you can't really be what you aren't, especially under intense pressure in a high-stakes environment. His habit of blowing kisses to the crowd at the end of a match made me uncomfortable. It wasn't real or necessary. I always wanted him to be the villain of the piece rather than trying to curry favour with gimmicky acts. I admire him greatly for what he is and who he is and hope to see the 'authentic Novak' for the remainder of his stellar career.

One thing I'm not an advocate of is the screaming and shouting, not to mention grunting, we've become so accustomed to. It's an increasingly ugly side of the game I'd like to see reined in but, equally, a sport without emotion is not a sport worth watching. Oh, how we frowned and disapproved of John McEnroe's madness, yet still we talk about his eruptions with fondness more than 40 years later. I was sitting courtside that famous afternoon in June 1981 when he launched into his immortal 'You cannot be serious' tirade at umpire Edward James, going on to call him 'the pits of the world' and 'an incompetent fool'. Tournament referee Fred Hoyles, officially described as a 'gentleman farmer' by trade, didn't know how to take the bull by the horns but it was the making of Mac, who went on to become champion for the first time at the end of that fortnight. It was also the beginning of the end for poor old Fred who didn't last much longer in his role before returning to the sanctuary of the countryside. We all laugh about that incident now but I do remember his opponent Tom Gullikson commenting afterwards, 'Everyone's afraid of these guys. If it was the 120th player in the world, they would have defaulted him.' And that's very true. Andy Murray got away with murder at times as well but I guess that's the advantage of being a star name and I'm sure it's the case in all walks of life.

Which brings me on to coaching during a match and the fact it's now permitted. A little like the pre-Open Era of shamateurism, when everyone knew players were receiving under-the-table payments but nothing was done about it, so the antics of coaches during a match were often referred to but seldom acted upon. For many it remains a contentious topic. I'll never forget Mark Petchey and Annabel Croft having an almighty row about whether or not on-court coaching should be allowed a few years back, live on Sky Sports during their coverage of the ATP Finals at the O2. I understand the view of those who feel it's up to a player to work out what he or she needs to do in the heat of battle. Equally, I see the advantages of a coach being able to offer advice and for it to be audible on TV. Watching Jack Draper at the US Open in 2024 provided that opportunity. Every word of his coach, James Trotman, came across crystal clear, prompting lots of debate. The instructions on that occasion were pretty basic in terms of the message being sent out. It was supportive more than anything else but, while I would prefer a silent coach in the Darren Cahill mould, it's another tweak I have no issue with and I was interested to see how the players' boxes were repositioned closer to the court at the 2025 Australian Open.

The stuff of dreams. Steve Rowe and Tony Mitchell with Bjorn in '79.

Greig gets to grips with the basics. Portugal 1982. Copyright Derek Rowe

A great place to grow. With Zoe, Greig and Katriona. Portugal 1982.

Buster and I teamed up for an exhibition match to officially open the centre in Portugal. May 1980. Copyright Leo Mason Photography

It wasn't all about hard work! Portugal 1981.

We are superstars! With Bobby Moore, Tony Jacklin, David Hemery, Barry John and Joe Bugner ahead of the 50-metre swim. Jackie Stewart didn't compete in that event. Crystal Palace. August 20th 1973. Copyright BBC

There weren't too many smiley moments with David Lloyd. Davis Cup teammates but never mates. Copyright Barnaby Studios

Questionable fashion sense for Paul Hutchins Davis Cup team of 1976. From top: me, John Feaver and Roger Becker (assistant coach). Bottom: David Lloyd, Paul Hutchins, John Lloyd. Copyright Barnaby Studios

Battered and bruised. The 1978 USA Wightman Cup team, including Tracy Austin, Chris Evert and Pam Shriver, left reeling by their defeat at the Royal Albert Hall. November 1978. Copyright Tommy Hindley

A winning combination! Trying not to look too tense alongside Virginia and Sue in the deciding doubles. November 1978. Copyright Tommy Hindley

Trying to hit the heights down under. Left to right: Nick Fulwood, Mike Walker, Stuart Bale, Andrew Castle, Jeremy Bates, Stephen Botfield, David Felgate, Jason Goodall. Adelaide, Christmas Day 1986.

Sweet revenge! Tim and Greg share my delight as Ecuador are beaten. September 2001. Copyright LTA.

Wedding day 2. 2005.

I suppose the other Roger won enough Wimbledon titles for the two of us. Alison looks extremely happy! Wimbledon. 2003.

My son Alex with his girlfriend Rachel enjoying a day out at the Championships in 2024.

Simply the best – and Rod Laver was pretty good too. Champions dinner at the Guildhall in July 2019.

A great player and top man. Laver Cup at the O2 in September 2022.

So near to that trophy again but I snared top prize with Alison. Champions dinner at Raffles hotel, July 2024.

An artistic touch. My son Greig had many talents.

In truth, you can't take too much on board in the middle of a match anyway but I do have one suggestion that would definitely help. Interminably long toilet breaks and injury time-outs have become a joke when we're trying to speed things up. My idea is simple. If your opponent does go off, or has to receive lengthy physio courtside, you should then be allowed to meet your coach on court and talk privately for as long as you have to wait. You can even hit with him or her if you fancy. This would enable a much more strategic conversation and, I'm sure, hasten the return of the other player!

Another significant change in recent years has been the scoring system at slams. There's the traditionalist part of me that rues the scrapping of the 'never-ending' final set. It should be survival of the fittest but I appreciate that after John Isner and Nicolas Mahut's three-day battle followed by the Isner-Kevin Anderson semi-final, something had to be done. In an ideal world I'd like all tie-breaks to be sudden-death, first to five points – the so-called nine-point tie-break we used to play. It's more exciting and less time-consuming so making it better for fans, organisers and the sponsors. Failing that, let's at least have sudden death at six-all.

There is another obvious way to quicken things up in slams during week one that I'd happily accept. Make rounds one to three the best of three sets before switching to five-setters from the last 16 onwards. Do it for the men and women, who are correctly paid the same prize money and therefore need to adhere to the same format. I know many of you will throw your arms up in the air at the prospect of that but hear me out. The players left in the draw come week two would be fresher and I'm sure we'd have many more memorable women's matches. I don't think the majority of the players would complain at the prospect either. Billy Jean King, who famously won her best-of-five-set 'battle of the sexes' against Bobby Riggs in 1973, said quite recently, 'I think the women should play three out of five sets or everyone should play two out of three. But if they play three out of five, then that means they have more content.'

Martina Navratilova has also been a supporter of the best-of-five formula. 'It gives us more of a chance to showcase our talent.' Andy Murray, one of the great advocates for equality between men and women in sport, has also highlighted the current inconsistency of the respective formats. 'I'm not saying the men work harder than the women,' he told the *New York Times*, 'but if you have to train to play five sets, it's a longer distance. It's like someone training to be a 400m runner and someone training to be a 600m runner.'

To me this is an obvious area crying out for reform and I sincerely hope we see it sooner rather than later. It may require a close look at the scheduling come week two of a slam but I don't see any problem with starting play on Centre and Number One earlier each day at Wimbledon and the other majors could easily factor in the possibility of longer matches. So much has been said and written about the duration of women's matches at slam level. I find it fascinating and fully agree with sports journalist Emily Salley who in a 2023 *Give Me Sport* article wrote, 'The best-of-three format in women's tennis is a result of tradition and the belief that women cannot handle the physical demands of five sets. Female tennis players have advocated for best-of-five matches in the past, but tournament organisers have been against the idea. The discrepancy in sets played between men and women reinforces gender inequality and prevents women from producing epic five-set performances. Women's tennis will always fall short of the men when there isn't even an opportunity to produce the same kind of compelling performance witnessed in the 2008 Wimbledon final between Rafael Nadal and Roger Federer for example.'

She is absolutely right. Female players voted for best-of-five-set matches in 1976 but tournament organisers immediately shut the idea down. I wonder how many of you know women did play best-of-five from 1891 to 1901 in the finals of the US National Championships. More recently, the end-of-season WTA final was contested over five sets from 1984 to 1998. Steffi Graf was involved in a couple of thrillers against Anke Huber and Martina Hingis and I genuinely think it's a real shame we are deprived of that potential excitement today.

While I continue to wear my 'Roger the Revolutionary' hat, how about doing away with the warm-up? We waste so much time between and during matches so I'd like to experiment with players coming out and starting straightaway. After all, a batsman doesn't march on to the pitch at Lord's in the middle of a Test match and ask for a few looseners. Likewise, top golfers don't walk on to the first tee and play a series of mulligans. On match day during my years competing at Wimbledon I used to go to Queen's to warm up. There were far fewer practice facilities available back then so I'd prepare on the fast indoor wood, often in the company of Roy Emerson who employed the same strategy. Those intensive bursts worked well for me but irrespective of how you prepare it's just a pattern you become accustomed to and, in my mind, I was ready the moment I walked out for the match.

It crossed my mind a few times to tell the umpire I didn't want the five-minute warm-up. There was absolutely no need to go through the motions of a few volleys and a couple of practice serves. Most of the players today never volley anyway so why bother trying out a few beforehand? On one occasion at Wimbledon I seriously considered planting a friend, dressed in tennis gear, in the front row to be my warm-up substitute. It would have been very interesting to see how my opponent coped. I just hope somebody has the guts to actually try it out one day. Being realistic, I can't see the warm-up being scrapped but we could at least insist on exactly five minutes from the moment the second player walks on to court with a shot clock clearly visible enabling everyone to see exactly how long there is to go before play has to start. That would definitely speed the process up.

The towel routine is another time-wasting exercise. Of course, you need to wipe away the sweat every now and then but not after every point. We had sweat bands and some of my contemporaries favoured a little towel you could tuck into the back of your shorts. Sawdust was another popular tactic. Today's constant wiping down, sometimes after an ace has just flown past you, is ridiculous and totally unnecessary.

Wimbledon's decision towards the end of 2024 to do away with line judges after 147 years captured plenty of headlines. While I feel sympathy for those directly affected by the loss of those roles, it's a good move from a players' point of view and effectively ends the notion of a 'bad' call. That represents progress and removes one area of stress and concern for those whose livelihoods are ultimately at stake. I'm not sure what it means regarding the future of umpiring in this country and how junior officials plot a career. What I would like to see is a referee on every court to back up the umpire if necessary. Then, if there is a serious dispute relating to a double bounce or something unforeseen, there'd be an opportunity to resolve the matter quickly and efficiently.

While we're on the subject of change, I have to mention equipment. Technology has transformed rackets as we all know, from the solid wooden ones of my generation to the steel and aluminium of the late 20th century and the composite materials with fibreglass reinforcements now being overtaken by carbon. The evolution of rackets and strings is well documented elsewhere. All I will say is that players from each generation would perform equally well with whatever's put in their hand. You may look back at matches in the 60s and 70s and compare them unfavourably with today's game but class is permanent irrespective of the conditions.

So, having examined the contenders, assessed the changes and suggested possible improvements in the rules and regulations of tennis, here's what you really want. The Taylor Top Ten based on slam titles, weeks at number one, career longevity – and a touch of subjective judgement.

Top Ten Men in the Open Era

1. **Novak Djokovic** – most weeks at number one and 24 slam titles.
2. **Roger Federer** – 20 slams. An icon and superb ambassador.
3. **Rafael Nadal** – 22 slams. Greatest clay court player ever.
4. **Bjorn Borg** – 11 slams before retiring aged 25. The Ice Man.
5. **Pete Sampras** – Pistol Pete won 14 slams.
6. **Andre Agassi** – won all the slams, eight of them in total. Pure ball striker.
7. **Jimmy Connors** – Eight slams, 109 ATP titles, 1,274 career wins!
8. **Ivan Lendl** – ten slams. 'Father of modern tennis.'
9. **John McEnroe** – eight slams. Brilliant and volatile in equal measure.
10. **Boris Becker** – six slams and the youngest male champion in Wimbledon history.

* It's probably only a matter of time before **Carlos Alcaraz** and **Jannik Sinner** surpass some of these players. Sinner has dominated the headlines while I've been collating this list. His three-month ban for the 'clostebol controversy' has prompted plenty of debate, and understandably so. The first thing to say here is that I don't pretend to know exactly what happened. The Italian comes across as a clean-cut, honest individual who was inadvertently caught up in a mess of his physio's making. That may well be so but it's the lack of consistency when it comes to the treatment of players accused of doping that worries me and, by the looks of things, a number of current stars are equally concerned.

When Jessica Pegula is quoted as saying 'none of the players trust the process' and Stan Wawrinka proclaims tennis is 'not a clean sport anymore', you realise there's trouble ahead. Liam Broady compared Sinner's ban, which began after the Australian

Open and conveniently ended just before Roland-Garros – in time for him to compete in front of his own fans at the Rome Masters – as 'like a Premier League footballer being banned over the summer'. I think the apparent leniency of the suspension and impression that the world number one had the financial clout to 'negotiate a settlement' has done him no favours long term. There will always be an asterisk against his name no matter what he goes on to achieve. Sure, every doping case is different, and it may well be that Sinner has merely paid a (small) price for the negligence of one of his team but, as Yevgeny Kafelnikov wrote, 'If you're 100 per cent sure of your innocence as he has always claimed to be, why would you accept a three-month ban and the inference that you are guilty?' I just hope some good comes out of it all in terms of lower-ranked players being better funded to fight similar accusations and that greater levels of transparency and consistency accompany all such cases in future.

NB: I'd like to give **Andy Murray** an honorary place in the Top Ten for his three slam titles, Davis Cup and Olympic heroics and magnificent fighting qualities that saw him reach number one in the world during an extraordinary era in the men's game.

Top Ten Women in the Open Era

1. **Serena Williams** – 23 slams (plus 14 doubles). Global impact, power and athleticism.
2. **Martina Navratilova** – 18 singles slams and 41 doubles! Revolutionised training.
3. **Steffi Graf** – 22 Grand Slam titles. Fraulein Forehand!
4. **Chris Evert** – 18 slams. Greatest clay court player.
5. **Monica Seles** – won ten slam titles, nine before the age of 20.
6. **Venus Williams** – ten slam singles titles and 14 doubles.
7. **Martina Hingis** – teenage superstar who finished with 25 major titles, five singles, 13 women's doubles and seven mixed.

8. **Justine Henin** – seven slams with arguably the best single-handed backhand in the men's and women's game.

9. **Aryna Sabalenka** – three slams and counting. I'm tipping her to rule the game for the next few years.

10. **Iga Swiatek** – five slams, four at Roland-Garros. Yet to shine on grass.

Top Ten Men in My Era and Slightly Before

1. **Rod Laver** – 11 slam titles and two calendar slams despite being banned for seven years: 198 titles altogether.

2. **Ken Rosewall** – faced an 11-year ban but still won eight slams and 147 titles in all.

3. **John Newcombe** – seven singles slams and world number one in singles and doubles (17 slam wins plus two mixed).

4. **Arthur Ashe** – three slams and one of the most influential players in the history of tennis.

5. **Ilie Nastase** – Maverick genius.

6. **Roy Emerson** – 12 slams, countless doubles titles and a record eight Davis Cup wins.

7. **Manuel Orantes** – underrated left-hander who reached two in the world. US Open champion in 1975.

8. **Pancho Gonzales** – won 14 pro majors and the US Open twice. Fabulous entertainer.

9. **Lew Hoad** – two-time Wimbledon champ. Superb doubles player and a Davis Cup champion four times.

10. **Stan Smith** – Wimbledon and US Open champ. Five doubles slams and a number one in singles and doubles.

Top Ten Women in My Era and Slightly Before

1. **Margaret Court** – 24 Grand Slam titles and had the edge over Billie Jean King.

2. **Billie Jean King** – Wonderful player who transcended the game with her fight for gender equality and social justice. Founder of the WTA.
3. **Evonne Goolagong** – seven-time slam champion and seven doubles slam titles too.
4. **Maria Bueno** – graceful player who won Wimbledon three times and the US on four occasions. The first woman to win the doubles calendar Grand Slam, in 1960.
5. **Ann Jones** – Wimbledon champion of 1968 and a two-time French Open champion. A hugely successful doubles player too and the best female player Britain has produced.
6. **Virginia Wade** – her 1977 Wimbledon triumph in the year of the Queen's Silver Jubilee was a stand-out moment in the history of the sport. Also won the Australian and US Open and picked up four Grand Slam doubles titles. The only British woman in history to have won titles at all four majors.
7. **Francoise Durr** – unorthodox French player who claimed 50 singles titles including the French Open in 1967, 60 doubles titles, five at Roland-Garros, six at Wimbledon and two more at the US Open.
8. **Darlene Hard** – powerful American who won the French Open in 1960 and the US crown in 60 and 61. Won 13 women's doubles titles at slam level with eight different partners, reflecting her wonderful volleying skills.
9. **Lesley Turner** – top-class Australian and two-time French Open Champion, beating Ann Jones in the 1963 final. She won seven women's doubles titles at slam level.
10. **Angela Mortimer** – the third 'home-grown' player on this list, Angela beat Christine Truman in the 1961 all-British final. She was also Australian and French Open Champion and won the Wimbledon doubles title in 1955.

So, that's my personal view. I'm sure you'll disagree with the order and indeed some of the names listed. The beauty of sport is that we can all have our own opinions and favourites and enjoy a bit of fun making a case for those choices. I've been struck by the intense support given to certain players of late. The Rafa, Roger and Novak fan clubs clearly don't see eye to eye. I'm all for a bit of tribal passion as long as it doesn't get out of hand. Demonstrate your support but never lose respect for a rival.

I look forward with interest to seeing if I'm right about Sabalenka as the player to beat over the next few years and just how high up my list Alcaraz and Sinner can climb. Even more importantly, I'm intrigued to see what happens to the new breed of Brits.

Chapter 34

Super Brits or Super Brittle?

JUST LIKE everyone else, I sat open-mouthed in front of my television as Emma Raducanu emerged from nowhere to enjoy her New York fairy tale in 2021. It was a remarkable achievement that understandably captured the imagination of the whole country and suggested a golden future for the Kent-based teenager.

So, what's gone wrong since then? There are plenty of theories. Did the dramatic leap to stardom go to her head? Was she distracted by the numerous business deals that made her a multi-millionaire? Is it correct to state she was poorly advised behind the scenes, particularly when it came to coaching appointments and scheduling?

I suspect that, to a degree, the answer to all those questions is yes. She found herself in a unique situation and it looks as though nobody around her knew how to deal with all the challenges. You have to constantly remind yourself that what happens on court should always be the priority, even if someone's offering you a fortune to wear their jewellery or drive their car. Once you lose focus it's very hard to get it back. There are those who point to who she beat at the US Open that year and say she got lucky. It's true the draw opened up but you still have to win those matches and deal with the extraordinary attention and expectation that comes with such a high-profile run.

Something shocked her afterwards and I have my doubts as to whether she'll ever scale such heights again. I don't know what kind of person she is but her strength of character will become clear over the next year to 18 months. Does she really want it? Is her love and passion for the sport strong enough? And is she surrounding herself with, and listening to, the right people?

It struck me that she played with no fear during that three-week run at Flushing Meadows which, don't forget, included having to come through qualifying, something she appears reluctant to do these days. The ball striking was crisp, the serve impressive, her demeanour a delight. And yet, almost instantly, those strengths deserted her. She looked nervous and increasingly despondent. A succession of coaches didn't help. Stability is a key ingredient for a successful player and the decision to replace Andrew Richardson within days of the US Open triumph was bizarre, so too the choice of a number of his replacements. Then came the injuries that left her sidelined for so long. We saw glimpses of brilliance during the middle part of 2024, and a really encouraging run to the last eight at the Miami event in March 25. She seems to enjoy playing opponents who hit hard which is what she's so good at herself. Coming to terms with those who like to loop it up remains a work in progress but in Miami there were definite signs that she has tightened up her game, is serving better and has that bounce back in her step. I just hope she has the belief to keep fighting, irrespective of what challenges lie ahead. Being a grand slam champion means there's a target on your back. All she can do is keep running and keep fighting no matter how long it takes to win and how awkward it may sometimes look.

And remember that retirement lasts forever. You don't want to hang up your rackets with any regrets.

Katie Boulter has made giant strides over the past couple of years and I'd love to see her continue in that direction. She was in the gym at the All England Club when I popped in recently and looks in great shape. Katie is working with Matt Little who made a name for himself as one of the best strength and conditioning coaches in the business during his rewarding 12-year spell as part of 'Team Andy Murray'. I've known Matt since way back and he reminded me that a reference letter I wrote on his behalf many moons ago secured him a good job at the Australian Institute of Sport in Canberra, which kick-started his career. Always happy to be of assistance! Add in Sonay Kartal, Harriet Dart, Jodie Burrage and Fran Jones and there is a nucleus of talented players who have the ability to achieve good things both individually and as part of the Billy Jean King cup squad.

Then, of course, there's Jack Draper. A lefty like me, it's perhaps not surprising I have a lot of time for him. At the age of 23 he's already a very talented, complete player and with his physique, good looks and charm has all the ingredients to become a superstar. He's powerful, looks comfortable with his double-hander, plays with purpose and moves well with a reassuring balance. His run to the semis at the US Open in 2024 took him into the world's top 20 and that first Masters 1000 title at Indian Wells in March 25 made him a top tenner and demonstrated what terrific progress he has made. He served brilliantly and I really like his attitude. Can he go on to win some slams? Well, yes, but again there are no guarantees. He's going to be there or thereabouts but come the semis of the big tournaments he'll have to find a way past the likes of Sinner, Alcaraz and whoever else emerges, someone like a Jakub Mensik who came from seemingly nowhere to beat Jack on his way to winning Miami. Just as the big three never let Andy Murray have the stage to himself so will it be for Jack and the big beasts roaming the jungle during his prime years. He has the weapons though. Big serve, a cracking forehand and increasing physical stamina. He volleys well too and needs to keep working on that aspect of his game. So often it comes down to the tie-breaks. Trying to break the big servers is incredibly difficult. To win four, five or six points when the ball is flying towards you at speed is a massive challenge but in a breaker it's all about snaring those big points when half a chance presents itself.

I was amazed by Mensik. He ticked every box on his way to denying Novak Djokovic a 100th title in the Miami final. He reminds me of an old Hollywood film star, someone like Cary Grant, and I'm really excited to see how he and the young Brazilian Joao Fonseca continue to develop.

From a British point of view Draper's rise towards the summit of the game is perfect timing. There we all were, coming to terms with Andy Murray's retirement and up steps Jack to fill a void and suggest another glorious era.

Along with him, I'm hopeful Jacob Fearnley builds on his quick-fire rise to somewhere just inside the world's top 100, at the time of writing. Will Henry Searle continue to make giant strides? In 2023 he became the first British junior to win the boys' title at Wimbledon since Stanley Matthews more than 60 years before and has posted some encouraging results on the main tour. Henry is another lefty and formed an excellent partnership with one of the best coaches in the country, Morgan Phillips. Blessed by a huge serve and forehand, he definitely possesses the tools for a bright future. Keep an eye out for Mark Ceban and Charlie Robertson too. Mark is still young but I've heard some good reports about him. Charlie's a small-framed Scot who has received plenty of support from the Murray family. He reached the semis of the Boys' Singles at the US Open in 2024 and has compiled some fantastic results on all three surfaces as a junior. Oliver Bonding is another player I've heard encouraging things about.

On the girls' front, Ealing-based Mika Stojsavljevic won the junior title in New York aged 15 the week Charlie made it to the last four. Heather Watson was the last Brit to claim that title in 2009 and with Hannah Klugman, Mimi Xu and Isabelle Lacy also catching the eye at junior level recently there's justifiable cause for optimism.

Strength and best wishes to them all and may they make the most of whatever wonderful opportunities come along. Their development is a far cry from my journey but they share the same dreams that inspired me and I sincerely hope some of them come true.

Chapter 35

Me in the 2020s!

WHAT ABOUT me in the 2020s, you may wonder. Well, for a man lucky enough to have stayed fit for the majority of his life, I have to inform you, and I'm sure it will come as no surprise, that getting old is not without its challenges.

Through a mixture of hard work and good fortune I barely felt a twinge until well into my 40s. The first relatively serious issue was a cartilage injury picked up in Portugal. Though no longer playing professionally, I still used to hurl myself about the place, diving for volleys and being as competitive as ever against any youngster who fancied their chances of claiming my scalp. One evening I landed awkwardly during a match and knew straight away there was some damage. My right knee kept clicking and I eventually went to see someone about it. In those days they simply took the cartilage out and left you with bone on bone, which often led to great pain if something slipped at an inopportune moment. Medical science has developed to an extraordinary degree since then but it took another 17 years before I was able to have that knee replaced.

I kept playing and learnt to handle the pain as best I could, though by the early 2000s it was clear the time had come to find a remedy. Around then, I took a young GB team that included Alex Bogdanovic to Vail in Colorado, the home of world-renowned surgeon Richard Steadman. He specialised in microfracture knee surgery, which essentially repairs cartilage by poking tiny holes near the defective area. I'm sure it's a lot more complicated than that but whatever he did yielded fantastic results for a number of sports stars including Martina Navratilova, Lindsay Davenport, Ronaldo and American football greats Dan Marino and Joe Montana. Through the LTA I managed to secure an appointment with Dr Steadman and was delighted to hear him tell me I could be as good as new after undergoing surgery. Unfortunately, my private health insurance company, Western Provident Association, wouldn't cover the costs in the States along with all the rehab and I was back to square one.

Eventually, after a great deal of research I tracked down David Hunt at the Wellington Hospital in London - he'd had some training under Steadman. He duly operated on me in 2005 and did a fantastic job. With the joint replaced it wasn't long before I was back on court, feeling like a spring chicken again. Surgery of that magnitude tends to take its toll, though. Your body often finds itself out of sync and I started to develop a limp. Over the next couple of years other parts of my body became increasingly sore. That led to the replacement of one hip in 2009 and then the other 12 months later. Finally, to complete the set, as it were, my left knee was replaced in 2017. Throughout that eight-year period I could hardly get on court at all, which was incredibly frustrating. In fact, it reached the stage where I began to fear I'd never play again. Despite that, I stayed as fit as possible, such was my desire to return to action at some point.

Around this extended period yet another part of my body retaliated after years of loyal service, though I really only had myself to blame. Shortly after the first knee operation in 2005 Alison and I went on holiday to Anguilla in the Caribbean. We were outside the villa, waiting for our friends Stacey Allaster and her husband John Milkovich to arrive before checking in. Now, Alison and I have always been rather competitive in each other's company. Actually, let me re-phrase that: Alison and I have always been ridiculously competitive in each other's company! It can be anything from who can do the most press-ups and run faster to which of us has the better ticket for a certain day at Wimbledon or who can order the most delicious-looking meal in a restaurant! She hates being beaten. And, of course, so do I!

While waiting for Stacey we jogged down to the beach and began a mini-Olympic competition. Determined to beat her in the press-up battle I foolishly tried one too many. Cue a burning sensation followed by an agonising pain in my left shoulder as I collapsed on to the sand; not exactly an ideal start to our break. Completing even the most basic of tasks became a challenge for several days after that. It's amazing how we take everything for granted until a key part of the body packs up. Over the next few months I was unable to lift anything heavy and even a game of social tennis was more or less out of the question. I could barely raise my arm beyond 45 degrees and felt bloody useless. Finally, a friend suggested I go and see Andrew Wallace, an Australian working out of Oxford Street, who was reputed to be one of the best shoulder men in the world. I made an appointment but wish I hadn't bothered. He barely looked me in the eye before conducting a series of incredibly painful tests. Wallace had me holding my arms out in various directions before banging my shoulders with no warning whatsoever. The shock was severe but, I suppose, necessary. Not being the type of person to say, 'Do you know who I am?', I hadn't mentioned anything about my background and he'd clearly done no research before meeting me. Come the end of the consultation Wallace finally looked me in the eye before saying, 'As long as you can make a cup of tea, and look after yourself, you'll be alright.' And that was it! Make a cup of tea! What, and shuffle around in my slippers watching old episodes of *Countdown*? I could not believe what I was hearing. Okay, I **WAS** struggling to lift a cup of tea at the time but there was no way I wanted, or was prepared, to accept that as the summit of my ambitions. Had there been a cup of tea in the room I might have tried to throw it all over him. Instead, I wrote out a cheque for £250, marched out and never went back.

My mind was in turmoil. What on earth should I do now? I tried to rehabilitate myself as best I could, all the time remembering how my old pal Jonah Barrington had done the same thing after tearing his Achilles tendon. Jonah, such an amazing mover on a squash court, never fully recovered and was left with a permanent limp. With that in mind I eventually went to see another shoulder specialist, at Parkside Hospital in Wimbledon. Mark Proctor was highly regarded but honest enough to admit he didn't have the experience to operate on my left shoulder because it was so badly damaged. In the end he did the right one, which was also showing plenty of wear and tear and that led to a very dramatic switch in the way I played tennis.

Having genuinely feared I'd never contest another point in anger again, it crossed my mind that if I learnt to serve right-handed with my new improved shoulder, all might not be lost after all. By now I'd become good friends with Dr Bob Murphy, an expert in the world of mental health who, as touched upon earlier, spent some time with my son, Greig, trying to work out the source of the issues that had troubled him for a number of years. Bob is a deep thinker and useful player with a crafty touch. We started hitting together on a regular basis and, aged 70-plus, I began my transformation into a right-hander.

It helped that I threw with my right hand. Developing a forehand proved to be reasonably straightforward but the backhand was a different matter altogether. I spent hours studying the technique and realised the key was to punch your fist into the shot before releasing the head. Gradually, I was able to rely on a reasonably acceptable top-spun single backhand but, to my intense frustration, there was absolutely no potency to it. Now, I know this will sound strange bearing in mind how we all came to worship at the altar of the single-hander, and I am a huge admirer of the likes of Roger Federer, Stan Wawrinka, Richard Gasquet and Grigor Dimitrov, but throughout my life I yearned to possess a two-hander! Had I developed one of those as a youngster I genuinely believe I would have been a much, much better player.

The new single-hander with my right hand did enable me to play again but did not have the zip to win points on a regular basis. So, the next stage in the Taylor 'ageing body revolution' was to mix things up, literally. I continued to serve right-handed before switching hands to play out the point. And that worked pretty well, except for one thing. Problems arose whenever I had to deal with a drop-shot. I'd often reach the ball in time but would then, invariably, be lobbed. Unable to smash or reach an overhead with my left hand, I'd have to switch hands again while back-peddling, which proved rather confusing. For a while I kept falling over, probably giving the impression to anyone watching that I'd had a couple of drinks pre-match, silly old fool. However, I eventually mastered the strategy and am quite chuffed by what was achieved in the twilight of my career. Without wishing to blow my own trumpet too loudly, there was no shortage of success at senior amateur level. From the age of 45 I was national champion six years running during which time I didn't drop a set and it was a similar story with the indoor championships. I won that event seven years in a row, also without dropping a set. Once the injuries set in I simply couldn't play on a regular basis but the right-handed renaissance reintroduced that winning feeling at national and international level quite late in life. Alongside Henk Nieboer I reached the final of the senior World Championship late into my 70s. Henk is a super-fit Dutchman who I could never get the better of when I started playing right-handed. That was annoying because he's an arrogant little so-and-so in the nicest possible way and didn't hide his satisfaction when coming out on top against me. For the first time in my life I had to accept losing more matches than I won, which wasn't easy. Yet at least I was playing again.

Life was rosy until, soon afterwards, other more serious concerns blotted the landscape.

Chapter 36

Life and Death for Real

THE IMAGE of being fit has always been of paramount importance to me. It's something I learnt from the Aussies, who always prioritised their physical conditioning, aside from when indulging in a pint or two of the amber nectar. Their strict regime made a real impression on me during the winters I spent down under when legendary coach Harry Hopman put the top players through their paces.

Alas, it doesn't matter how fit you are when the dreaded C comes to call. Approaching 80, a constant need to get up in the night for a pee provided a signal that something untoward was occurring in my prostate. I had a number of PSA tests and feared the worst before sitting down to be told I did, indeed, have cancer. The prognosis wasn't a massive shock but my world stood still for a moment as I realised nothing would ever be quite the same again.

The biggest concern was whether the cancer had already spread to other parts of my body. I underwent an intensive course of radiotherapy, which left some horrid side effects. That treatment took place at the Royal Marsden hospital in Chelsea for 40 straight days, bar Sundays, and knocked me sideways. The doctors were generally encouraging, suggesting the cancer wasn't aggressive, hadn't spread and I'd outlive it, whatever that meant, but it was still a real shock to the system. As sod's law would have it, all this came about shortly after we'd decided to cancel my private health insurance. I'd been with Western Provident Association for 38 years and never really forgiven them for refusing to cover that knee operation Richard Steadman had wanted to do in the States. As most of you with health cover will know, the premiums start going through the roof come a certain age. I'd been forking out in excess of £6,000 a year for ages and called time on that just before the cancer made its presence felt.

It meant I was left in the hands of the NHS, which, for all the criticism levelled at it, has looked after me remarkably well under the guidance of Doctor Vincent Khoo. Sure, the process hasn't been perfect, but after some oestrogen shots to supress the tumour and lower my PSA levels, I was accepted on to a special course that has continued to monitor my blood markers and keep things ticking over satisfactorily. All well and good, I thought.

Except there was more to come.

Part of the course included having a CAT scan to examine my whole body. Lo and behold, the scan revealed a shadow by the heart in the left ventricle which, even with my limited medical knowledge, I knew to have a rather important role in everyday life. If you want to breathe properly, the ventricle has to be functioning effectively. The discovery of the shadow led to a number of tests around the heart but no immediate conclusion as to what might be causing it. After several months I was finally diagnosed with a very rare condition called amyloidosis. In essence, that's caused by a protein called amyloid building up inside you, affecting the heart, kidneys, liver, spleen, nervous system and digestive tract. Doesn't sound very nice and just happens to be terminal. Apart from that, it's totally harmless!

My symptoms vary from day to day. I go from being fine to feeling as though I've hit a brick wall. There have been a couple of times coming back from Portugal, and also in Wimbledon village, when it's suddenly felt as though I'm not moving at all while everyone bustles past me. So disconcerting, and I find it very difficult to get my strength back after an episode like that.

Though there is no cure at present, a tremendous amount of research is taking place, all related to gene editing, which will, I'm sure, provide plenty of answers in the years to come, though probably not in time to help me. The experts in this field are the sort of people who go on to win Nobel prizes. A number of clinical trials have taken place in the United States and one of the men at the centre of the studies, Professor Julian Moorhouse, actually examined me in London. I don't really understand a word of what they do but wish them all enormous success with their research.

Throughout the whole medical saga I have tried to remain philosophical with regards to the direction my life is taking, and the prospect of never hitting another tennis ball in anger. Given the chance I would play every day but all good things must come to an end. I'm hanging on to the belief that a cure for this little-known disease is just around the corner and that I will be able to walk on court again one lovely, sunny afternoon, experiencing the sense of peace and satisfaction that hitting a few fluffy balls over a net in some form of competitive environment brings. Realistically, it's not going to happen but while it's still a possibility I will continue to hope and dream.

Although my playing days have been curtailed, for now at least, Alison has gone from strength to strength with her coaching and competitive fixtures. She has represented Canada with great success at every age group since turning 40 despite having the disadvantage of not being a tournament player from a young age. That's when you pick up the tricks required to win ugly when necessary and on a regular basis. She gives her all, though, and never throws in the towel, which is exactly what you want from someone you're coaching. I've done what I can to help and am thrilled to see her representing her country with such distinction, something she never even dreamed of until a few years ago. It's been a terrific ride and fun for me to be involved in a different way.

Not that it's always been plain sailing, particularly on the coaching front. She worked her socks off when head coach at the Westside Club near Wimbledon but finally had enough of the political infighting that soured the atmosphere there. Most notably, Alison has shown just how accomplished a coach she is at high-performance level. Hannah Klugman, a hugely talented young Brit on the junior tour, is one of a number of potential star names to have benefitted from her wisdom and guidance early on. Hannah, I might add, also had a lesson with me some years ago when Alison was away. My brief was to help her develop an effective backhand slice. It was fascinating to appreciate what a quick learner she was and how easily the technical side of the game came to her at the age of six or seven. I could immediately see she wasn't cutting across the ball with sufficient impact to create enough spin. It has to be a bit like a karate chop and you don't want to decelerate through the motion. The backhand slice will never be as good as the topspin version but is an important part of a top player's armoury and Hannah can now boast a 'Taylor-made' version. And if she doesn't, I will!

Alison also worked with Hannah's older sister Alice who won the prestigious Road to Wimbledon junior championship. Alice had a great deal of potential but hockey was her main love and she switched to that full-time in her early teens. It wasn't a bad decision either as she went on to represent Great Britain at under-16 level. Hannah was an excellent hockey player too but nailed her colours to the tennis mast when Covid came around. Her love for the sport was apparent from the age of four. Back then she would have a 15-minute private lesson with her coach, Austin Coventry, while Alison worked alongside Alice. But she'd hang around the club all day asking anyone who'd give her the time of day if they'd practise with her. She could already hit the ball pretty well by then, showing real focus and natural athleticism. Hannah competed officially for the first time when aged five in one of the red-ball events held at the Westside Club and more than held her own against much older children despite barely knowing how to score.

Ben Haran, head of performance tennis at Reed's school in Surrey, came aboard when she was ten and is alongside her now as the journey continues, with so many possibilities but absolutely no guarantees. What makes her so good at such a tender age? Well, it's a mix of key ingredients. An innate confidence in her ability means she backs herself in any situation. Her incredible athleticism is so important in the modern era, likewise a fantastic understanding of the game, which I was lucky enough to have too and is such an advantage. Trying to predict how a player will develop, even one as good as Hannah, is so difficult, though. Clearly, she's on the right path to something special but there are pitfalls aplenty. Everything has fallen into place for her so far. She's never been injured and has been able to live at home while making giant strides. What I will say is that she has a terrific family to lend whatever support may be required and her work ethic is outstanding, so good luck and bon voyage.

Another player to have gone through the Alison Taylor school of coaching is Arthur Fery. Arthur, who has frustratingly spent more than his fair share of time on the sidelines through injury, was ranked just outside the world's top 200 at 22 when I wrote this. It was from the age of four to 12 that he worked closely with Alison before enjoying a very successful junior career that saw him peak at number 12 in the singles rankings and included runs to the semi-finals of the Wimbledon Boys' Doubles event in 2019 and the Australian Open juniors a few months later.

More recently, Alison has teamed up with another promising youngster, Tommy Gabor. Despite all her success as one of the most respected junior coaches in the country she still listens to me, sometimes at least, though come to think of it she has become a little more bolshy of late! The key thing for a coach at any level is to explain clearly why you are advocating a certain move and make sure the technical side is understood. It's not rocket science but the more a player appreciates why they should be doing something, the easier it is for them to execute the plan.

Having fun is so important as well. Creating a bond with any player, particularly junior ones, is imperative. I've also encouraged

Alison to deal with the parents as shrewdly as possible. Don't push them away; bring them in and keep talking to them. Mums and dads have a huge role to play in the process but need educating, like their kids. If they want to be on court, that's fine but only if they learn to be actors. Any negative displays of emotion will have an adverse effect on their sons and daughters – you see it all the time. Parents are key to the process but some of them actually need more coaching than the players!

Chapter 37

Roger and Out

I'VE STARTED this final chapter on the eve of another birthday. It's lucky I don't like cakes because we'd never find one big enough to fit 83 candles; 83! Where have the years gone? I guess that's a question asked by so many of us as we reach a certain age. That and what's it all been about?

In truth, my career was a million to one shot. You don't grow up hitting balls in a Sheffield park with your mother until an advanced age and then go on to become a top-ten player and British number one. Logic dictates that's simply not feasible.

I was tenacious and resilient, though, and never afraid of hard work. Those qualities coupled with some natural ability proved a winning combination. Three Wimbledon semis, another in Australia, two US Open doubles titles, and prolonged success in the Davis Cup were the end result, along with famous wins over the likes of Rod Laver, Bjorn Borg and Arthur Ashe.

Of course I'd have liked more titles and that elusive Wimbledon crown but there could easily have been a lot fewer.

I took chances. Becoming one of the Handsome Eight proved a wise move but could have finished my career in its prime. Embracing the tennis holidays business was risky too but gave me a new lease of life as I searched for something to replace the buzz of being a professional athlete. Receiving an MBE from the Queen in 1977 during her Silver Jubilee was affirmation I'd done okay since climbing aboard that Sheffield-to-London steam train with Dickie Dillon in the late 50s. It was a huge thrill to come face to face with Her Majesty. Not a big tennis fan, she asked me a few questions about Billie Jean King as I looked into the eyes of the most famous woman in the world and tried to answer as coherently as possible.

In terms of regrets, I've had a few, both professionally and personally, but who hasn't? I just hope my story might inspire some youngsters not blessed by their background to see what can be achieved in any profession with the right mindset and work ethic. Tennis itself is a brutal sport that invariably requires a lot of physical, mental and financial investment. But it also teaches you so much about yourself, the day-to-day challenges we all have to face and the rollercoaster ride of emotions experienced on tennis courts and way beyond.

Keep putting one foot in front of the other, stand firm and do the right thing. That was always my mantra and would be if I had a chance to do it all again.

Accepting my destiny and looking forward to whatever is left keeps me on an even keel today. I may not have won Wimbledon but I hit a million balls and had my chance. Yes, some proper coaching at an early age might have made all the difference. Had the boycott never happened, those lost years in the mid-70s could have panned out very differently. And who knows what the outcome might have been had I made the effort to attend that second James Bond audition at Pinewood Studios.

Ifs, buts and maybes. We use those three words every day but the most important thing is to be able to live with yourself. Like 007, I never backed down. For better or worse I stuck to my principles irrespective of the cost. You know that by now. Staying true to what you believe in isn't always as easy as it sounds. Yet, be it overturning a call in my favour when match point up against Bjorn Borg, standing my ground during the boycott or making unpopular decisions as Davis Cup captain, I always wanted to be able to look in the mirror afterwards and feel no shame or anguish. I'm pleased to say I can.

Whether or not I'm the man who saved Wimbledon, I'm certainly the man who loves everything to do with it. So, if my battles on and off court there are remembered every once in a while, and if a few people occasionally look back on their tennis holidays in the sun with fond memories, I can rest easy. Us Sheffield folk tend not to get carried away but should that prove to be the case, then, to borrow an old-fashioned Yorkshire phrase favoured by my father, 'It would be proper champion, lad.'

Index

Alcaraz, Carlos 50, 222, 229
Allaster, Stacey 205, 239
Ali, Muhammad 138
Alexander, John 48, 103
Anderson, Malcolm 120
Anderson, Kevin 225
Annacone, Paul 156
Anne, Princess 147,
Applewhaite, Charlie 65
Arazi, Hicham 182–183
Ashe, Arthur 40, 42, 44, 111, 122, 212, 231, 249
Austin, Tracy 185, 189, 191, 197
Bacall, Lauren 197
Bale, Stuart 156, 159–160
Baily, James 153
Baranyi, Szabolcs 51
Barrett, John 44–45, 156–157
Barker, Mark 136
Barker, Sue 66, 169, 185, 188–189
Barrington, Jonah 204, 241
Barthes, Pierre 46, 90–91, 93–95, 130
Bassett, Carling 205
Bates, Jeremy 145, 159–160, 177, 184
Baxter, Hedley 98
Becker, Boris 62, 82, 160, 177, 221, 229
Becker, Roger 177
Bedard, Bob 99
Beecher, Colin 35
Belkin, Michael 99
Bellamy, Rex 69
Benedikte, Princess 129
Bennett, Mickey 68, 89
Bennett, Reg 68, 89
Benson, George 147
Berner, Vicki 191
Bergelin, Lennart 50
Berry, Mary 204
Berryman, Noel 132
Bishop, Bert 21
Bjorkman, Jonas 176

Blanke, Ernst 98
Bloxham, Dan 216
Bogdanovic, Alex 155, 180, 238
Bolton, Sally 218
Bond, James 132–134, 250
Bonding, Oliver 237
Bone, Derek 196
Boogert, Kirstie 172
Borg, Bjorn 50, 72, 192, 195, 198, 220, 229, 249–250
Botfield, Stephen 159
Boulter, Katie 235
Bowrey, Bill 125
Bowles, Stan 136
Broad, Neil 170
Broady, Liam 229
Broccoli, Cubby 133–134
Bromwich, John 222
Brook, Phil 217
Brown, Nick 154
Buchholz, Earl (Butch) 90–91, 95–96
Bueno, Maria 203, 232
Bugner, Joe 138–141
Bungert, Wilhelm 31, 86, 96, 106
Butler, Gloria 35
Button, Dick 136
Cahill, Darren 224
Capriati, Jennifer 136
Carmichael, Bob 34
Carpenter, Keith 99
Carreno-Busta, Pablo 110
Casals, Rosie 188
Castle, Andrew 156, 159
Ceban, Mark 237
Chang, Michael 62
Charles, Lesley 186
Charles, Ray 147
Childs, Lee 174, 212
Chaplin, Charlie 79
Clement, Arnaud 172
Clerk, Jose Luis 157

Index

Coe, Sebastian 204
Cohu, Heidi 178
Coles, Glynis 186
Collins, Robert 159
Connery, Sean 132
Connors, Gloria
Connors, Jimmy 42, 49, 70, 113, 116, 197, 229
Cooper, Henry 138
Cornejo, Patricio 109
Correia, Eurico 202
Corretja, Alex 167
Court, Margaret 231
Coventry, Austin 246
Cowan, Barry 166, 170, 172, 174
Cox, Mark 9, 44–45, 68, 83, 97, 129, 151, 177
Cox, Susie 71
Croft, Annabel 154, 224
Crookenden, Ian 119
Crowther, John 163–164, 184
Curtis, Peter 83
Darmon, Pierre 35
David, Herman 44–45, 56, 96
Davenport, Lindsay 239
Davidson, Owen 42, 48, 109, 131
Day, Doris 197
Deford, Frank 90
Delgado, Jamie 153–154, 163, 168
Del Potro, Juan Martin 61
Dell, Dick 109
Dell, Donald 42, 48, 113
Diepraam, Keith 35
Dietrich, Marlene 36
Dimitrov, Grigor 153, 241
Dillon, Dickie 9, 20, 28, 63, 187, 250
Dixon, Dave 89, 92–95, 98
Djokovic, Novak 39, 55, 60, 84, 102, 129, 147, 229, 236
Dominguez, Patrice 122
Douglas, Kirk 197
Draper, Jack 213, 224, 236–237
Drysdale, Cliff 41–44, 48, 56, 86, 90, 92, 108–109, 131, 133, 212
Durr, Francois 232
Dyke, Broderick 156
Edberg, Stefan 118, 221
Edmund, Kyle 19
El Aynaoui, Younes 182–183
Elschenbroich, Harald 50
Emerson, Roy 65, 97, 221, 227, 231
Enqvist, Thomas 176
Evans, Leon 9, 15, 80, 152, 199, 209
Evans, Michael 9, 15, 80, 152, 199, 209
Evans, Richard 9, 15, 80, 152, 199, 209

Evert, Chris 91, 161, 185–191, 230
Evert, Jeanne 91, 161, 185–191, 230
Fairlie, Brian 103
Fearnley, Jacob 237
Feaver, John 127, 129
Federer, Roger 39, 60, 90, 104–105, 129, 220, 222, 226, 229, 241
Felgate, David 154, 159, 167, 183–184
Felner De Costa, George 192, 195
Ferreira, Wayne 35
Fery, Arthur 247
Fillol, Jaime 109
Finney, Albert 203
Flatman, Barry 164
Fleming, Ian 133
Fletcher, Gavin 178
Forbes, Sir Hugh 43–44
Francome, John 204
Franklyn, Bill 109
Fraser, Neale 103
Frazier, Joe 136, 138
Fulwood, Nick 159
Gabor, Tommy 247
Gainford, Philip 159
Garcia-Lopez, Guillermo 110
Gasiorek, Wieslaw 124
Gasquet, Richard 222, 241
Geraghty, Barry 32
Geraghty, Rex 32
Gerulaitis, Vitas 109
Gibson, Mike 24, 53, 55
Gimeno, Andres 90, 96, 109
Gisbert, Juan 127
Goodall, Jason 159
Goolagong, Yvonne 232
Gorman, Tom 83, 122
Gonzales, Pancho 87, 90, 96–97, 221, 231
Gottfried, Brian 73
Graebner, Clark 84, 105
Graham, Colin 65, 83, 99, 196, 202
Graf, Steffi 226, 230
Gray, Andy 204
Griffiths, Eldon 43
Gullikson, Tom 224
Gulyas, Istvan 98
Hackman, Gene 197
Hagelauer, Patrice 163
Haillet, Jean-Louis 50
Hampson, Ernest 26
Hancock, Julie 202
Hannah, Bob 205, 237, 246–247
Haran, Ben 246
Hard, Darlene 18–19, 30, 35–36, 41, 51, 57, 62, 65, 69, 71, 76, 79, 82, 84,

100, 113, 129, 144, 146, 152, 155, 157, 160–161, 169, 179, 192–193, 199, 212, 223, 232, 234–235, 238, 249
Haring, David 127, 197
Harvey, Mike 21
Heldman, Julie 186
Hemery, David 137, 139–141
Henin, Justine 230
Henman, Tim 55, 100, 153–154, 160, 162, 166–167, 170–171, 177, 181, 215, 217
Heston, Charlton 197
Heyman, Allan 44
Hewitt, Bob 74, 108, 116, 122
Hewitt, Lleyton 34, 90, 180
Higueras, Jose 127
Hill, Al (junior) 90, 92
Hill, Bob 9, 21, 64
Hill, Frank 64
Hingis, Martina 227, 230
Hirst, David 200
Hoad, Lew 36, 88, 96, 207, 221, 231
Hobbs, Anne 186, 189
Hoey, Kate 170, 172
Holdsworth, Sally 48
Hopman, Harry 243
Howarth, John 202
Howey, John 202
Hoyles, Fred 224
Hrebec, Jiri 50
Huber, Anke 227
Hughesman, Patrick 158
Hunt, David 239
Hutchins, Paul 73, 127, 156, 162, 185, 197
Hunt, Lamar 89–90, 92–93
Ickringill, Simon 202
Isner, John 125, 225
Ivanisevic, Goran 55, 62
Jacklin, Tony 137
Jacks, Brian 140
Jacques, Warren 88, 162
James, Edward 224
Jennings, Pat 140
Jevans, Debbie 218
Jessup, Peter 199
Johansson, Thomas 176
John, Barry 137, 139–141
Jones, Alan 146
Jones, Ann 130, 216, 232
Jordan, Michael 42
Kalogeropoulos, Nick 131
Kavelnikov, Yevgeny 172, 230
Keating, Frank 40
Keldie, Roy 131
Keegan, Kevin 136–137

Keothavong, Anne 85
Kent, Duke and Duchess 50
Khoo, Dr Vincent 244
King, Billie Jean 157, 185, 189–190, 231, 250
Klugman, Alice 237, 246
Klugman, Hannah 237, 246
Konta, Jo 85
Kovac, General Dusan 40
Kodes, Jan 49, 81, 106, 108
Knight, Billy 64–65
Kramer, Jack 41, 44, 68, 83, 88
Krajicek, Richard 62
Kucera, Karol 171
Kuhnke, Christian 86
Kyrgios, Nick 80
Lacy, Isabelle 237
Lane, Terry 17, 29, 132
Lapentti, Giovani 168, 175
Lapentti, Nicolas 7, 165–166, 168–169, 173–175
Laver, Rod 42, 65, 67, 70, 87, 90, 96–97, 100, 102, 117, 221, 231, 249
Lazenbury, Gordon 9, 137
Lazenby, George 134
Leconte, Henri 82
Lee, Martin 168, 174, 178–179
Lendl, Ivan 42, 62, 90, 217, 221, 229
Lewinshon, Max 158
Lewis, Richard 169
Little, Matt 235
Lloyd, David 73, 150, 154, 161–162, 164–166, 173, 201
Lloyd, John 57, 74, 120, 127, 161
Lloyd, Robin 143
Lloyd, Scott 161
Lloyd, Tony 150
Lockwood, Beverley 201
Lutz, Bob 108
Mackin, Alan 180
Maclagan, Miles 168, 179–180
Maclennan, Frances 142
Maclennan, Keith 150
Maclennan, Lindsey 142, 150, 208
Maclennan, Veronica 142, 150, 208
Macpherson, Don 62
Mahut, Nicolas 125, 225
Maker, Ali 38
Mantle, Mickey 104
Mappin, Sue 9, 186, 188–189, 191, 196
Margetts, John 194
Marino, Dan 239
Maris, Roger 104
Markson, Jonathan 205
Marray, Johnny 180

Index

Martin, Bill 70
Maskell, Dan 22, 26, 74, 203
Matthews, Stanley 237
Mauresmo, Amelie 61
Maybourne, Richard 132
Mayer, Sandy 49
McCormack, Mark 135
McEnroe, John 34, 73, 78, 80, 223, 229
McGrath, Vivian 222
McKinley, Robert 50
McManus, Jim 44, 49
McMillan, Frew 75, 103, 108
Medvedev, Daniil 104
Meiler, Karl 51
Metreveli, Alex 56, 148
Mezzadri, Claudio 156
Milkovich, John 239
Mills, Alan 66–67, 177
Mitchell, Tony 9, 196
Moore, Bobby 137–139
Moore, Ray 77, 100
Moore, Roger 134
Moorhouse, Professor Julian 245
Morejon, Luis 165, 167, 175
Montana, Joe 239
Mortimer, Angela 232
Mottram, Christopher (Buster) 9, 71-74, 126–127
Mottram, Linda 72
Mottram, Tony 72
Moya, Carlos 62
Mukerjea, Chiradip 103
Mulligan, Martin 132
Munoz, Antonio 109
Murphy, Bob 144, 241
Murray, Andy 58, 60, 84, 100, 153, 160, 181, 224, 226, 230, 235–237
Murray, Jamie 110
Nadal, Rafael 39, 55, 60, 104–105, 226, 229
Nagelsen, Betsy 186
Nastase, Ilie 39, 49, 79, 86, 117, 203, 212, 231
Navratilova, Martina 145, 190, 226, 230, 239
Nestor, Daniel 172
Newberry, Janet 186
Newcombe, John 42, 49, 69, 86, 90–91, 96, 100, 106–107, 117, 131, 165, 212, 231
Nicklaus, Jack 135
Nieboer, Henk 242
Niland, Ross 213
Noah, Yannick 74, 91
Offenheim, Joseph 67
Okker, Tom 129–131

Olmedo, Alex 88
Orantes, Manuel 109, 117, 127, 231
Orchard, Alan 159
Oremans, Miriam 172
Pacino, Al 65
Paige, Elaine 147
Palmer, Arnold 135
Panatta, Adriano 74, 99, 130, 198, 203
Parmar, Arvind 61, 163, 166, 178
Parsons, John 44
Parun, Onny 82, 97
Pasarell, Charlie 43, 103, 108
Pattison, Andrew 121
Pecci, Victor 203
Penman, Derek 99
Pernfors, Mikael 156
Perry, Fred 28–30, 32, 58, 69, 72, 100
Perry, Penny 59-60
Petchey, Mark 154, 224
Peterson, Oscar 147
Philippoussis, Mark 180
Phillips, Morgan 237
Phillips, Tim 22, 48
Pickard, Tony 162
Pickering, Ron 136, 140
Pignon, Laurie 103, 187, 190
Pilic, Niki 40, 56, 90–91
Pinsent, Matthew 171
Player, Gary 135
Pod, June 199
Pokorny, Peter 98
Powell, Enoch 73
Proctor, Mark 241
Pullin, Julie 155, 170, 172
Querrey, Sam 61
Raducanu, Emma 234
Rafter, Pat 34
Ralston, Dennis 90–91, 93–96, 100
Reay, Basil 22
Richardson, Andrew 235
Richey, Cliff 43
Riessen, Marty 100, 129
Rigg, Diana 134
Riggs, Bobby 40, 197, 225
Riordan, Bill 117
Roberts, Arthur 66
Robertson, Charlie 237
Roche, Tony 69, 73, 90, 97, 107
Rosen, Barney 18
Ronaldo 239
Rose, Justin 120
Rosewall, Ken 43, 87, 90, 96–97, 100–101, 106, 114, 221, 231
Rossiter, Leonard 109
Rowe, Steve 196–197

Rublev, Andrey 62, 84
Ruffles, Ray 86
Rusedski, Greg 70, 152, 162, 166, 178
Ruth, Babe 104
Sabalenka, Ayrna 231, 233
Sabatini, Gabriela 91
Safin, Marat 172
Saila, Pekka 133
Salah, Mo 137
Salley, Emily 226
Sampras, Pete 221, 229
Sammel, Dave 169
Sanders, Robin 35
Sangster, Mike 65, 67, 98–100, 123, 125, 177, 212
Sayers, Sarah 184
Schallau, Mona 186
Seagren, Bob 136
Searle, Henry 237
Seewagen Butch 103, 109
Seixas, Vic 125
Seles, Monica 230
Segura, Pancho 88, 197
Sellar, David 198
Seruca, Marco 202
Sherwood, David 180
Shock, Penny 199
Shriver, Pam 134, 185, 188, 190–191
Simcox, Adrian 202
Simpson, Russell 156
Sinner, Jannik 199
Slater, Jim 153–154
Smith, Stan 11, 42, 44, 56, 83, 108, 197, 212, 231
Soares, Bruno 110
Sorrell, Martin 194
Spadea, Vince 166
Spencer, Kyle 170, 172
Spitz, Mark 136
Srichaphan, Paradorn 179–180
Stakhovsky, Sergiy 61
Steadman, Richard 238–239, 244
Steele, Chauncey 132
Stewart, Jackie 138–139, 141
Stich, Michael 118, 145
Stillwell, Graham 65, 83, 99, 202
Stolle, Fred 87, 96, 122, 173, 193
Stojsavljevic, Mika 237
Stove, Betty 32, 185
Swiatek, Iga 231
Szikszay, Andras 98
Taylor, Alison (nee Hannah) 9, 144, 205–210, 239, 245–246
Taylor, Anastasia 143–144
Taylor, Claire 145

Taylor, Frances 27, 47, 130, 132-133, 142-145, 148, 150, 152, 192-194, 204, 207-208
Taylor, Greig 143-146, 208, 215–216, 241
Taylor, Katriona 144, 146-148, 165
Taylor, Lilian 15-18, 26-27, 35, 130
Taylor, Mark 15-17, 26-27, 130
Taylor, Vivian 16-17, 27, 32, 149
Taylor, Zoe 144-145
Threlfall, Bill 79
Tiafoe, Frances 62
Tilden, Bill 87
Timms, Linda 97
Tiriac, Ion 82–84, 130
Trotman, James 213, 224
Truman, Christine 232
Turner, Leslie 232
Tyler, Michelle 186, 188
Udomchoke, Danai 179
Ulrich, Lars 147
Ulrich, Torben 147
Van Alen, Jimmy 118–119
Van Binst, Gilbert 137
Van Dillen, Erik 108
Van Gelder, Sander 195, 207
Vazquez, Tito 212
Velasco Senior, Jairo 121
Vilas, Guillermo 82
Wade, Virginia 185, 189–190, 232
Wadge, Herbert 26
Wagner, Tibby 29
Walker, Mike 156, 159–160, 164
Walden, Nick 9, 201
Wallace, Andrew 240
Watson, Heather 237
Wawrinka, Stan 229, 241
Wayne, Jeff 147
Wayne, John 197
Wayne, Marisa 35
Weatherley, Ken 216
Wilander, Mats 156, 158, 221
Williams, Serena 39, 62, 230
Williams, Venus 230
Wilson, Bobby 66, 99, 123–124, 177, 212
Wilson, Peter 103
Woodbridge, Todd 180–181
Woodroffe, Lorna 170, 172
Wooldridge, Keith 48
Worthington, George 26, 28
Xu, Mimi 237
York, Andy 159
Zverev, Mischa 61
Zverev, Sascha 62